ROUSSEAU AMONG THE MODERNS

# ROUSSEAU AMONG THE MODERNS

MUSIC, AESTHETICS, POLITICS

*Julia Simon*

The Pennsylvania State University Press
University Park, Pennsylvania

Library of Congress Cataloging-in-Publication Data

Simon, Julia, 1961–
Rousseau among the moderns : music, aesthetics, politics / Julia Simon.
    p. cm.
    Summary: "Reevaluates Jean-Jacques Rousseau through the lens of music theory to question his contribution to thinking about music as an aesthetic force in social life. Links Rousseau's understanding of concepts in music to the problem of the individual's relationship to the social order"—Provided by publisher.
    Includes bibliographical references and index.
    ISBN 978-0-271-05958-7 (cloth : alk. paper)
    ISBN 978-0-271-05959-4 (pbk : alk. paper)
    1. Rousseau, Jean-Jacques, 1712–1778—Knowledge—Music.
2. Rousseau, Jean-Jacques, 1712–1778—Criticism and interpretation.
    3. Music—Philosophy and aesthetics.
    4. Music—Political aspects.
    I. Title.

ML410.R86S56  2013
780.92—dc23
2012047292

Copyright © 2013 The Pennsylvania State University
All rights reserved
Printed in the United States of America
Published by The Pennsylvania State University Press,
University Park, PA 16802-1003

The Pennsylvania State University Press is a member of the
Association of American University Presses.

It is the policy of The Pennsylvania State University Press to use acid-free paper. Publications on uncoated stock satisfy the minimum requirements of American National Standard for Information Sciences—Permanence of Paper for Printed Library Material, ANSI Z39.48-1992.

TO MY MOTHER, *Renée Simon*

2

CONTENTS

*Acknowledgments* / ix
*A Note on the Text* / xi

Introduction / 1

1
Performance, Rhythm, and the Constitution of Community / 19

2
Singing Democracy: Music and Politics / 47

3
Rameau and Rousseau on Absolute and Relative Value:
The Theory/Practice Problem / 75

4
Folk Music: Authenticity, Primitivism, and the
Uses of Roots Music / 115

5
Rousseau and Aesthetic Modernity:
Music's Power of Redemption / 147

Conclusion: Rousseau Sings the Blues / 173

*Notes* / 187
*Bibliography* / 217
*Index* / 227

ACKNOWLEDGMENTS

This book is dedicated to my mother, Renée Simon, who made sure I was exposed to music at an early age. My mother was the impetus behind the presence of the baby grand piano in our house growing up. I have fond memories of listening to her play a wide variety of music, from waltzes to popular songs. In some ways, she inspired my own desire to play. And once I started, she dutifully took me to music lessons, listened to hours of practicing and, most especially, attended every band concert and solo I ever performed. My mother provided the nourishing and supportive environment for my early musical proclivities.

Academic studies and an initially nonmusical career path moved my interests away from music. No longer a performer, I was content to listen. My return to music was sparked by my husband, Charles Oriel, who has been an inspiration to me in reconnecting with this passion that had become submerged. Playing and performing together has inspired a great deal of the thinking that forms the backdrop of this project. I am grateful to Charles for bringing me back to my passion for music. Performing has enabled me to experience many of the feelings and emotions that are central to my conceptualization of this project. Charles has also patiently listened to hours of musings on a wide variety of topics, read draft after draft, always with the cheerful support and encouragement of someone who truly believes along with me. His thought-provoking comments and insights have added immeasurably to the project.

My daughter, Sabina, also inspired the return to music. Singing to her, taking her to music lessons, and generally watching a passion for music develop in her reminded me of how much it meant to me. I am especially happy to be able to share a love of music with her.

Reconnecting with playing music led to thinking about Rousseau's writing on music. I want to thank Claude Dauphin from the Université du Québec à Montréal for organizing the 2001 Rousseau Association meeting dedicated to "Musique et langage chez Rousseau." The conference afforded me the occasion to get my feet wet writing about Rousseau's work in music. I also wish to thank my wonderful colleagues and friends from the Rousseau Association who have inspired and challenged me over the last ten years to think about Rousseau in so many fruitful ways: Chris Bertram, Mira Morganstern, Ourida Mostefai, Michael O'Dea, John Scott, and Byron Wells.

My colleagues at The Pennsylvania State University and at the University of California, Davis, have also helped me to think carefully about the thorny questions of interdisciplinary research. I am especially grateful to Vera Mark and Joan Landes at Penn State and to Juliana Schiesari, Noah Guynn, and Anna Maria Busse Berger at UC Davis. I also wish to thank wonderful graduate and undergraduate students who have inspired me throughout the project. Finally, I am especially grateful to Tracy Strong for helpful criticism of early drafts of the manuscript and to Dick Terdiman for his support and encouragement over many, many years of professional and personal growth.

Two chapters of this book represent versions of earlier articles. I thank *The Journal of the History of Ideas* for permission to reprint a revised version of "Singing Democracy: Music and Politics in Jean-Jacques Rousseau's Thought," which originally appeared in volume 66 (2005): 433–54. I also thank *Eighteenth-Century Music* and Cambridge University Press for granting permission to reproduce a revised version of "Rousseau and Aesthetic Modernity: Music's Power of Redemption," which originally appeared in volume 2, no. 1 (2005): 41–56. Finally, I am grateful to several librarians who helped me to track down an eighteenth-century edition of Rousseau's *Dictionnaire de musique* in order to be able to reproduce plate N: Mike Winters at UC Davis, Eunice Schroeder and Tom Moon at UC Santa Barbara, and Sarah M. Allison, Caitlin St. John, and Gwido Zlatkes at UC Riverside.

# A NOTE ON THE TEXT

All parenthetical references to works by Rousseau are to Jean-Jacques Rousseau, *Œuvres complètes*, edited by Bernard Gagnebin, 5 vols. (Paris: Gallimard, 1959–95). Internal citations refer to volume and page number. Translations are my own unless otherwise indicated.

The *Encyclopédie ou dictionnaire raisonné des sciences, des arts et des métiers*, edited by Denis Diderot and Jean LeRond d'Alembert, is available online at the ARTFL Encyclopédie Project website (http://encyclopedie.uchicago.edu/). All references to the *Encyclopédie* in the notes are to this website, which can be searched by keyword.

# Introduction

> Je parle de la musique. Il faut assurément que je sois né pour cet art, puisque j'ai commencé de l'aimer dès mon enfance, et qu'il est le seul que j'aye aimé constamment dans tous les tems.
>
> —Jean-Jacques Rousseau, *Confessions,* book 5

The history of the critical reception of Rousseau's corpus bears the traces of interests conditioned by historical circumstance. While this is true of most writers, it is all the more true of the author of *Du contrat social* and the *Discours sur l'origine de l'inégalité parmi les hommes*. In the wake of the French Revolution, Rousseau's work was reductionistically viewed with skepticism and even fear as the philosophical inspiration behind Robespierre and the Terror.[1] As the threat of a repeat of the atrocities of the Terror receded in collective consciousness and the experiments with forms of political authority—empire, constitutional monarchy, republic, empire—unfolded in nineteenth-century France, the critical condemnations of the late eighteenth and early nineteenth centuries gave way to more nuanced readings of Rousseau's work, although still largely focused on the political theory. The corpus provided sufficient fuel in all of its internal contradictions for an array of critical readings from positions situated all along the political spectrum.

While the critical reception of Rousseau's corpus has broadened gradually to include all of the major works attended to by scholars in disciplines as diverse as political science, philosophy, literature, and musicology, the slow addition of texts to the canon has often followed specific critical readings. In other words, a seminal reading has often elevated a particular text to the status of "worthy of critical attention," followed by heated debate. One such example is Jacques Derrida's pathbreaking *De la grammatologie*.

In the late 1960s, Derrida pushed the *Essai sur l'origine des langues* from its relative obscurity as a marginal text into the limelight of twentieth-century critical theory. As I will discuss in detail below, Derrida's reading of the *Essai* changed the categories of perception of Rousseau's work, offering a reading that highlighted his place in the history of thinking about language. Derrida's close examination of the *Essai* sparked a wave of interest by an array of critics intrigued by the philosophical stakes of not only the *Essai* but also a variety of works in the corpus, now read through the lens of literary-philosophical concerns.[2]

Overall, the history of Rousseau's critical reception traces a gradual widening of the corpus from an early narrow focus on the political theory toward the integration of fictional and nonfictional works of a decidedly more literary bent. Although the types of works subjected to scholarly attention has grown, the difficulty remains in moving among the various disciplinary fields represented. Rousseau's corpus taken as a whole presents the critic with the challenge of working and synthesizing across multiple disciplinary domains. Most significant in this regard is the relatively scant attention paid to the works dedicated to music by scholars outside of musicology.[3] Oddly enough, and in spite of the full title of the famous *Essai sur l'origine des langues où il est parlé de la mélodie*, few critics outside of musicology have sought to integrate a consideration of the works on music into the broader whole.[4] *Rousseau Among the Moderns* undertakes just such an approach.

If historical circumstance conditions critical reception, why integrate the work on music now? A number of factors determine this choice. First is the state of the field. The publication of *De la grammatologie* ushered in a period of intensely theoretically oriented readings of most of the major authors of the French Enlightenment, Rousseau included. Derrida, de Man, Starobinski, and others contributed to a wave of critical attention informed by a range of theoretical approaches. In short, theory was all the rage and Rousseau provided grist for the mill. In the wake of the theory wave, the field of eighteenth-century studies (and literary studies more generally) experienced a period of uncertainty.[5] Interdisciplinary studies—both of the highly theoretical and the more empirically driven varieties—have become increasingly prevalent in the field. This is not to say that all scholarship has taken a turn toward interdisciplinarity, but since the "theory wave," eighteenth-century studies has become increasingly marked by an interest in expanding the narrow bounds of national literatures and histories to encompass work that charts new paths across the disciplinary divides.[6] One clear symptom of this interdisciplinary movement is the increase of scholarship on material culture from a variety of critical perspectives. As an example of this phenomenon, there has been a surge of interest in *cabinets de curiosités* and nascent museum culture, producing work that straddles the boundaries of traditional literary, historical, and art historical analysis. This interdisciplinary work has challenged scholars to move beyond the boundaries established by canonical texts within their traditional fields of specialization to examine what have been considered marginal or peripheral areas.

Concomitant with the shift toward interdisciplinary scholarship has been a need for methodological innovation. Much like the earlier theoretical wave pushed critics to explore questions conditioned by the interests of continental philosophy, the new interest in other disciplines has necessitated another shift in approach. Scholars working in a variety of disciplines have been drawn to acquaint themselves with the theory and methods of related fields, entailing forays into a broad range of subject areas.

And yet music has not been prevalent in this interdisciplinary movement. Perhaps because of its highly specialized vocabulary and analytical methodology, scholars from other fields have not made significant inroads into musicology. Likewise, musicologists have been slow to integrate their scholarly work into interdisciplinary venues, limiting exchange between musicology and the rest of eighteenth-century studies and literary studies more generally. But these barriers are starting to come down. Rousseau's corpus seems to me to be the ideal site for an interdisciplinary approach that can integrate another form of cultural study: texts devoted to music and music theory can be brought into fruitful dialogue with a broad range of texts from a number of other disciplines.

I am not a musicologist. My training and research have followed the trajectory of eighteenth-century studies that I have just traced. Influenced by the theoretical wave of criticism from the late 1960s through the 1980s, my interdisciplinary focus has expanded in line with the interests of continental philosophy into the fields of social and political philosophy, epistemology, metaphysics, aesthetics, and ethics. Rousseau's corpus has provided and continues to provide a rich field of exploration for these interests. And yet the aesthetic piece of the puzzle remained elusive. Limiting my reflections on aesthetic theory to the *Lettre à d'Alembert sur les spectacles* or the prefaces to *Julie, ou la nouvelle Héloïse* seemed inadequate in the context of Rousseau's contributions to social and political theory and ethics. Turning my attention to the work on music offered a glimpse at another world of thought on aesthetic questions, one largely ignored by scholars outside of musicology. This project grew slowly out of forays into the texts devoted to music, integrating themes and concerns from my previous work into the broader context of the musical theory.

The methodological approach integrates literary, philosophical, and especially social and political concerns into an analysis of texts devoted to musical themes and ideas. My aim is not to contextualize Rousseau's work in aesthetics as represented in the texts on music within broader themes in eighteenth-century aesthetics, but rather to bring these texts into dialogue with concepts central to the rest of his corpus. By reading these works as part of Rousseau's corpus, I seek to create a kind of dialogue between the theoretical positions taken in these texts with other, better-known theoretical positions in ethics, politics, social theory, and aesthetics with a view to introducing scholars largely unfamiliar with the work on music to new ways of conceptualizing central principles in Rousseau's thought.

When I speak about Rousseau's "music theory," I designate his reflections in the field of aesthetics that take music as their privileged object. Rousseau did not write music theory in the traditional sense: there are no major treatises on harmony,[7] nor do there exist texts dedicated specifically to the question of the role of music in social and political life. Nonetheless, many texts that I shall discuss in the following pages offer glimpses into philosophical positions about the relationship of aesthetics to ethics and morality, social and political formations, community, epistemology, and metaphysics. In short, when I use the term "music theory," I refer to these philosophical reflections in the aggregate, gleaned from multiple passages across numerous works in Rousseau's corpus. For this reason, I have chosen not to situate my readings of Rousseau's work on music within the context of eighteenth-century debates in aesthetics, with the important exception of Rameau. I strongly believe that moving away from the terms, definitions, and debates of the eighteenth century enables connections to be forged between the musical concerns as aesthetic arguments and the broader debates in philosophy.[8] In this respect, I choose to situate Rousseau "among the moderns," insofar as his reflections on the role of music as an aesthetic form may be read as a precursor to later developments in aesthetic theory.[9]

In the following study, I develop an extended reading of several key concepts in Rousseau's work viewed from the perspective of his work on music. I hope to shed new light on old debates concerning the relationship among, for example, the individual and the community, theory and practice, relative and absolute value, and reason, imagination, judgment, and feeling. Ultimately, my focus on the work on music aims to argue in favor of an aesthetic theory in Rousseau's work that differs markedly from interpretations and understandings conditioned by readings of *Julie, ou la nouvelle Héloïse* or the *Lettre à d'Alembert*. In the course of the proposed dialogue between musical texts and other works, I also seek to reopen questions concerning the general will, freedom, interest, political practice, democracy, and, most important, the relation between theory and practice in Rousseau. Ultimately, using the musical texts as a foundation for a new understanding of Rousseau's aesthetic theory, I offer a reading that seeks to integrate political, ethical, and aesthetic concerns.

The Works on Music

Creating a dialogue between the works in music and the broader corpus presents a number of difficulties. For readers unacquainted with the body of work on music, I offer a brief overview of these texts before addressing methodological questions related to reading these works alongside of other texts in Rousseau's oeuvre.[10]

Rousseau begins his musical writing in 1741 with the *Projet concernant de nouveaux signes pour la musique* and continues writing on music in one form or another through the *Dictionnaire de musique* of 1767–1768.[11] Well into the 1770s, he continued copying music for a living. Bernard Gagnebin gives an account of this final phase of his life:

> Se jugeant persécuté, incompris, malheureux, il ne trouvait d'apaisement et de réconfort que dans la musique et la botanique. Après son retour à Paris, il a composé des herbiers pour ses amis et copié plus de trois cents morceaux. Son Registre de copies, mentionné au XIXe siècle mais aujourd'hui disparu, révélait qu'entre septembre 1770 et février 1777 il n'avait pas copié moins de 11 200 pages. (5:xxviii)

> Judging himself to be persecuted, misunderstood, unhappy, he found appeasement and comfort only in music and botany. After his return to Paris, he composed herbaria for his friends and copied more than three hundred pieces. His Copy Register, mentioned in the nineteenth century but lost today, reveals that between September 1770 and February 1777 he copied no less than 11,200 pages.

While the output of copied music, as well as the number of texts specifically engaged with questions concerning music, is prodigious, it certainly represents only part of the story. As Rousseau recounts in the opening of the

*Confessions*, he attributes his passion for music to his Aunt Suzon, tying early childhood memories to his aunt's singing.[12] In Annecy and Chambéry as well as in Venice, we know from the *Confessions* that he continued his musical education.[13] Whether studying, teaching, composing, or copying music, whether performing or working as a tuner, nearly the entire span of Rousseau's life is engaged in one form or another with music.[14]

The textual output begins, as I mentioned above, with the *Projet*, written in 1741 and presented to the Académie des sciences in 1742. From that point forward, Rousseau produced a number of texts directly engaged with musical debates in fairly quick succession, including the *Lettre sur l'opéra italien et français* (1745, unpublished), the *Dissertation sur la musique moderne* (1743), and the articles written for the *Encyclopédie* (1749). These articles inspired the famous composer Jean-Philippe Rameau to respond to perceived criticisms of his theoretical positions with *Erreurs sur la musique dans l'Encyclopédie* (1755), fueling the growing debate between the two. Rousseau penned a number of texts oriented toward musical considerations in the 1750s, including participating in the celebrated *querelle des bouffons*.[15] Texts from this decade include *Lettre à Grimm au sujet de ses remarques sur Omphale* (1752), *Lettre sur la musique française* (1753), *Lettre d'un symphoniste de l'Académie royale de musique à ses camarades de l'orchestre* (1753), and, likely, *Examen de deux principes avancés par M. Rameau*.[16] The 1760s saw a continuation of his output in musical theory. Although dating the *Essai sur l'origine des langues* is famously problematic, many believe the date of composition to be around 1761.[17] Finally, the articles originally written for the *Encyclopédie* were reworked and expanded in the late 1760s.

Thus, the textual production spans from 1741 until the late 1760s, while the engagement with music—as either conscious listener, reader of theory, performer, or copyist—stretches from roughly 1719 almost until his death in 1778. This kind of sustained engagement with music cannot help but condition one's thinking in a number of areas. The present study seeks to tease out these areas of connection, arguing for analogical relationships between key concepts in social, political, and ethical theory, and music theory. In other words, by taking the similarities seriously, for example between tuning and democratic procedure, I seek to refine and nuance our understanding of Rousseau's thought as a whole.

Given Rousseau's lifetime engagement with music, I have not sought to detail specific stages of his thinking about music by attending to a strict chronology. Rather, guided by the central concepts of his philosophical thought, I have rather created a dialogue between what I take to be salient similarities and conceptual parallels in the different subject areas. In this respect, I have not sought to read texts that date from roughly the same time period together, but have instead organized the argument according to general theoretical questions central to the history of Rousseau criticism. In so doing, I have called on texts from various periods of composition to create an argument driven by key concepts. While I have sacrificed an adherence to strict chronology, I believe that I have gained in being able to construct an argument centered on philosophical principles. Moreover, I believe that Rousseau's sustained engagement with music over the course of his lifetime, demonstrated not only by his textual output but also by his return to the articles written for the *Encyclopédie* and their revision for the *Dictionnaire*, could not help but to have influenced his thinking in other areas. As a practicing musician, his passion for music necessarily colored his perceptions of other spheres of life.

Reading the texts devoted to music alongside the better-known works of the corpus offers a new vantage point on often well-trod critical territory. It is my hope that this perspective will bring into focus details that have been neglected or unnoticed by Rousseau scholars in the past. Likewise, my reading of the musical texts in the context of the rest of the corpus also seeks to interject some interdisciplinary perspective on the reception of texts that have been largely relegated to specialized analysis by musicologists. By way of example, I turn to Derrida's celebrated reading of the *Essai* in *De la grammatologie* as an entry into the kinds of unexpected turns my attention to music produces.

Reading Derrida Reading Rousseau

As I have indicated, Derrida's analysis of the *Essai* sparked a storm of critical attention for this formerly neglected and marginal text. Reading the *Essai* from the perspective of Lévi-Strauss's attachment to Rousseau, Derrida famously highlights the privileging of speech over writing as part of the phonologocentric tradition of Western metaphysics. Framing his reading with a chapter devoted to "A Writing Lesson" from *Tristes Tropiques*, Derrida reads Lévi-Strauss's concerns with the power relations inscribed within the ability to write as part of Rousseau's philosophical legacy. As Derrida reads Lévi-Strauss's account of how he taught the Nambikwara chief "to write," he highlights Lévi-Strauss's understanding of "writing [as] the exploitation of man by man" (*Grammatology*, 119).[18] In the episode, the anthropologist attempts to show the leader how to write, only to find that the leader uses this "knowledge" to wield power over his people:

And now, no sooner was everyone assembled than he [the leader] drew forth from a basket a piece of paper covered with scribbled lines and pretended to read from it. With a show of hesitation he looked up and down his "list" for objects to be given in exchange for people's presents. To so and so a bow and arrows, a machete! and another a string of beads! for his necklaces—and so on for two solid hours. What was he hoping for? To deceive himself, perhaps; but, even more, to amaze his companions and persuade them that his intermediacy was responsible for the exchanges, that he had allied himself with the white man, and that he could now share in his secrets. (Derrida, *Grammatology*, 125–26; quote from Lévi-Strauss, *Conversations*, 289)

Lévi-Strauss concludes from this episode among the Nambikwara that "the primary function of written communication is to facilitate slavery."[19] Derrida rightly attributes to Lévi-Strauss a "Rousseauist theme" in his account of the advent of writing among the Nambikwara, writing, "only a microsociety of non-violence and freedom, all the members of which can by rights remain within range of an immediate and transparent, a 'crystalline' address, fully self-present in its living speech, only such a community can suffer, as the surprise of an aggression coming from without, the insinuation of writing, the infiltration of its 'ruse' and of its 'perfidy'" (*Grammatology*, 119). Derrida attributes to Lévi-Strauss a "Marxist theory of writing" (119), arguing that "the power of writing in the hands of a small number, caste, or class, is always contemporaneous with hierarchization, let us say with political differance; it is at the same time distinction into groups, classes, and levels of economic-politico-technical power, and delegation of authority, power deferred and abandoned to an organ of capitalization" (130). The episode among the Nambikwara provides an opportunity to expand on a Rousseauist theme opposing a "before" and "after" of writing that attributes to the advent of writing the possibility of exploitation, domination, and enslavement. In reading Lévi-Strauss with Rousseau (and Rousseau with Lévi-Strauss), Derrida maps an argument about the political uses of writing onto themes in the *Discours sur l'origine de l'inégalité* and the *Essai*.[20]

While neither Derrida's nor Lévi-Strauss's reading of Rousseau touches on the question of music, their analyses are nonetheless consistent with arguments he makes in the *Projet concernant de nouveaux signes*. In this early text, as I will argue in chapter 2, Rousseau proposes to simplify the musical notation system in order to make reading music easier and thus

Introduction    9

more widely accessible. In parallel with the argument concerning an initiated elite capable of reading and writing in Lévi-Strauss and Derrida, Rousseau maintains that the current system of musical notation stands as an obstacle to learning to read and perform music. By extension, a simplified system might reverse whatever hierarchy exists in the world of musical performance, enabling greater participation by greater numbers, a conclusion fully consistent with Lévi-Strauss and Derrida. What remains less clear in the case of reading and writing music are the political stakes.[21]

While this aspect of Derrida's reading of Rousseau via Lévi-Strauss—related to social and political theory—works across the divide between language and music, such is not always the case with the remainder of the argument concerning the status of writing. As we will see, the attention to the dichotomy "speech/writing"—in which, according to Derrida, "speech" is the privileged term for Rousseau and Lévi-Strauss—yields an interpretation that is not fully applicable to the case of music. Indeed, focusing attention on music rather than language disrupts some of the interpretations of the binarisms that Derrida perceives in Rousseau's text.

To return to Derrida's argument, reading the *Essai* with Lévi-Strauss in mind, he finds in Rousseau "a classical ideology according to which writing takes the status of a tragic fatality come to prey upon natural innocence, interrupting the golden age of the present and full speech" (*Grammatology*, 168). While overstated, the characterization does point out a general elegiac structure in Rousseau's genetic accounts of origins that tends to romanticize earlier periods and condemn later ones as comparatively corrupt and denatured.[22] Derrida's reading ultimately highlights two sets of terms in Rousseau:

> We thus see two series working themselves out: (1) animality, need, interest, gesture, sensibility, understanding, reason, etc. (2) humanity, passion, imagination, speech, liberty, perfectibility, etc. It will gradually appear that, under the complexity of strands tangled in Rousseau's texts among these terms, requiring the minutest and most careful analyses, these two series always relate to each other according to the structure of supplementarity. All the names of the second series are metaphysical determinations—and therefore inherited, arranged with a laborious and interrelating coherence—of supplementary difference. (*Grammatology*, 183)

What Derrida seems to be suggesting as a relation between the two series—"supplementary difference"—amounts to a structure underlying Rousseau's thought. Animality in the state of nature is replaced by humanity in social life through the transformations described in the *Discours sur l'origine de l'inégalité* and *Du contrat social*. Whereas natural man is isolated, independent, and free in a limited sense—closer to an animal—the appearance of social groups enables the progression to a more meaningful type of freedom through interaction. In this sense, the pair "animality/humanity" signals the genetic structure of Rousseau's thought that Derrida characterizes as "supplementary differance."[23] One term comes to replace the other by adding onto what was previously asserted, while at the same time operating a fundamental transformation. The earlier state is lost forever; however, the state that supplants it represents both an improvement of sorts and a decline as human history "progresses."

The opening sentence of the *Essai* supports Derrida's reading in the realm of language: "La parole distingue l'homme entre les animaux" (5:376) [Speech distinguishes man from the animals]. Humans are separated from animals through the use of language, losing their prior innocence but also gaining access to social and moral life. Likewise, the pair "need/passion" corresponds to the distinction that gives rise to spoken language for Rousseau. In the *Essai* he writes, "Il est donc à croire que les besoins dictérent les premiers gestes et que les passions arrachérent les prémiéres voix" (5:380) [It is therefore to be believed that needs dictated the first gestures and that passions tore out the first voices]. While simple gestural indicators are sufficient to communicate needs, passions spark the development of spoken language to facilitate communication of feeling and, ultimately, the kind of sharing that is foundational for meaningful human relationships.[24]

For Derrida, the next pair in the series, "interest/imagination," reveals Rousseau's alignment of reason with interest and imagination with pity and the passions. It is this dichotomy that produces the privileging of speech over writing, according to Derrida's reading. As Derrida sees it, imagination is required to ignite the passions in Rousseau (*Grammatology*, 183).[25] Reason alone is insufficient to move either the passions or elicit the feeling of pity. Indeed, Rousseau's elaboration of the mechanism of pity in the *Essai* highlights the necessity of both the understanding and the imagination to aid in the process of identification in a way that is missing from the account in the *Discours sur l'origine de l'inégalité*:[26]

> Les affections sociales ne se développent en nous qu'avec nos lumières. La pitié, bien que naturelle au cœur de l'homme resteroit éternellement inactive sans l'imagination qui la met en jeu. Comment nous laissons-nous émouvoir à la pitié? En nous transportant hors de

nous-mêmes; en nous identifiant avec l'être souffrant. Nous ne souffrons qu'autant que nous jugeons qu'il souffre. (5:395)

[The social affections only develop in us with our knowledge/reason. Pity, while natural in the heart of man, would remain eternally inactive without the imagination that puts it into play. How do we allow ourselves to be moved by pity? By transporting ourselves outside of ourselves; in identifying with the suffering being. We only suffer as much as we judge that s/he suffers.]

Rousseau's use of the word "lumières" as necessary for social affections does not rule out reason's role in the operation of pity. Nonetheless, Derrida reads Rousseau's position as maintaining that without the imagination cold reason can only appeal to interest, which is insufficient for moral and political life.

Derrida's reading, focused closely on Rousseau's treatment of writing, draws from Rousseau's condemnation of the influence of reason on language through the medium of writing to conclude that reason drains passion from certain forms of expression.[27] Rousseau writes in the *Essai*, "L'écriture qui semble devoir fixer la langue est précisément ce qui l'altére; elle n'en change pas les mots mais le génie; elle substitue l'exactitude à l'expression. L'on rend ses sentimens quand on parle et ses idées quand on écrit" (5:388) [Writing, which seems should fix language, is precisely what alters it; writing doesn't change the words but rather the genius, it substitutes exactitude for expression. One renders one's sentiments when one speaks and one's ideas when one writes]. Likewise, languages that have adopted writing, especially with phonetic alphabets, become conditioned by the analytical attitude that writing engenders (5:392–93). Relying on this condemnation of the inability to move listeners through a form of speech overly conditioned by the rationality of writing, Derrida detects a broader pattern of the privileging of speech in the *Essai*. For Derrida, this privileging of speech is related to Rousseau's belief in its ability to excite the passions using the imagination. Derrida understands the way in which the imagination operates through speech to excite the passions in Rousseau as a form of mimesis.[28] As he develops his reading of mimesis in Rousseau, Derrida emphasizes the role of imitation in artistic production. With respect to music, Derrida writes,

> In the living arts, and preeminently in song, the outside imitates the inside. It is expressive. It "paints" passions. The metaphor which

makes the song a painting is possible, it can wrest from itself and drag outside into space the intimacy of its virtue, only under the common authority of the concept of imitation. Painting and songs are reproductions, whatever might be their differences; the inside and the outside share them equally, expression has already begun to make passion go outside itself, it has begun to set it forth and paint it. (*Grammatology*, 203)

Derrida suggests that music operates in the same way as painting: both forms provide reproductions based on an imitation of subjective states. Song and painting represent exteriorizations of inner life, mimetic articulations of passion that enable the subject to share feelings with other subjects. Yet this is not what Rousseau actually says about music in the *Essai*. As we will see in the following chapters, Rousseau is careful to distinguish between painting and music in the *Essai*, and specifically their very different economies of space and time.

Without delving into too much detail here in the introduction, suffice it to say that music and painting are distinctly different in terms of the ways in which they engage the imagination for Rousseau.[29] As Derrida describes song as "painting" passions, he narrativizes and spatializes the structure of the imagination in Rousseau. According to the Derridean reading, if music moves the listener, it is through the same type of narrative and spatial structure (inside/outside; intimacy/expression) used by painting, theater, and other forms of literature.

As I will argue in the following chapters, I do not believe that this is the case. Rousseau reserves a special place for music, which operates according to a different economy from that of painting. And while paintings exist in a spatial economy of presence, music's sequential nature resides in a temporal economy that is both present and absent.[30] That is to say, each piece of music requires presence for performance (musicians playing), but within its very structure works against this presence because of the ephemeral quality of its performance: what was played at the beginning no longer exists at the end. Indeed, the entire piece only exists within the perception and imagination of the listener.

Paying careful attention to the privileging of live music changes the character of our understanding of the privileging of speech over writing in Rousseau from the one diagnosed by Derrida. Where Derrida reads Rousseau as favoring a form of communication that enables more stability of meaning through the presence of the speaker as opposed to writing, I will argue that taking into account Rousseau's preference for live music over the written score yields a different interpretation. Rousseau's privileging of music highlights the accents, tones, and rhythms that come into being through performance. These same qualities are also applicable to spoken language. And yet, in the privileging of live music, it is the variety of possible interpretations realized through minute differences in accent, tone, tempo, and rhythm that provide the richness of musical expression. If we were to extend the same argument, the privileging of spoken language relates less to its stability than to the kind of variety that Derrida identifies with writing. In other words, the valorization of the infinite variety of musical performance runs counter to the notion that speech is more stable than written language. If Rousseau understands speech and music in the same way, then spoken language embodies choices about tone, accent, and rhythm that are unrepeatable, ephemeral, and not fundamentally stable.[31]

Derrida does not comment on the dichotomy between performed music and score in the way that he analyzes Rousseau's distinction between speech and writing. It would seem likely that Derrida would interpret Rousseau to privilege performance over written music for its "immediate presence" (*Grammatology*, 237). And indeed, as I have suggested, Rousseau does privilege performance over score, but for reasons that do not line up with the argument concerning writing. In discussing what he diagnoses as Rousseau's ambivalent attitude toward writing, Derrida argues, "Rousseau speaks the desire of immediate presence. When the latter is better represented by the range of voice and reduces dispersion, he praises living speech, which is the language of the passions. When the immediacy of presence is better represented by the proximity and rapidity of the gesture and the glance, he praises the most savage writing, which does not represent oral representation: the hieroglyph" (237).

Derrida identifies Rousseau's tendency to privilege forms of representation that stand a better chance of engaging the passions without disrupting the power of oral communication. In the realm of music, the choices are not as various as they are with language: Rousseau is limited to live performance and written score. Whereas in the linguistic example, in one instance he may privilege communication with gestural language, in another he may privilege specific forms of writing, such as hieroglyphics. Through this uncovering of the logic of supplementarity, Derrida seeks to demonstrate the fundamental instability of Rousseau's system in its reliance on dichotomies and distinctions that are constantly destabilized and often effaced. Such is not the case with music: without the intermediary form of recorded music in the eighteenth century, music is trapped in the neat binarism of live performance/written score, without the possibility of slippage and supplementarity adduced by Derrida in the case of writing.

Ultimately, Derrida's argument with respect to the status of writing in Rousseau asserts the presence of the visual even within speech. Derrida writes, "The metaphoric origin of speech opens an eye, one might say, at the center of language. And the passion that draws out the first voices relates to the image. The visibility inscribed on the act of birth of the voice is not purely perceptive, it signifies. Writing is the eve of speech" (237). For Derrida, Rousseau's insistence on the distinction between speech and writing is ultimately meaningless: writing is always already both inside and outside of speech. Even in the moment of its first appearance, speech demonstrates its reliance on the visual, undermining the dualistic logic that subtends Rousseau's philosophical system, as Derrida reads it.[32]

In much the same way that he equates painting and song in Rousseau, Derrida reads the birth of speech as simultaneous with the appearance of visual forms of communication and, specifically, writing. For Derrida, speech's reliance on the visual betrays its fundamental inseparability from writing. But is the same true for music? I would argue that it is not the same. The privileging of musical performance in Rousseau, while it does emphasize the ability to move the listener by exciting the interests and the passions, does not contrast specifically with written music. For one thing, few people are able to pick up a score and hear the notes in their heads. For those who are able to hear notes while looking at a written score, clearly the experience is something akin to reading a text, but for the majority of people this is not a possibility.[33] But beyond this superficial distinction between written music and written language, the privileging of musical performance, as we will see in the chapters that follow, has as much to do with its ephemeral quality, its unrepeatability, and the realization of the myriad possibilities inscribed on any sheet of music as it does with its immediacy for those listening. Rather than focus on fixity, stability, or permanence, Rousseau praises the infinite variety that performance brings to the virtual reality of the written musical score. In other words, performance, rather than fix the inherent instability of the written text, instead celebrates that variety by realizing one of an infinite number of possibilities inscribed on the paper. And while the presence of performers and audience is significant for social and political reasons, I hope to demonstrate that the notion of presence departs radically from the kind of privilege accorded to the stability of meaning that Derrida identifies with the Western metaphysical tradition.

Performance, Politics, and Aesthetics

Derrida's influential reading of the *Essai* in *Of Grammatology* focused attention on what had been a largely ignored text and an area of

Rousseau's thought that had also been long overlooked. His argument concerning the privileging of the presence of speech has had an enormous impact on the way that scholars perceive Rousseau's corpus. In this respect, my readings owe a great debt to Derrida's attention to the speech/writing binary in Rousseau. Yet at the same time, as is no doubt already clear, the shift of attention from language to music changes the terms under consideration. Instead of the speech/writing dichotomy, my study opens with an examination of the central concept of performance. As the discussion above has already indicated, one of my central concerns in the opening chapter is the realization of tone, meter, accent, and rhythm through performance. In reading Rousseau's privileging of performance in music, I turn away from the opposition with the written score and rather seek to uncover a different conception of community. I argue that the performance of music understood as the coming together of a community of sorts has implications for notions of interest that bind the community together. In addition to the reappraisal of the social and political conceptions of community in Rousseau, this aesthetic reading also comments on the understanding of aesthetic reception in ways that differ markedly from readings focused on *Julie, ou la nouvelle Héloïse* and the *Lettre à d'Alembert sur les spectacles*. In thinking about the community that comes together for the performance of live music—musicians and listeners—I seek to examine the ways in which music moves the individuals to embody a community, and in so doing to offer a new interpretation of the grounds of community in Rousseau.

Chapter 2 continues the interrogation of the concept of community, but argues for an analogical relationship between singing and democracy in Rousseau. Beginning with the *Projet concernant de nouveaux signes* and following through the articles in the *Encyclopédie* and *Dictionnaire*, I argue for a democratic impulse in Rousseau's musical thought. Paying careful attention to Rousseau's privileging of the human voice and capacity for song, I argue for a reading of the general will that takes account of the realities of performance, both musical and political. Ultimately, reading the music theory with the political theory in this instance creates a bridge between theory and practice that reveals striking forms of compromise not normally associated with the conception of the general will in the *Social Contract*. In the final analysis, the idea of democratic song questions the notions of relative and absolute value in Rousseau, ingrained within the traditional theory/practice problem.

The following chapter continues the discussion of absolute and relative value, now in the context of Rousseau's extended debates with the composer Rameau. By examining the theoretical debates in music, I draw on the previous chapters to expand the debate over absolute and relative value, from the domains of aesthetics and social and political theory into epistemology and metaphysics. Reading the debates between Rameau and Rousseau in the context of the problem of relative and absolute value yields surprising results. Whereas the mathematically and scientifically oriented Rameau would seem to be more absolutist in his leanings than Rousseau, careful analysis leads to an interpretation that demonstrates the limits of Rameau's absolutism as well as Rousseau's relativism. Ultimately, pushing the debate onto the terrain of epistemology and metaphysics reveals the moral stakes in aesthetic issues for Rousseau. I argue that when music moves the passions, humans are oriented toward moral action for the good.

Chapter 4 analyzes Rousseau's understanding of folk music in the context of the previous chapter's emphasis on music's service to the moral good. Beginning with accounts in the *Confessions* and moving to the *Encyclopédie* and *Dictionnaire*, I uncover Rousseau's formal categorization of music as more or less primitive. Turning to Rousseau's own *Devin du village*, I argue that Rousseau self-consciously wrote a form of "primitive" music with moral and political ends in mind. My discussion encompasses considerations of the representations of music in *Julie* as well as the uses of celebration in the *Projet de constitution pour la Corse* and the *Considérations sur le gouvernement de Pologne* to uncover a potential use for music in social engineering.

The final chapter of the book attends to the broader question of Rousseau's aesthetic theory in light of the readings of the works on music. Placing Rousseau within the trajectory of the history of aesthetics, I argue for a reading of him as a modernist. Returning to the themes of the ephemeral quality of music, and its temporal and sequential nature that were present in the opening chapter on performance, I examine the understanding of the aesthetic object for Rousseau. Ultimately, the consideration of Rousseau's aesthetics takes account of his uses of music, as seen particularly in the chapters on democracy and folk music, to argue in favor of a redemptive function for the aesthetic realm in Rousseau. This reading brings his thought in line with a tradition that stretches from the nineteenth century through the Frankfurt School to identify within the aesthetic realm the possibility of a cure for modernity's ills. In this respect, I place Rousseau "among the moderns."

The conclusion of *Rousseau Among the Moderns* takes the unconventional path of speculation about what Rousseau would have to say about the genre of the blues. His own methodology in texts such as the *Discours sur l'origine de l'inégalité* relies on the construction of hypothetical and conditional fictions in order to gain access to what he claims are deeper truths. Although his hypotheses always entail a fictionalized and original past, I think that imagining his hypothetical reception of the blues in a different kind of temporal fiction does not deviate significantly from the goal at hand, namely, to offer a way of imagining philosophical problems in concrete ways. Indulging my own passion, I seek to bring together numerous strands of thought in the book in a way that celebrates creativity but also specificity. In thinking about how Rousseau might react to the blues, I return to the themes of performance, rhythm and accent, democratic impulse, community, formal structure, "primitive" music, and the social and political uses of the aesthetic to provide a somewhat speculative yet concrete example of the implications of his thought in a broader context.

# I

## Performance, Rhythm, and the Constitution of Community

With the musical experience, the expectation is that something musical will *happen* in the playing of the music, and it is the *something* that fascinates, that elevates the expectation and places the hearer in a critical mode.

—FLOYD, *The Power of Black Music*

There is a strong dialectical tension throughout Rousseau's work between the individual and the community. Whether in the social and political writings, the works dealing with education, or even in fictional representations, Rousseau seems to struggle between championing the rights of the individual over and against the claims of the multitude and maintaining the rights of community against dissenting voices.[1] Perhaps most representative of this emblematic tension is the gulf between the insistence on independence and isolation in the *Discours sur l'origine de l'inégalité* and the primacy accorded to the community in *Du contrat social*.

Rousseau's theoretical writings on music are not exempt from this tension. His privileging of melody over harmony seems to align nicely with the arguments in favor of individual rights. Self-expression and the cries of passion override mathematical considerations of harmony or polyphony.[2] On the other side, his system of musical notation, as we will see in the following chapter, strives for accessibility by rendering harmonic relationships easier to comprehend—enlarging the community of musicians. Likewise, his opera implies and even requires a group effort, a community of sorts, for performance. The tension between individual and community that is present in other works runs throughout the discussions of music. I would like to begin by reopening the individualist/collectivist debate in

Rousseau, but from the vantage point of music theory and practice. Specifically focusing on the dynamics and demands of performance and reception, I would like to probe Rousseau's understanding of the tension between individual and community within the context of musical performance with a view to a different understanding of what underlies and motivates group dynamics in Rousseau.

I wish to emphasize the role of performance in Rousseau's work on music for a number of reasons. To begin with a historical contextualization, as a twenty-first-century reader of Rousseau, I have sought to remind myself continually of the wide gap during the eighteenth century between the written notes on the page and the music's performance.[3] To state the obvious, without recording technology, music only has two modes of existence: virtual and realized. The intermediary state of recorded performance does not mediate between the two. As a listener or as a musician, one must be in the company of others in order to appreciate music as sound (except in the case of soloists playing for themselves). Clearly, in the case privileged by Rousseau of a singer performing with accompaniment, or even of opera, the music requires live performance, including cooperation between players for its realization. This makes the disjuncture between written and performed music even greater in his world than it is today—a fact that is oddly difficult to bear in mind.

If we take Rousseau's own entrée into the intellectual scene in 1742 as a point of departure—his presentation of the *Projet concernant de nouveaux signes pour la musique* to the Académie des sciences—the emphasis on performance seems justified. Indeed, the *Projet* foregrounds the importance of performance, especially for vocalists, by insisting on making key transposition and sight-reading easier.[4] Rousseau argues, and I will develop further in the next chapter, that a notation system that fosters transparency would enable more people to learn to sing and perform earlier in life.

Foregrounding performance privileges music's temporal existence over its spatial one. From Rousseau's perspective, the virtual life of music (notes on a page) is less important than the live sound generated through performance for an audience of listeners. While this might seem obvious and intuitive in our age of easy access to recorded performances, such was not the case in the eighteenth century. As I will argue in chapter 3, many composers and even performers, such as Rameau, privilege the notes on the page over live performance because they make the entire system visible. The written score externalizes and concretizes the harmonic system, whereas live performance makes such things apparent only for the most skilled listeners.[5] Privileging performance thus is consistent with Rousseau's privileging of melody over harmony, for harmony is best understood and appreciated on the written page, while melody stands out in live performance for the average listener.[6]

In addition to the accentuation of melody that tends to occur in live performance, other aspects of musical composition are transformed through the process of performance. As Rousseau argues in the textual fragment "L'origine de la mélodie,"[7] performance requires assigning temporal values to sequences of notes. While at the very least some proportional indication of these note values is given in scores, there is nonetheless a great deal of artistic liberty possible both in the interpretation of tempo and the execution of sequences of notes. The musician creates a rhythmic pattern based on the indications in the score, all the while introducing interpretive elements that make any particular performance unique.

In "L'origine de la mélodie," Rousseau stresses the artist's freedom in creating melody out of sequences of notes specifically through the application of rhythm:

> Qu'on présente au Musicien une suite de notes de valeur indéterminée, il en va faire cinquante melodies entiérement différentes, seulement par les diverses maniéres de les scander, d'en combiner et varier les mouvements; preuve invincible que c'est à la mesure qu'il appartient de déterminer toute mélodie. (5:337)
>
> [Present a musician with a series of notes of indeterminate value and he will make fifty entirely different melodies from them, solely through the different ways of scanning them, of combining them and of varying their movements; irrefutable proof that meter determines all melody.]

While clearly this example of a series of notes with indeterminate value represents an extreme case, it is also true that all performance requires some degree of rhythmic interpretation.[8]

Before moving forward in the analysis of the importance of rhythm in Rousseau, I think it important to point out that his own notation system fails miserably in this regard.[9] The sequence of numbers separated by commas provides no quick and easy way to grasp relative value relations among the notes.[10] Furthermore, his reduction of meters or time signatures to two ("tous les mouvemens de ces différentes mesures se reduisent à deux, savoir: Mesure à deux tems, et mesure à trios tems" (5:147) [all the movements of these meters may be reduced to two, namely: duple-time and triple-time]) indicates a lack of subtlety with respect to the nuances of different time signatures.[11] Finally, his condemnation of the use of notes with the same relative value in different tempi—for example, quarter notes in adagios and allegros (5:148)—points to a lack of sophistication concerning rhythmic variety, although one consistent with those of his day. While the desire to simplify musical notation is a laudable goal, within his proposed notation system rhythmic relations were sacrificed in order to facilitate the easy comprehension of tonal relations. In spite of these shortcomings, I nonetheless propose to emphasize the place of rhythm, timing, measure, and meter in Rousseau's conception of music in view of highlighting the centrality of live performance.

Music in Time

Rousseau privileges music as a temporal phenomenon in his emphasis on performance. In the *Essai sur l'origine des langues*, Rousseau's preference for music over painting clearly reveals his preoccupation with the temporal quality of music. In an extended passage comparing music to visual stimulus, he maintains,

> Toutes les richesses du coloris s'étalent à la fois sur la face de la terre. Du prémier coup d'oeil tout est vû; mais plus on regarde et plus on est enchanté. Il ne faut plus qu'admirer et contempler sans cesse.
> Il n'en est pas ainsi du son: la nature ne l'analyse point et n'en sépare point les harmoniques; elle les cache, au contraire sous l'apparence de l'unisson; ou si quelquefois elle les sépare dans le chant modulé de l'homme et dans le ramage de quelques oiseaux, c'est successivement et l'un après l'autre. . . . *Ainsi chaque sens a son champ qui lui est propre. Le champ de la musique est le tems, celui de la peinture est l'espace.* Multiplier les sons entendus à la fois ou developer les couleurs l'une après l'autre, c'est changer leur économie, c'est mettre l'oeil à la place de l'oreille, et l'oreille à la place de l'oeil. (5:419–20, my emphasis)

> [All the riches of coloration are spread out all at once over the surface of the earth. From the first glance everything is seen; but the more one looks the more one is enchanted. Nothing more is necessary than to admire and contemplate without end.
> Such is not the case with sound: nature does not analyze it nor separate out the harmonics; on the contrary, it hides them under the

appearance of unison, or if sometimes it separates them in the modulated song of man and in the call of some birds, it is successively and one after another. . . . *In this way, each sense has its proper field. The field of music is time; that of painting is space.* To multiply the sounds heard at the same time or develop colors one after another is to change their economy, it would be to put the eye in place of the ear and the ear in the place of the eye.]

The contrast with painting in the passage from the *Essai* comes close to negating the validity of the existence of music in spatial form as notes on a page. The simultaneous presence of notes and the relative transparency of harmonic relations in scores runs counter to Rousseau's definition here that stresses the temporal sequencing of music that conditions its perception.

As Barbara Barry summarizes the distinction in *Musical Time*, "music objects differ from spatial ones in the mode of their existence as well as in constantly changing identity. Space is three-dimensional, reversible, symmetrical and there 'all at once.' Time is asymmetrical, irreversible, one-dimensional, and constantly changing" (46). These constraints neatly define what Rousseau describes as two separate economies: sight and sound. The score, for Rousseau, would dwell in the realm of a spatial economy, negating or at least resisting what he considers to be music's defining features. In this respect, I would argue that Rousseau considers scores to be virtual representations of music's actual form: they are not realized until performed.

So how do notes on a page come to life through performance? What is the process involved? As we saw in the citation from "L'origine de la mélodie" above, Rousseau highlights the necessity of assigning temporal value to notes in performance. While the passage above represents an extreme case of improvisation with a sequence of notes of indeterminate value, it is also true that all performance requires temporal interpretation.

Returning to Barry's masterful discussion, she explains the different levels on which musical time exists, drawing the parallel to hours, minutes, and seconds:

> It is striking that the stratification of physical clocks has precise analogs in musical time-keepers. Music also has large-scale rhythms of ebb and flow, dynamic impulse and tension recession; within these, at intermediate levels, interlocking rhythmic strata, such as pulse, metrical rhythm, harmonic and phrase rhythm, elements which fill the span of duration shaped by musical events—motifs and melodies,

harmonic progressions and contrapuntal interplay between lines. In turn, these intermediate level events contain infinitely minute microrhythms. They are not notated (and perhaps only computers may be able to record with such precision), but they are crucial in the expressive interpretation of notation. They affect the spacing between beats and constitute the music's fine-grained nuance in performance. (7)

Barry's formulation highlights all the ways in which time inflects the performance of music by requiring an interpretation from the musicians. At the broadest level, she suggests that pieces of music contain sections that shape time in what she terms "rhythms of ebb and flow." At the next level, smaller units of temporal measure determine the experience of time in "motifs and melodies." Finally, she suggests that these interpretations also exist at the micro level.

To give a concrete example of what this might mean in Rousseau's time—when arguably, aesthetic constraints on music were much more restrictive than they are today—let us take a performance of *Le devin du village*. Corresponding with Barry's "large-scale" stratum, we might consider the overall effect of the entire opera: how do the relative tempi of the different pieces of music that form the opera create a feeling of "ebb and flow"? At the next level, how does the recurrence of motifs from the overture in the arias condition our perception of the music? Does familiarity with the motifs alter our response? Within a specific aria, how does the return of motifs condition our sense of time? Finally, comparing performances, how does one soprano's performance of, for example, "J'ai perdu tout mon bonheur" differ from another's? Does the elongation of a syllable or the holding of a trill or grace note affect our perception of the music? This final consideration would correspond to what Barry calls "the music's fine-grained nuance in performance."

Performance necessitates making decisions on all of these levels in order to bring the notes on the page into temporal existence. Rousseau's understanding of time in music depends on a few key concepts that reveal the stakes in the insistence on temporality and performance. In the article "Mesure" from the *Dictionnaire de musique*, Rousseau attributes the development of meter in music to the ancient Greeks, arguing that song is not possible without rhythm: "chanter sans *Mesure* n'est pas chanter; et le sentiment de la *Mesure* n'étant pas moins naturel que celui de l'Intonation, l'invention de ces deux choses n'a pû se faire séparément" (5:889) [singing without meter is not singing, and the feeling of meter being no less natural than that of intonation, the invention of these two things could not have been done separately].¹² The accounts in both the version in the *Encyclopédie* and the later *Dictionnaire* underscore the importance of meter in prosody, linking the development of rhythm in music to the metrical conventions of poetics.

Beyond the developmental/historical account of music's links to the metrics of poetry, Rousseau provides other indications that rhythm and meter are essential to our apprehension and understanding of music. In the same article, "Mesure," from the *Dictionnaire*, he asserts in the opening definition the necessity of meter for our perception of music: "Division de la durée ou du tems en plusieurs parties égales, assez longues pour que l'oreille en puisse saisir et subdiviser la quantité, et assez courtes pour que l'idée de l'une ne s'efface pas avant le retour de l'autre, et qu'on en sente l'égalité" (5:889) [Division of duration or of time into several equal parts, long enough so that the ear is able to grasp and subdivide the quantity, and short enough so that the idea of the one is not erased before the return of the other, so that one may feel the equality].¹³ Meter in music provides a kind of internal structure for our perception of the parts that make up a piece of music. Rousseau stresses equality in his definition of meter, suggesting that rhythm helps us to subdivide a piece of music into equal constituent parts that guide our perception and experience of structure through repetition.¹⁴

In the *Lettre sur la musique française*, he develops the relation between meter and musical structure further, here arguing for an analogical relationship between music and language: "Passons maintenant à la mesure, dans le sentiment de laquelle consiste en grande partie la beauté de l'expression du chant. La mesure est à peu près à la mélodie ce que la Syntaxe est au discours: c'est elle qui fait l'enchaînement des mots, qui distingue les phrases et qui donne un sens, une liaison au tout" (5:293–94) [Let us now proceed to meter, in the feeling of which consists in large part the beauty of expression in song. Meter is approximately to melody as syntax is to discourse: it is what constitutes the link among the words, what distinguishes phrases, and what gives meaning, a connection to the whole]. While in the article "Mesure" he stresses the perception of equal parts, in the *Lettre* Rousseau attributes to meter a kind of syntactic function in music: rhythms help us perceive several elements of musical structure, including the ties between notes, motifs, and the relationship between the various parts and the whole. Beyond the cognitive function, meter provides the framework for the perception of beauty in music at least in so far as expression is concerned, echoing the earlier claim that singing without meter is impossible. The analogy to syntax is only approximate—the order of notes being determined by other factors in music—but the significance behind the parallel drawn is clear: without meter to structure music, we would only perceive an amorphous blob of sound without expression or meaning. Pleasing though it might be, without meter it would not *mean* anything to us.

Rousseau's strongest statement about the central role of rhythm in music occurs not surprisingly in the article "Rhythme." In the final paragraph of the entry in the *Dictionnaire*, he relates rhythm not only to structure and melody, but to imitation as well:

> Le *Rhythme* est une partie essencielle [sic] de la Musique, et surtout de l'imitative. Sans lui la Mélodie n'est rien, et par lui-même il est quelque chose, comme on le sent par l'effet des tambours. Mais d'où vient l'impression que font sur nous la Mesure et la Cadence? Quel est le principe par lequel ces retours tantôt égaux et tantôt variés affectent nos ames, et peuvent y porter le sentiment des passions? (5:1026)

> [*Rhythm* is an essential part of music, and above all of the imitative. Without it melody is nothing, and through it, it is something, as one can feel in the effect of drums. But where does the impression that meter and cadence has on us come from? What is the principle through which these sometimes equal, sometimes varied turns affect our souls and bring the feeling of the passions to it?]

Meter and cadence not only structure melody, but they are also responsible for the communication of feeling in music. In Rousseau's account, we are more affected by the flow of musical beat than the colors of the sound palette. Although Rousseau does attribute the usual ability to evoke specific emotion to certain types of sound, he does not neglect meter and rhythm in the process.[15] Continuing in his discussion, he again draws the parallel to prosody in poetics—as many in the French tradition had before him[16]—but highlighting the rhythmic dimension:

> Tout ce que nous pouvons dire ici est que, comme la Mélodie tire son caractère des accens de la Langue, le *Rhythme* tire le sien du caractère de la Prosodie; et alors il agit comme image de la parole: à quoi nous ajoûterons que certaines passions ont dans la nature un caractère rhythmique aussi bien qu'un caractère mélodieux, absolu et indépendant de la Langue; comme la tristesse, qui marche par Tems égaux

et lents, de même que par Tons rémisses et bas; la joie par Tems sautillans et vîtes, de même que par Tons aigus et intenses: d'où je présume qu'on pourroit observer dans toutes les autres passions un caractère propre. (5:1026)

[All that we can say here is that, as melody derives its character from the accents of language, *rhythm* derives its from the character of prosody; and in so doing acts like an image of speech: to which we will add that certain passions have a rhythmic character in nature as well as a melodic character, absolute and independent of language; like sadness that moves by equal and slow tempos, as well as by attenuated and low tones; joy by hopping and quick tempos, as well as by sharp and intense tones: from which I presume that one could observe in all the other passions a particular character.]

Rousseau does not depart from the standard wisdom that associates specific keys with specific emotions. He does, however, add the word "tems"—here perhaps best understood as a combination of tempo, meter, and measure, providing a pulse to music—to the equation, signaling the necessity of rhythm to evoke emotion. In the article "Tems" from the *Dictionnaire*, he further underscores the effect of rhythm and tempo on emotion: "Ce sont les durées relatives et proportionnelles de ces mêmes Sons qui fixent le vrai caractère d'une Musique, et lui donnent sa plus grande énergie. Le *Tems* est l'ame du Chant; les Airs dont la mesure est lente, nous attristent naturellement; mais un Air gai, vif et bien cadencé nous excite à la joie et à peine les pieds peuvent-ils se retenir de danser" (5:1112) [It is the relative and proportional durations of the same sounds that fix the true character of a piece of music and give it its greatest energy. *Time/tempo* is the soul of song; airs with slow meters naturally sadden us; but a gay, lively, well-cadenced air excites us to joy and our feet can barely be refrained from dancing]. The pulse of music creates an almost irresistible urge to move in time with the beat.

The dependence on rhythm for the expression of accent and passion in melody draws attention to the necessity of performance for the perception of beauty and emotion in music. While it seems fairly obvious that performance is required to move a listener—few are able to read scores and hear the music in their heads—Rousseau's account of rhythm suggests that performance enables the addition of several crucial elements to music's aesthetic existence. Performance requires the interpretation of the notes on the page and their transformation into a temporal sequence of sounds with fixed duration. Moreover, performance necessitates interpretation down to the minutest level of detail to create the emotion that exists in a virtual state in the score. Musicians create sound by applying rhythm, meter, tempo, and cadence based on notations in the score. This, in turn, helps to communicate movement and passion to the audience.

Accent, Passion, and Prosody

Music's existence in time stresses not only its performance, but also its effects on listeners. As others have shown, Rousseau's arguments in the *Essai sur l'origine des langues* stress the ways in which music moves listeners.[17] While other critics have underscored Rousseau's theory of the way in which music incites the passions through expression and imitation, I would like to consider this theory of the movement of the passions in relation to time and rhythm.

In his exhaustive study of time in musical performance entitled *Shaping Time*, David Epstein traces the similarities between our experiences of time and of music. Specifically with relation to motion, he argues that music is a specialized form of controlling motion, and time, through pacing and structure. In other words, the experience of motion or movement in music is a result of pacing that takes place through rhythm, meter, accent, beat, tempo, and pulse.[18] Epstein draws an analogy between the composer and the architect of a rollercoaster:

> Imagine commissioning an architect to build a roller coaster of any shape, length, curves, and contours that creativity might demand. The resulting structure would have to fulfill two conditions: first, that the sole source of power for its car be gravity. Thus, the car would have to start from on high, where the kinetic energy of its initial descent would "fuel" the rest of the ride. Second, the car would have to conclude its ride precisely at the end of the track, fully expending its energy by that point. . . . The parallel with musical time structure is obvious. By its network of rhythmic, metric, harmonic, melodic, and other constructs, all cofunctioning and intersecting upon various levels, a musical work likewise moves until its scheduled point of conclusion. Its time structure is the undergirding that controls motion. (27)

Our experience of music is conditioned by its structural components that allow us to feel it move through time and, in effect, control our experience of time. But what is the nature of this feeling or experience of time in music? Epstein asserts that motion has a direct effect on emotion. As is evident from the rollercoaster metaphor, music's development over time, with its twists, turns, bends, speeding up, and slowing down, produces an emotional response. As complexity develops, Epstein argues, there "are tensions that impel the music forward, that snare us in the uncertainties they create, carrying us along emotionally and physically as their interlocking complexities expand, ultimately to resolve at some future structural downbeat" (35).[19]

As we have just seen in his discussions of rhythm and meter, Rousseau attributes to the pulse of music the ability to move the listener. While he believes that the best music expresses something meaningful about the human condition through an imitation of the cries of passion or the accents of nature, he also suggests that the structuring of time that takes place through musical performance has an emotional effect on the listener. In the *Lettre sur la musique française*, part of the condemnation of French music lies precisely in the choice of tempo and meter conditioned by the constraints of French prosody. Rousseau rails against the dragging down of French opera by the lack of flexibility in the language:

> Le caractére traînant de la langue, le peu de flexibilité de nos voix, et le ton lamentable qui regne perpétuellement dans notre Opéra, mettent presque tous les monologues François sur un mouvement lent, et comme la mesure ne s'y fait sentir ni dans le chant, ni dans la Basse, ni dans l'accompagnement, rien n'est si traînant, si lâche, si languissant que ces beaux monologues que tout le monde admire en bâillant; ils voudroient être tristes et ne sont qu'ennuyeux; ils voudroient toucher le cœur et ne font qu'affliger nos oreilles. (5:317)

> [The dragging character of the language, the little flexibility of our voices, and the lamentable tone that perpetually reigns in our opera sets almost all French monologues in a slow movement, and as the beat does not make itself felt either in the song, or in the bass, or in the accompaniment, nothing is as dragging, as slack, as languishing as these beautiful monologues that everyone admires while yawning; they would like to be sad and are only boring; they would like to touch the heart and only afflict our ears.]

Such music, in Rousseau's estimation, cannot touch the heart, for it fails to engage the emotions because of the rhythmic choices. While many critics have examined the relation between language and music in this account, none have turned their attention to the metrical component. Rousseau maintains that the audience needs to be able to feel the pulse of the music in order to be moved by this form of expression. Strikingly, Rousseau claims that the meter (*mesure*) does not make itself felt to the audience, resulting in a boring and painful sound experience.[20]

How would such a feeling come about? How does time or pulse in music move listeners? The key in vocal music is what Rousseau calls accent, defined in the article from the *Dictionnaire* as "toute modification de la voix parlante, dans la durée, ou dans le ton des syllables et des mots dont le discours est composé; ce qui montre un rapport très-exact entre les deux usages des *Accens* et les deux parties de la Mélodie, savoir le Rythme et l'Intonation" (5:613) [any modification of the speaking voice, in its duration or in the tone of the syllables and the words of which the discourse is composed; which demonstrates a very precise relationship between the two uses of *accents* and the two parts of melody, namely, rhythm and intonation]. He goes on to develop the analogy between music and language, maintaining that there are types of accent appropriate to grammatical, logical, and oratory considerations (5:614). The first focus of the analysis thus privileges accent as a regulatory principle, providing a support for structure in language. The last category, the accent appropriate for oratory, enables the communication of emotion, "par diverses inflexions de voix, par un ton plus ou moins élevé, par un parler plus vif ou plus lent, [qui] exprime les sentimens dont celui qui parle est agité, et les communique à ceux qui l'écoutent" (5:614) [through the diverse inflections of voice, through a more or less elevated tone, through faster or slower speech, [that] expresses the sentiments by which the one who is speaking is agitated and communicates them to those who listen]. This last category of accent is most helpful to the musician attempting to express feeling.

According to Rousseau, the difficulty in composing moving music is in making the accents particular to discourse accord with the constraints of harmonic systems. In Rousseau's estimation, certain languages, like German and French, make this more difficult than, say, Italian. Nonetheless, all composers are faced with the same dilemma: how to observe the accents in discourse without sacrificing the accents required of the musical system. Rousseau concedes,

> On ne peut douter que la Musique la plus parfaite ou du moins la plus expressive, ne soit celle où tous les *Accens* sont le plus exactement observés; mais ce qui rend ce concours si difficile est que trop de regles dans cet Art sont sujettes à se contrarier mutuellement, et se

contrarient d'autant plus que la langue est moins musicale; car nulle
ne l'est parfaitement: autrement ceux qui s'en servent chanteroient au
lieu de parler. (5:615)

[One cannot doubt that the most perfect music or at least the most
expressive would be the one in which all the *accents* are observed the
most precisely; but what renders this concord so difficult is that the
rules in this art are subject to thwart one another mutually, and
thwart each other all the more in cases where the language is less
musical; for none is perfectly musical: otherwise those who use it
would sing instead of speaking.]

While there is no perfect solution, Rousseau does offer the criterion of
judgment that enables us to distinguish between expressive and unexpressive music: consistency with the accents of discourse that enables the communication of passion. In the case of French opera, the combination of bad prosody and poor rhythmic choices undermines the concordance between accents in the discourse and accent in the music, resulting in dull, drawling monologues that leave the audience cold.

While it is clear what happens when music fails to move the audience—listeners yawn, or worse, go home early—what happens when music works in the way that Rousseau advocates? What does it mean to move the passions for Rousseau? As Allan Bloom explains, Rousseau follows contemporary thinkers in believing that "passion is the only real power in the soul and that there is nothing in it capable of controlling the passions. Passion must control passion."[21] The passions, understood in more or less Cartesian terms, are movements internal to the psyche.[22] With an empiricist inflection from Condillac, it is the passions that help us to focus our attention, form ideas, and make sense of the world.[23] As a form of directed interest, they also enable us to make value judgments—from the simple judgment of, for example, what type of food will satisfy hunger, to the more complex judgment of what type of remedy will offer a satisfactory solution to a given situation, for example, what lullaby to sing a child to sleep. While they may sometimes lead us in the wrong direction, they can also be trained for positive results.

In the *Essai sur l'origine des langues*, Rousseau offers an example from discourse that sheds some light on the mechanism that he imagines. Distinguishing between the visual and the auditory, he privileges sound over sight to ignite the passions, and especially pity. Returning to the temporal sequencing argument that I cited above, he describes the effects of discourse in a rhythmical way: "L'impression successive du discours, qui frappe à coups redoublés vous donne bien une autre emotion que la presence de l'objet même où d'un coup d'oeil vous avez tout vû" (5:377) [The successive impression of the discourse that strikes in repeated blows gives you a very different emotion than the presence of the object itself, whereby in a glimpse you have seen everything]. The beating of the discourse (*frappe à coups redoublés*) seems to create a movement inside the listener, as Epstein suggests. Rousseau goes on to describe moving scenes of tragedy that depend on accent more than gesture to communicate, that is, physically move, the emotion from speaker to audience:[24]

> Les passions ont leurs gestes, mais elles ont aussi leurs accens, et ces accens qui nous font tressaillir, ces accens auxquels on ne peut dérober son organe pénétrent par lui jusqu'au fond du coeur, y portent malgré nous les mouvemens qui les arrachent, et nous font sentir ce que nous entendons. (5:378)

> [Passions have their gestures, but they also have their accents, and these accents that make us shudder, these accents from which we cannot shield our organ penetrate through it to the bottom of the heart, carrying in spite of us the movements that wrest them, and make us feel what we hear.]

The violence of the description is unmistakable: Sounds penetrate our ears and forcibly stir us, making the physical properties of sound as relevant as the temporal sequencing. The repeated blows of discourse or music rap on our hearts through the entryway that cannot be shielded, the ears. This makes us *feel*, as an involuntary movement in our bodies (like the beating of the heart when a marching band passes), the passion of the music.

But the effect is not just physical. Rousseau is clear on this point: "Voyez comment tout nous ramêne sans cesse aux effets moraux dont j'ai parlé, et combien les musiciens qui ne considérent la puissance des sons que par l'action de l'air et l'ébranlement des fibres sont loin de connoitre en quoi réside la force de cet art" (5:422) [You see how everything continually brings us back to the moral effects of which I have spoken, and how far the musicians that only consider the power of sounds in terms of the action of the air and the shaking of the fibers are from knowing where the force of this art resides]. Stirring the emotions through sounds entails tapping into moral sentiments and moving the audience.[25] If accent is applied correctly, the sound will penetrate to the heart and awaken feelings of passion. Ideally, the experience should awaken the most positive of passions: virtue. As Bloom points out, virtue represents a "special kind of complex passion," for it enables human beings to overcome their particular self-interest and experience a form of passion that is other-oriented.[26]

Not unlike the famous passage from the *Essai* in which Rousseau describes the tropological and figurative use of language prior to its literal use (5:381–82),[27] he attributes to musical signs an affective component that, like figurative language, communicates emotion: "Les sons dans la mélodie n'agissent pas seulement sur nous comme sons, mais comme signes de nos affections, de nos sentimens; c'est ainsi qu'ils excitent en nous les mouvemens qu'ils expriment et dont nous y reconnaissons l'image" (5:417) [Sounds in melody not only act on us as sounds, but also as signs of our affections, of our sentiments; it is in this way that they excite in us the movements that they express and whose image we recognize]. When we are moved by melody the movement that is communicated to the heart functions as a sign. Rousseau cannot escape the visual metaphor of image, but seems to suggest that, like the primitive man who calls the first human he sees "giant" to communicate his fear, music carries an emotional charge that functions on a very basic level. Rhythmic, organized sounds can help us to feel sensations that go beyond the merely physical to the moral.

I would suggest that the emphasis on temporal sequencing, as well as the insistence on the physical beating of discourse and music, indicates a significant rhythmic component to the musical sign. Beyond considerations of prosody or accent in language, the necessity of rhythmic pulse to communicate passion foregrounds the importance of performance in order for music to realize its potential as a moral sign. In other words, the temporal existence of music necessitates the creation of a rhythmic pulse that enables the communication of movement vital to stirring the passions and moral sentiments.

## The Moral Dimension: Communication, Community, and Aesthetic Reception

If good musical performance touches an ethical chord in listeners and performers alike, it is because they are *moved* by the experience. And, as we have seen, music "moves" in terms of passions and emotions, but also through a common experience of time. Until now, I have not distinguished between the individual listening to music and the audience as a whole. Indeed, Rousseau does not make a distinction between the two experiences.

Returning to my warning at the outset to bear in mind the lack of recordings in the eighteenth century, the distinction between a single person listening to a performance and an audience seems almost meaningless in the historical context: only the soloist performing alone could experience what we routinely feel while listening to MP3 players. A soloist performing for an audience of one—no doubt a rare occurrence—still constitutes a group of two sharing a musical experience. Most often, a small group of musicians plays for a small audience, creating a group dynamic.

As we have seen, performance requires tempo, metrical, and rhythmic choices that help to bring music to life. If these choices are made in effective ways, the regular motion of the music will move the audience, touching them in their hearts. In the ideal performance, musicians and listeners, conditioned by the structures of tempo, meter, accent, and rhythm feel time together, all at once. I would suggest that the experience of music enables a shared experience of time. Taking their cue from the musicians, the audience experiences the flow of time conditioned by all the temporal elements defined by Barry that together create the pulse of the music. The musicians enable the conditions through which the social group—audience and performers—shares a common experience of time. In this respect, the social group bonds over the regular, rhythmic movement, feeling, almost as if in one body, the rhythmic pulse of the music.

The act of listening to music together enables them to share a common structure for experience, at least temporarily binding them together.[28] Turning to *Du contrat social*, the common experience of time by musicians and audience sheds new light on some of the more difficult passages related to group formation and the general will. Rousseau famously describes the social contract as resulting in the creation of a collectivity bound by a single identity:

> A l'instant, au lieu de la personne particuliere de chaque contractant, cet acte d'association produit un corps moral et collectif composé d'autant de membres que l'assemblée a de voix, lequel reçoit de ce même acte son unité, son *moi* commun, sa vie et sa volonté. (3:361)
>
> [At that moment, instead of the individual person of each contractor, this act of association produces a moral and collective body composed of as many members as the assembly has voices, which receives from this same act its unity, its common *self*, its life and its will.]

In the instance of live musical performance, the same kind of association takes place as the listeners and musicians form a *moi commun* that feels the pulse of the music together. The rhythmic pulse awakens feelings that the group shares, representing a kind of repeatable enacting of the primordial moment of the social contract.[29] Musicians and audience who share in the performance experience will feel the kind of common bond that serves as the foundation for all community.

It is significant that Rousseau insists that musical signs are more than physical and, indeed, carry a moral charge. The group dynamic absent the moral component would only create the conditions for a shared pleasurable experience. The *moi commun* might feel that beating of its common heart in the music and simply experience the pleasure and beauty of synchronicity. Instead, the communication of moral feeling in music has ethical and political implications. As a sign, music has the ability to excite the passions in each one of us, but it does more than just that. Returning to Bloom's contention that virtue represents a complex passion in Rousseau, Bloom's argument turns on the move from particular wills to a generalized will in the *Social Contract*. Bloom reads the general will as a generalized form of will in each individual contractor: a proto-Kantian impartial perspective. The social contract instantiates a situation in which each individual must struggle between the dictates of his or her "particular desire" and his or her "general will, a will recognized as nonarbitrary and good." According to Bloom, "self-overcoming is the essence of moral experience" for Rousseau ("Rousseau's Critique," 157). This Kantian reading of Rousseau, with its implication of a kind of *sensus communis* that enables shared moral experience, finds support in many passages from not only the *Social Contract* but also the *Second Discourse* and the *Essay on the Origin of Languages*.[30] The mutual and reciprocal demands of the social contract underscore the common experience that enables such a contract to exist in the first place: "Les engagemens qui nous lient au corps social ne sont obligatoires que parce qu'ils sont mutuels, et leur nature est telle qu'en les remplissant on ne peut travailler pour autrui sans travailler aussi pour soi" (3:373) [The engagements that tie us to the social body are only obligatory because they are mutual, and their nature is such that in fulfilling them one cannot work for another without also working for oneself].

Rousseau never makes an explicit connection between the arguments in the *Social Contract* and elsewhere concerning a common emotional and psychological makeup and the ability for music to function as a moral sign. However, I would argue that the formulations from the *Essai* clearly point to the notion that as humans we create language and music out of a shared need to communicate our inner lives: "Sitot qu'un homme fut reconnu par un autre pour un Etre sentant, pensant et semblable à lui, le desir ou le besoin de lui communiquer ses sentimens et ses pensées lui en fit chercher les moyens" (5:375) [As soon as a man was recognized by another as a feeling being, thinking and similar to himself, the desire or the need to communicate to him his feelings and his thoughts made him seek the means to do so]. Our common affective structures enable and indeed necessitate communication through language and music. Just as we all have *amour de soi* and *pitié*, we all have emotional lives that we feel the need to communicate through language and music.

When music in particular taps into these common affective structures, we experience the same emotions as those around us. In other words, while listening to a piece of music being performed as the member of an audience, we all shed a tear in response to the motion of the music. The more the music can express common feelings by moving us collectively through the structuring of time using meter, rhythm, accent, tempo, and beat, the more the audience will respond with a shared reaction: the creation of a *moi commun*. In these moments, I would argue, the general will is constituted as the group experiences its common humanity through shared emotional response.[31]

Rousseau's formulations of the ways in which the general will or common interest is fostered and created are notoriously problematic. Critics have long debated the totalitarian tendencies of the suppression of individual expression in favor of group cohesion in the *Social Contract*, *Project for Corsica*, and *Considerations on the Government of Poland*.[32] In the following chapter, I will examine the ways in which a reading of Rousseau's music theory may shed new light on the normative constraints that determine the general will. For now, I would like to raise the question of the conflict between particular and group interests in the formation of the community. The *Social Contract* famously leaves the conflict between particular and general interests unresolved, failing to provide a satisfactory answer to the question of how it is that the group comes to embody the general will.[33] Already, in the instance of musical performance, we have a situation in which particular and group interests merge, at least temporarily, insofar as the group simultaneously experiences the same emotional effects from the music.

If music succeeds in evoking the same passion in each individual in such a way as to help create a *moi commun* through this collective emotion, it may also help to mitigate the effect of particular interests in other ways. The simultaneous experience of a common moral feeling suggests that music elicits a moral group response. If music is able to help promote the formation of the general will, it must do so in part by helping to suppress particular interests. In some respect, in order to foster the constitution of a moral community, music must appeal to a transcendent form of passion that overcomes particular interests in favor of the common interest. In other words, the group response should engage each individual's virtue in such a way that a collective experience of virtue or general will may emerge.

In the "Profession de foi du vicaire Savoyard," Rousseau has the vicar espouse a doctrine of mind/body dualism that imagines human nature in a constant struggle between the dictates of the baser passions and a higher calling:

> En méditant sur la nature de l'homme, j'y crus découvrir deux principes distincts, dont l'un l'élevoit à l'étude des vérités éternelles, à l'amour de la justice et du beau moral, aux régions du monde intellectuel, dont la contemplation fait les délices du sage, et dont l'autre le ramenoit bassement en lui-même, l'asservissoit à l'empire des sens, aux passions qui sont leurs ministres, et contrarioit par elles tout ce que lui inspiroit le sentiment du prémier. En me sentant entraîné, combattu par ces deux mouvemens contraires, je me disois: non, l'homme n'est point un; je veux et je ne veux pas, je me sens à la fois esclave et libre; je vois le bien, je l'aime, et je fais le mal: je suis actif quand j'écoute la raison, passif quand mes passions m'entrainent; et mon pire tourment quand je succombe, est de sentir que j'ai pu resister. (4:583)

> [In meditating on the nature of man, I believe that I have discovered there two distinct principles, of which one elevates him to the study of eternal verities, to the love of justice and to moral beauty, to the regions of the intellectual world the contemplation of which constitutes the delights of the sage, and of which the other brings him basely back to himself, subjects him to the empire of the senses, to the passions that are its ministers, and thwarts through them everything that the first feeling inspired in him. In feeling myself pulled, beaten by these two contradictory movements, I said to myself: no, man is not one. I want and I don't want; I feel myself to be a slave and free at the same time; I see the good, I love it, and I do evil; I am active when I listen to reason, passive when my passions carry me away; and my worse torment when I succumb is to feel that I could have resisted.]

While there is nothing particularly striking about the mind/body dualism or the struggle that it engenders, this formulation reinforces Bloom's interpretation of moral experience in Rousseau as a form of self-overcoming.

Rousseau has the vicar go on to maintain that overcoming the baser passions by listening to the voice of conscience enables us to find contentment: "La suprême jouïssance est dans le contentement de soi-même; c'est pour mériter ce contentement que nous sommes placés sur la terre et doüés de la liberté, que nous sommes tentés par les passions et retenus par la conscience" (4:587) [The supreme pleasure is contentment with self; it is in order to merit this contentment that we are placed on this earth and endowed with liberty, that we are tempted by the passions and retained by conscience]. While this struggle is noble and defines human beings as moral beings, certain experiences might help us to move closer to self-contentment and reconciliation.

If music can facilitate the overcoming of baser passions, then it represents an aesthetic experience that, while pleasurable in itself (it resides in the realm of the senses), also provides access to the supreme (intellectual) pleasure of self-reconciliation. By sparking a type of moral feeling, it engages the passions not in the base form, but rather in the exalted form, nullifying the struggle between passion and conscience. In other words, the passions are redirected toward a moral goal when listening to music, enabling each individual to experience the supreme pleasure of self-contentment. And, because musical performance must happen in a group setting, the pleasure of self-contentment is replicated in each individual present, creating a group moral feeling. I believe that it is this feeling that comes closest to what Rousseau imagines for the general will. Ideally, the community bonded over common moral sentiment could act out of common interest and the general good.

The Problem of Identification

The common moral feeling evoked through musical performance depends, at least in part, on identical structures in all listeners. In other words, invoking a Kantian form of argument, the community formed through music comes into being because of similar psychological and moral faculties, geared toward this type of aesthetic reception.[34] I now turn to the texts in which Rousseau addresses aesthetic reception most explicitly in order to try to tease out the mechanisms for a positive aesthetic and moral response. The *Letter to d'Alembert* and *Julie* offer competing accounts of aesthetic reception.

The question of aesthetic reception implicitly raises the question of overcoming heterogeneity within the community. In other words, attempting to elicit a response from an audience—the same response in each individual—

necessarily addresses the issue of overcoming differences among individuals in order to create a group response. While at times Rousseau suggests that ensuring communal consensus depends on constructing identical interests and values, this solution begs the question of overcoming more fundamental forms of difference.[35] Imposing values in order to foster community does not eliminate the potential conflict within the community that always threatens to undermine it, and of which Rousseau is keenly aware, namely, between particular and general interests. Viewed from this perspective, Rousseau's republican community, although engineered to minimize difference, nonetheless is always already internally threatened by its dependence on individuals. Particular wills can always undermine the pronouncements of the general will: "En effet chaque individu peut comme homme avoir une volonté particuliere contraire ou dissemblable à la volonté générale qu'il a comme Citoyen. Son intérêt particulier peut lui parler tout autrement que l'intérêt commun" (3:363) [In effect each individual can as a man have a particular will contrary or dissimilar to the general will that he has as a citizen. His particular interest can speak to him entirely differently than the common interest]. Indeed, in this formulation each individual potentially leads a double life internally divided between self- and group-interest. Although Rousseau asserts repeatedly that acting in the common interest is ultimately the same thing as acting out of self-interest, the practical provisions for government made in *Social Contract*, *Project for Corsica*, and *Government of Poland* all belie the faith in the individual to overcome his or her own particular interests.

A theory of aesthetic reception offers the potential to overcome this difference that always threatens to shatter the republican community. If individuals can be brought together to experience the same feelings, at the same time, in the same place, then there is hope for the emergence of the general will. By forming a *moi commun* through aesthetic experience, the group may be in a better position to instantiate the general will in political deliberations.

To begin by way of negative example, *Lettre à d'Alembert* provides a clear indication of what Rousseau does not want to happen: the alienating effects of aesthetic experience in the theater.[36] Part of the problem resides in the need to please theater audiences, setting up situations in which vices and base passions are encouraged. In this respect, Rousseau asserts emphatically that theater cannot be used to "changer des sentimens ni des moeurs qu'il ne peut que suivre et embellir" (5:18) [change feelings or mores that it can only follow and embellish]. Rousseau does not view theater as a potential vehicle for change, but rather as a reinforcement of existing national character (5:19).

Rousseau's critique of the Aristotelian theory of catharsis relies on the notion that rather than being purged, the passions are instead excited by dramatic performance.[37] Spectators do not leave the theater cleansed of base passion, but rather animated by strong emotion. In response to the theory of catharsis, Rousseau asserts,

> Il ne faut, pour sentir la mauvaise foi de toutes ces réponses, que consulter l'état de son coeur à la fin d'une tragedie. L'émotion, le trouble, et l'attendrissement qu'on sent en soi-même et qui se prolonge après la pièce, annoncent-ils une disposition bien prochaine à surmonter et régler nos passions? (5:19)

> [It is only necessary, in order to feel the bad faith of all these responses, to consult the state of one's heart at the end of a tragedy. The emotion, the agitation, and the feeling of pity that one feels in oneself and that is prolonged after the play, do they announce a disposition close to surmounting and regulating our passions?]

Stirring the passions in this way, rather than promoting group cohesion and values, in the case of the theater tends to promote self-interest.[38] Due in part to the subject matter of French theater—Rousseau devotes many pages to discussions of specific plays—the audience cannot be expected to walk away with a morally uplifting experience. Instead, individual spectators identify with different characters and, famously, carry away lessons such as how to be a misanthrope without seeming like one.

Again, the problem lies in self-interest:

> Le coeur de l'homme est toujours droit sur tout ce qui ne se rapporte pas personnellement à lui. Dans les querelles dont nous sommes purement Spectateurs, nous prenons à l'instant le parti de la justice, et il n'y a point d'acte de méchanceté qui ne nous donne une vive indignation, tant que nous n'en tirons aucun profit: mais quand nôtre intérêt s'y mêle, bientôt nos sentimens se corrompent; et c'est alors seulement que nous préférons le mal qui nous est utile, au bien que nous fait aimer la nature. (5:22)

> [The heart of man is always correct on everything that does not relate to him personally. In quarrels to which we are purely spectators, we

instantly take the side of justice, and there is no act of meanness that does not give us sharp indignation, as long as we do not derive any profit from it: but when our interest is mixed up in it, soon our feelings are corrupted; and it is only then that we prefer the evil that is useful to us to the good that makes us love nature.]

Theater has a tendency to encourage the bad side of human nature by awakening self-interest rather than the nobler moral sentiments. As long as our self-interest is not engaged, we remain impartial spectators rooting for the side of justice. Unfortunately, our self-interest rarely lies dormant. Rousseau attributes this result not only to the content of French plays, but also to the circumstances of theatrical production and reception, as well as to the notoriously bad morals of actors. He famously criticizes the use of the theater as a kind of public sphere to see and be seen that promotes *amour propre*—directly opposed to the kind of civic space desirable in a republican democracy. But the problem goes beyond the potential cooptation of the public realm by the theatergoing audience. A kind of alienation occurs in theater reception that promotes, rather than suppresses, a self-interested response.

Rousseau makes it clear that although individuals come together to form an audience, they do not truly come together. Instead, they isolate themselves from one another: "L'on croit s'assembler au Spectacle, et c'est là que chacun s'isole; c'est là qu'on va oublier ses amis, ses voisins, ses proches, pour s'intéresser à des fables, pour pleurer les malheurs des morts, ou rire aux dépens des vivans" (5:16) [We believe that we gather together in the theater, and it's there that each one is isolated; it's there that one goes to forget one's friends, one's neighbors, one's relatives, to take an interest in fable, to cry over the misfortunes of the dead or to laugh at the expense of the living]. Moral feelings of relationship are forgotten before fictive tales that only exaggerate distance instead of overcoming it.[39] Toward the end of the *Lettre*, Rousseau contrasts this experience with public festivals that are held outdoors, suggesting that the confines of the theater contribute to the kind of reception that he imagines.[40] Echoing the platonic formulation in *The Republic*, the audience, "un petit nombre de gens dans un antre obscur" [a small number of people in a dark cave] are held "craintifs et immobiles dans le silence et l'inaction" (5:114) [fearful and immobile in silence and inaction].[41] Dramatic productions only *seemingly* create a group. Instead, Rousseau argues that theater produces alienated spectators isolated from one another, their passions enflamed by the spectacles to which they bear witness.[42]

The model from the theater serves as a warning and counterexample to what Rousseau seeks to create through musical performance. Combating self-interest with collective interest in order to foster the general will is key to promoting the right kind of group experience. As we have seen, the role of the passions is essential to ensuring that the group dynamic unites the community through common moral sentiment. If the passions are engaged in the wrong way, that is, in the way that they are in theater, performance runs the risk of undermining community by reinforcing self-interest.

*Julie, ou la nouvelle Héloïse* offers a potentially more satisfactory model for the kind of aesthetic experience that Rousseau envisions for music, one that would be more morally uplifting. Nicholas Paige has recently argued that readers of *Julie* were not as gullible as Robert Darnton's influential reading of the fan mail would lead many to believe.[43] Paige asserts that the readers did not believe "that the letters are real, nor even that Rousseau stumbled upon their story and wrote it up with his inimitable talent. They conclude, rather, that *La Nouvelle Héloïse* must be inspired by Rousseau's own experience."[44] Citing from the fan mail, Paige underscores a kind of identification that takes place between reader and author through the intermediary of the characters. Opposed to a theory of aesthetic contagion that would posit a movement of passion from character to reader, Paige instead highlights an identification with the author that places the reader within the narrative, but as a "compassionate observer" rather than as a fellow actor.[45] Paige describes a mechanism whereby readers are able to identify with the moral sentiments that gave rise to the fiction rather than with the fiction itself, enabling aesthetic distance from characters and events, while at the same time preserving the capacity to feel along with the characters.

Paige's reading of the contemporary reception of *Julie* responds to difficulties posed by the theory of aesthetic reception articulated in the two prefaces to the novel. Specifically in the second preface, R (Rousseau's mouthpiece in the dialogue) refuses to answer the question posed about whether the letters are real or fictive. While Rousseau answers for the letters, he will not say definitely whether or not the characters ever existed. The force of the letters, according to R, resides in their ability to communicate feeling to the reader. Distinguishing between a love letter written by an author and a real love letter, R maintains that while the former might be better written, it will not really move the reader. The real love letter will contain:

> Rien de saillant, rien de remarquable; on ne retient ni mots, ni tours, ni phrases; on n'admire rien, l'on n'est frappé de rien. Cependant on

se sent l'ame attendrie; on se sent ému sans savoir pourquoi. Si la force du sentiment ne nous frappe pas, sa vérité nous touche, et c'est ainsi que le cœur sait parler au cœur. (2:15)

[Nothing outstanding, nothing remarkable; one retains neither words, nor turns of phrase, nor sentences; one admires nothing, one is struck by nothing. Nonetheless, one feels one's soul softened; one feels moved without knowing why. If the force of the sentiment does not strike us, its truth touches us, and it is in this way that the heart knows how to speak to the heart.]

Lack of stylistic sophistication in fact enables the communication of true feeling. It is as if the ornaments of style impede the transmission of sentiment from the written text to the reader. And while the second preface never admits that Rousseau is the author of *Julie*, and the citation above continues to insist on a distinction between real and fictive letters, nonetheless the core of the argument maintains that letters containing authentic feeling will be able to communicate that feeling to their readers, if stylistic concerns do not impede that transmission. What seems to matter more than their fictional or nonfictional status is the truth of the feeling expressed in the letters. Rousseau's willingness to have his name appear on the collection of letters—to answer for it, as he says in the second preface (2:27)—underscores their truth value. In a sense, by vouching for the letters, he attaches his name to the sentiments expressed. Whether or not they are real or fictive does not matter in the end. Paige's reading of the fan mail suggests that readers felt that the feelings expressed in *Julie* were true, in the sense that they were authentic and readers associated those feelings with the author.

Paige further distances the reception of *Julie* from theater reception as described in the *Lettre à d'Alembert*, by highlighting places in the correspondence addressed to Rousseau where readers reference their own feelings and emotional lives. Whereas in the theater they are tempted to share the emotions of flawed and immoral characters, the identification with *Julie* is fueled by a kind of self-discovery. Paige writes, "The power of *La Nouvelle Héloïse* derives from its uncanny likeness to the inner world of its readers. Identification does not lie in becoming what you are not—as in the old model of emotional transport—but in recognizing what you already are."[46] Readers experience strong emotion because the world represented feels familiar to them.

Together, the identification with Rousseau as source of the moral feeling in the novel and the readers' self-discovery in the emotions of the characters creates a model for identification that does not require one-on-one match-ups between reader and work of art. Instead, the model from *Julie* suggests that readers could experience emotion and, in so doing, discover hidden emotions within themselves. The novel speaks to them and moves them because it taps moral sentiment in a way that gives them a clearer understanding of who they are.

But novels are usually read in private. Although in the eighteenth century it was not uncommon for novels to be read aloud to a group, novel reading and the response that it elicits does not offer a particularly effective model for group dynamics. We are left with a dilemma: the theater isolates and separates, encouraging self-interested passion, while the novel sparks moral feeling, but in individuals. In order to construct a model for music reception, it will be necessary to build on the positive aspects of novel reading while avoiding the pitfalls of theater reception.

Identification and the Overcoming of Distance: Rhythm

In nearly identical passages in the *Essai sur l'origine des langues* and the *Dictionnaire de musique*, Rousseau reveals how it is that composers tap into the emotions of listeners through a kind of imitation. I will discuss the problem of mimesis in music in detail in chapter 5, but for now let us look briefly at an articulation of the effect of imitation in music that parallels what we have just seen at work in *Julie*. Rousseau maintains that it is not actual sounds that are imitated, but rather the movements one experiences before particular objects that are imitated in the movement of the music.

> Que toute la Nature soit endormie, celui qui la contemple ne dort pas, et *l'art du Musicien consiste à substituer à l'image insensible de l'objet celle des mouvemens que sa présence excite dans le cœur du Contemplateur.* Non-seulement il agitera la Mer, animera la flamme d'un incendie, fera couler les ruisseaux, tomber la pluie et grossir les torrens; mais il peindra l'horreur d'un desert affreux, rembrunira les murs d'une prison souterraine, calmera la tempête, rendra l'air tranquille et serein, et répandra de l'Orchestre une fraîcheur nouvelle sur les boccages. *Il ne représentera pas directement ces choses, mais il excitera dans l'ame les mêmes mouvemens qu'on éprouve en les voyant.* (5:861, my emphasis)[47]

[Let all of nature be asleep, he who contemplates it is not sleeping, and *the art of the musician consists in substituting for the imperceptible image of the object the movements that its presence excites in the heart of the one who contemplates.* Not only will he agitate the sea, animate the flame of fire, make the streams run, the rain fall, and the torrents swell, but he will also paint the horror of an awful desert, darken the walls of an underground prison, calm the tempest, make the air tranquil and serene, and will spread a new freshness over the groves from the orchestra. *He will not directly represent these things, but he will excite in the soul the same movements that one feels in seeing them.*]

Listeners in a concert hall or in a salon do not hear imitations of the sounds of nature; instead the music moves them in the same way that they would be moved if they were before these natural scenes. Parallel to the experience of reading *Julie*, listeners "recognize" the movement of the passions that occurs while they listen and make associations, in this case with the feelings they have had before natural phenomena. Whereas in reading *Julie* they felt emotions that enabled them to recognize themselves, in listening to the right kind of music listeners feel familiar sentiments accrued from past experience. They feel the rhythmic pulse of the music in such a way that awakens feelings of fear, calm, joy, pain, anger, or security. The feelings are not merely physical sensations, but are also moral feelings, associated with experiences from the past.

What distinguishes this effect from the effect of theater, I would argue, lies precisely in the familiarity of the feelings.[48] Listeners in a concert hall and readers of *Julie* discover their own feelings in the feelings evoked by the music. In other words, what enables these aesthetic modes of expression to be received in the way Rousseau envisages is the reliance on the awakening of feelings the audience has already had. While listening to a piece of music, members of the audience enjoy the pleasure of self-discovery through the feelings set in motion by the work.

What also distinguishes the musical experience from the theatrical one is the presence of rhythm. By carefully controlling time, the performers are able to shape the audience's experience of the movement of the music in such a way as to create a common group pulse. This beating of the music works against the alienation experienced by theatergoers by overcoming the isolation of the individuals that compose the audience. Instead, the musical audience feels the common beat of the music and knows that his or her neighbor in the next seat feels the same thing. Rather than awaken self-interest and other negative forms of passion, music works to overcome self-interest through the group dynamic of a common pulse. In a sense, the passion awakened is shared by the community. Although Rousseau never uses the word to describe it, the shared passion resembles compassion: but rather than a shared form of suffering—like *pitié*—the group dynamic of aesthetic reception enables shared feelings of belonging. By simultaneously awakening moral feelings in the collective audience, I believe that Rousseau intends for music to work to create the bonds of community. As Samuel Floyd Jr. maintains for African American music, for Rousseau as well, "the expectation is that something musical will *happen* in the playing of the music."[49] What "happens" in the musical experience unites aesthetic performance and reception with moral sentiment and, as I shall argue, political community.

In the next chapter, I turn to the specific question of the democratic community in Rousseau to examine the functioning of the general will in relation to the group dynamics of musical performance. Attention to performance practice provides new insight into the normative function of the general will in group deliberations.

# 2

## Singing Democracy: Music and Politics

Ce qu'on appelle union, dans un corps politique, est une chose très équivoque; la vraie est une union d'harmonie, qui fait que toutes les parties, quelque opposées qu'elles nous paraissent, concourent au bien général de la société; comme les dissonances, dans la musique, concourent à l'accord total. Il peut y avoir de l'union dans l'Etat où on ne croit voir que du trouble; c'est-à-dire une harmonie d'où résulte le bonheur, qui seul est la vraie paix.

— MONTESQUIEU, *Considérations sur les causes de la grandeur des Romains et de leur décadence*

In American life, you have all of these different agendas. You have conflict all the time. And we're attempting to achieve harmony through conflict. Which it seems strange to say that, but it's like an argument that you have with the intent to work something out, not an argument that you have with the intent to argue. And that's what jazz music is. You have musicians and they're all standing on a bandstand. Each one has their personality and their agenda.... So you have that question of the integrity, the intent, the will to play together. That's what jazz music is. You have yourself, your individual expression and then you have how you negotiate that expression in the context of that group. And, it's exactly like democracy.

— WYNTON MARSALIS, *Jazz*, a film by Ken Burns

Democratic theory, and particularly Rousseau's, is suffused with the idealism and lack of pragmatism that make it both immensely compelling and extraordinarily frustrating. Conceived under the decaying edifice of the absolute monarchy, it strives toward perfection, offering theoretical formulations that often defy practical application. And yet this theory continues to inspire democratic practice and political debates even more than two hundred years after its writing.

One of the key problems of interpreting Rousseau's political theory concerns the conception of democracy. Indeed, in one passage of *Du contrat social* Rousseau asserts, "S'il y avoit un peuple de Dieux, il se gouverneroit Démocratiquement. Un Gouvernement si parfait ne convient pas à des hommes" (3:406). [If there were a people of Gods, it would govern itself democratically. Such a perfect government is not suited to men]. And yet the thrust of the work and the critical force of Rousseau's corpus encourage and challenge us to strive toward democracy, as impossible a goal as it may be for mere mortals.

Music in the eighteenth century suffers from many of the same difficulties that political theory does, chief among them the tendency toward a level of abstraction that defies practical application. Like the problem of democracy in the eighteenth century, music also presents the temptation of retreat into a world of abstract perfection based on mathematical certainty with little relation to practical reality. Perhaps nowhere is the tension as acute between the ideal and the real in music as in the domain of tuning and, specifically, in keyboard tuning and the question of tempering. So, as in the political domain, there is a potentially wide gulf between music theory and music practice.

Unlike his political theory, however, Rousseau's work in music was founded in practice, as we have just seen with respect to performance. In the following pages, I propose to explore the relationship between singing and the political practice of democracy in Rousseau's work. If there is any hope of realizing democracy in the way that Rousseau understood it, then an exploration of his work on music may provide the crucial bridge between theory and practice.

Rousseau's theoretical work in music—and singing in particular—covers a number of distinct subject areas. First, his proposal for a new system of musical notation links directly to democratic impulses in his political and social theory. Second, the kinds of emotions that music stirs are related in Rousseau's thought to forms of expression that remain closer to their natural origins. Finally, I will demonstrate that Rousseau's preference for melody, as opposed to harmony, relates directly to his conception of the political sphere and, specifically, to the relationship between the general will and the workings of the body politic in a democracy. Unexpectedly, reading Rousseau's musical theory alongside his democratic theory produces a nuanced and moderate view of the social contract, one that deepens our understanding of the relationship between relative and absolute values, in politics as well as in music, while offering a model for practice.

## Musical Notation and Democracy

A distinctly democratic impulse motivates the *Projet concernant de nouveaux signes pour la musique*: Rousseau's revision of the musical notation system is designed to increase accessibility to music. With characteristic rhetoric, Rousseau introduces his project for "simplifying" musical notation with a short, to-the-point paragraph: "Ce projet tend à rendre la Musique plus commode à notter, plus aisée à apprendre, et beaucoup moins diffuse" (5:133). [This project tends to make music easier to write down, easier to learn, and much less diffuse]. Following this statement of purpose, Rousseau relates, in a contrastive rhetorical style—replete with specialized vocabulary—the current state of affairs in musical notation:

> Cette quantité de lignes, de Clefs, de transpositions, de dièses, de bemols, de bécarres, de mesures simples et composées, de rondes, de blanches, de noires, de croches, de doubles croches, de triples croches, de pauses, de demi pauses, de soupir, de demi soupir, de quarts de soupir, etc. donne une foule de signes et de combinaisons d'où résultent deux inconvéniens principaux: l'un d'occuper un trop grand volume, et l'autre de surcharger la mémoire des Ecoliers de façon que l'oreille êtant formée et les Organes aiant acquis toutte la facilité nécessaire longtems avant qu'on soit en état de chanter à Livre ouvert, il s'ensuit que la difficulté est bien plus dans l'observation des régles que dans l'exécution du chant. (5:133)

> [This quantity of lines, keys, transpositions, of sharps, flats, naturals, of simple and complex measures, of whole notes, half notes, quarter notes, eighth notes, sixteenth notes, thirty-second notes, of rests, half rests, quarter rests, eighth rests, sixteenth rests, etc., gives a quantity of signs and combinations from which result two principle inconveniences: the first, to occupy too great a volume, and the second, to overload the memory of schoolchildren in such a way that the ear being formed and the organs having acquired all the necessary facility long before one is capable of singing from a book, it follows that the difficulty is more in the observation of rules than in the execution of the song.]

Already in the opening paragraphs, it is apparent that the new system is designed to bring music to a greater number of people. The enumeration of technical terms in the description of the traditional system for musical notation highlights the difficulties of penetrating what appears to the noninitiate to be a secret code.[1] Moreover, his claims about schoolchildren—that musical notation actually inhibits their ability to sing—imply that "natural ability" is being hindered by the current system. In contrast, his new system offers wider accessibility to a broader public, due to material advantages related to the reduction in printing costs and easier transport, and to the pedagogical advantages related to greater ease in reading music (5:154).[2] Rousseau suggests that if his system for musical notation were adopted, more people would have access to music: they would learn to read music and gain an understanding of its principles more easily and quickly, as well as have easier access to musical texts. The result would be an enlarged community of musicians who could perform music together.[3]

What are the advantages of an enlarged community of individuals capable of reading music and singing together? It seems clear that the egalitarian impulse here echoes Enlightenment themes of bringing technical knowledge to the people. This type of "enlightenment" supports the political goals of democratic theory to create the most egalitarian and homogeneous populous possible.[4] But the desire to create a broader "singing public" seems to go beyond the desire to dismantle an elitist form of culture, although clearly that desire is present as well. Rousseau wants to return singing "to the people" and, in so doing, restore something that is missing from contemporary music.

In practical terms, adopting Rousseau's new system will enable individuals to learn to read music and then join with other musicians in order to perform together.[5] The new system of musical notation will help to unify or create more tangible bonds between members of a "musical community." But this desire does not go far enough in explaining the democratic aspects of Rousseau's music theory. Singing together, clearly facilitated by a system of musical notation that is easier to learn, leads to something more: the act of singing together helps to create and reinforce more fundamental communal relationships.

Music and Emotion

As we saw in the preceding chapter, the link between music and emotion is a profound one and is associated, in Rousseau's thought, with something "natural." While chapter 1 explored the connection between music and emotion in relation to meter, rhythm, accent, and pulse in music, here I would like to focus on Rousseau's claims with respect to music's "natural" origin. In the *Essai sur l'origine des langues*, he sketches a hypothetical model for the development of language along with music. For Rousseau, music represents a form of sound production that remains closer to its natural origin than language. For this reason, music has the ability to move the listener, to make the listener share the emotion of the one who performs.

In Rousseau's developmental account, music's ability to move the listener relates to its origins: like speech, music owes its existence to the passions and not to needs. Rousseau asserts, "Il est donc à croire que les besoins dictérent les premiers gestes et que les passions arrachérent les prémiéres voix" (5:380). [It is therefore to be believed that needs dictated the first gestures and that passions tore out the first voices]. While gestures are always referential, and for Rousseau, primitive man could point to things that satisfied needs, speech entails a higher order of cognition.[6] Indeed, for Rousseau, the first language is figurative. Insofar as speech entails a signifying system that always exceeds mere referentiality, it is always tinged by emotion for Rousseau. As Rousseau relates it, emotions and passions inspired the first sounds:

> Toutes des passions rapprochent les hommes que la nécessité de chercher à vivre force à se fuir. Ce n'est ni la faim ni la soif, mais l'amour la haine la pitié la colére qui leur ont arraché les prémiéres voix. Les fruits ne se dérobent point à nos mains, on peut s'en nourrir sans parler, on poursuit en silence la proye dont on veut se repaitre; mais pour émouvoir un jeune cœur, pour repousser un aggresseur injuste la nature dicte des accens, des cris, des plaintes: voila les plus anciens mots inventés, et voila pourquoi les prémiéres langues furent chantantes et passionnées. (5:380–81)

> [All the passions bring together men that the necessity of finding a means of subsistence forced to flee from one another. It is neither hunger nor thirst, but rather love, hate, pity, anger that pulled from them the first utterances. Fruits do not hide themselves from our hands, one can nourish oneself without speaking, one pursues the prey that one wishes to feed on in silence; but to move a young heart, to repulse an unjust aggressor nature dictates accents, cries, pleas: here are the most ancient words invented, and this is why the first languages were singing and passionate.]

Speech was born of the passions and still theoretically retains the ability to communicate emotion. The accents, cries, and pleas that Rousseau mentions are at once speech and song in their original indistinguishable form.

It is this depth of emotion that is lacking, in his opinion, in contemporary forms of language, overly determined by the practice of writing.[7] But these primordial accents can be retrieved in music. If contemporary language is doomed to the emotionless monotones produced by an overdependence on writing and reason, music is not. As we saw in the preceding chapter, within music is the possibility to accede to this fount of emotion and unleash the accents of passion.

Indeed, it is not the sounds themselves that move the listener and excite the passions, but rather the passions behind the sounds. In a passage cited in the previous chapter, Rousseau makes a comparison between painting and music to explain that it is not the materials of composition, that is, colors and sounds, that stir the emotions in these forms of art.[8] It is the formal qualities of painting and music that bring these arts to life and move their audiences. Chords and notes are the building blocks of music; melody is the formal arrangement of these materials that enables emotion to be communicated through a kind of imitation.[9]

Although music has a "natural" origin, as we have seen, it is also true that, for Rousseau, music is a kind of language, a conventional sign system that requires knowledge for decoding and understanding: "Les sons dans la mélodie n'agissent pas seulement sur nous comme sons, mais *comme signes de nos affections, de nos sentimens*; c'est ainsi qu'ils excitent en nous les mouvemens qu'ils expriment et dont nous y reconnoissons l'image" (5:417, my emphasis). [Sounds in melody act on us not only as sounds, but *as signs of our affections, of our feelings*; it is in this way that they excite in us the movements that they express and of which we recognize the image in them].[10] Rousseau's emphasis on melody, a formal attribute of music and not necessarily a feature of "natural" musical sounds, highlights the importance of understanding music as a convention.

As with painting, music derives its ability to move the passions from its ability to imitate: mimesis is the privileged aesthetic mode.[11] But Rousseau's understanding of musical mimesis takes account of the fact that music is also a conventional sign system. Although music imitates, it does so through formal means. The voice or an instrument cannot simply imitate sounds and touch the listener's emotions. The musical sounds operate within a system, structured by melody, to elicit an emotional response. The listener must be at least somewhat familiar with the musical signifying system in order to be moved. This explains why music from other cultures does not always sound beautiful or move members of other cultures.[12]

Rousseau characterizes music's movement of the passions as a "moral effect," as we saw in chapter 1. To distinguish the mere physical effects of vibration (associated with hearing or the senses) from the more profound effect music has on the "soul," and to further develop the distinction between the content of music (sounds) and its form (melody), Rousseau stresses the animate quality of music. To really move the emotions literally requires motion.[13] Motion can only come from an animate object. What music communicates is the motion of life from one being to another. It is a form of contact and connection that relies on the perception of another sentient being. Insofar as it taps into sentience in this way, music surpasses the realm of sensation and enters the realm of the moral. "Les couleurs sont la parure des êtres inanimés; toute matière est colorée; mais les sons annoncent le mouvement, la voix annonce un être sensible; il n'y a que des corps animés qui chantent" (5:420) [Colors are the ornament of inanimate beings; all matter is colored; but sounds announce movement, the voice announces a sentient being; only animate bodies sing]. In this respect, music's moral effects bear a resemblance to the way in which pity functions in humans: both evoke feelings that result from the perception of sentience in another being.[14] Pity derives from human beings' experience of suffering and their awareness that others suffer. While the accounts in the *Second Discourse* and the *Essay on the Origin of Languages* differ in their estimation of the psychological mechanisms necessary for the feeling of pity, nonetheless both stress the capacity for and recognition of suffering as the underlying causes that enable this form of identification among humans. In *Emile*, Rousseau outlines maxims for pity in the section preceding the "Profession of Faith of the Savoyard Vicar." These maxims, particularly the third one, stress the emotional identification with suffering in another as the foundation for moral life.[15] Pity amounts to a kind of vicarious emotional sharing occasioned most often by the perception and awareness of physical suffering in others.

Music, while not dependent on the recognition of suffering, does hold in common with the experience of pity a kind of emotional sharing through a form of communication. We recognize suffering through certain external signs (cries, gestures, etc.) and feel pity. Likewise, we recognize emotional expression when we hear musical sounds. When such feelings are stirred through a form of recognition, they exert a moral force. For Rousseau, music and pity elicit moral feelings through the recognition, albeit intuitive or instinctive, of another moral being. But whereas pity merely causes one to suffer at the sight of another suffering being, music requires communication of a sort between the one emitting the sounds and the one being moved by them. In other words, the musician communicates emotion to the listener and moves him or her to experience emotion.

## Democratic Music

At first glance, it would not appear that music has any particular link to democracy. Particularly well suited to move the passions, music might seem out of place in a democracy, or at least at the site of democratic political deliberations. The ability to move the passions might cloud judgment and inhibit the proper functioning of the general will.[16] The relationship of music to democracy is a complex one in Rousseau's thought. Though it is true that music can be used to move the passions and therefore has the potential to be abused by a tyrant to subdue a people, it is also true that music enables patriotic expression. In this section, I explore music's relations to Rousseau's theory of the social contract, and particularly the functioning of the general will. I argue that music serves as a practical model for democracy and, as such, an aid to its effective practice.

One of the most glaring trouble spots in Rousseau's social contract is his conception of the general will. Much ink has been spilled in attempting to define precisely what Rousseau means by the general will and how it functions within the context of a democratic republic. Most disturbing is the absolute nature of the general will, causing some critics, most famously J. L. Talmon, to charge Rousseau with instituting the conditions for a dictatorship.[17] It is Rousseau's infamous contention that the general will is never in error, that only people make mistakes, that has raised the specter of despotism:

> La volonté générale est toujours droite et tend toujours à l'utilité publique: mais il ne s'ensuit pas que les délibérations du peuple aient toujours la même rectitude. On veut toujours son bien, mais on ne le voit pas toujours: Jamais on ne corrompt le peuple, mais souvent on le trompe, et c'est alors seulement qu'il paroit vouloir ce qui est mal. (3:371)

> [The general will is always right and always tends toward public utility: but it does not follow that the deliberations of the people always have the same rectitude. One always wants one's own good, but one does not always see it: The people is never corrupted, but often fooled, and it is only then that it seems to want what is bad.]

Coupled with Rousseau's seeming distrust of the workings of democracy, a picture of the general will emerges in which a leader may impose an absolute principle of the public good on a willing or unwilling people.[18]

It is not my intention here to defend against the absolutist readings of the general will in the social contract, but rather to offer a reinterpretation of the general will in light of Rousseau's musical theory. I would like to read the social contract as if the democratic republic born of it were a musical one, that is to say, that the social contract brings into being not only a *moi commun* or body politic with a single will, but also with a single voice: a musical body, echoing my argument concerning the mechanisms underlying performance in chapter 1.

This interpretation is not as far-fetched as it might first appear. Many of the passages of the *Social Contract* that speak of the body politic as a whole address the issue of its moving and acting as a whole:

> A l'instant, au lieu de la personne particuliere de chaque contractant, cet acte d'association produit un corps moral et collectif composé d'autant de membres que l'assemblée a de voix, lequel reçoit de ce même acte son unité, son *moi* commun, sa vie et sa volonté. (3:361)

> [In that moment, instead of the private person of each party to the contract, this act of association produces a moral and collective body composed of as many members as the assembly has voices, which receives from this same act its unity, its common *self*, its life, and its will.]

This moral person that is the body politic acts together, in concert, I will argue, in much the same way that an orchestra or chorus does: it moves as a single entity composed of smaller entities, each executing individual parts. Whether it is the body politic deliberating about the common good, or a chamber group performing one of Rameau's *Pièces de clavecin en concert*, the individuals bind themselves together in such a way that they, at least temporarily, function as a cohesive unit.

Rousseau himself hints at an ancient coincidence between singing and the political realm in his article "Chanson" for the *Dictionnaire de musique*. Recounting a history of song that runs parallel to the account in the *Essai*, he asserts, "les anciens n'avoient-ils point encore l'art d'écrire qu'ils avoient déjà des *Chansons*. Leurs Loix et leurs histoires, louanges des Dieux et des Héros, furent chantées avant d'être écrites. Et de-là vient, selon Aristote, que le même nom Grec fut donné aux Loix et aux *Chansons*" (5:690) [the ancients did not have the art of writing, but already they had *songs*. Their laws and their histories, their praise of Gods and heroes, were sung before they were written. And from this comes, according to Aristotle, the fact that the same Greek name was given to laws and to *songs*].[19] Like the original coincidence that exists between speech and song in Rousseau's developmental history in the *Essai*, here, in ancient Greece, the overlap extends to include the laws.

Other than this brief reference to political life in the *Dictionnaire de musique*, there are no other explicit connections drawn between singing and politics in Rousseau's work, although my epigraph from Montesquieu's *Considérations sur les causes de la grandeur des Romains et de leur décadence* does suggest one possible source of inspiration.[20] That is not to say that Rousseau does not recognize the potential political implications of the performing arts. Indeed, the *Lettre à d'Alembert* links the aesthetic and political life of a republic, focusing specifically on the spectacle of theater. Rousseau's concern with the potential political effects of theater is not surprising, given the historical association of the performing arts with the court and systems of patronage, making them easy targets for his suspicions concerning their use as vehicles for propaganda. Within the eighteenth-century context, the performing arts are viewed as rife with political implications in part because of Louis XIV's deft use of theater, dance, and music in the context of his spectral reign in the preceding century, and the continuing associations between the court and the royal academies.[21]

Specifically in the realm of music, the Paris Opéra became a political battleground during the *querelle des bouffons*. According to historians of cultural life under the Old Regime, the potential political ramifications of aesthetic choices fuel many debates from midcentury forward.[22] As James Johnson convincingly argues, at the heart of the *querelle des bouffons*—in which Rousseau participated—are ideological differences that go beyond aesthetics to engage broader philosophical and political issues.

For Rousseau, the connection between aesthetics and politics, and especially the performing arts, is part of the context of their reception and interpretation. In hierarchical societies with monarchs, patronage often ensures the controlled dissemination of politically motivated messages through theater, opera, and ballet. Even debates about style and taste, such as the *querelle des bouffons*, are seen as having political overtones in such a cultural context. Likewise, singing in the context of popular culture may have other political connotations for Rousseau. As Laura Mason argues, under the Old Regime, the street singing of the *chansonniers* was often associated with political and critical messages dating back to the religious wars of the sixteenth century and continuing throughout the eighteenth century.[23] Thus, from the standpoint of both elite and popular culture, there are strong ties between musical performance and a political message.

The cultural context of eighteenth-century life provides an important tool for understanding how and why Rousseau's political theory may be better understood in tandem with his music theory, yet my argument does not involve the political implications of the performing arts in this way. For the present argument, I am less concerned with Rousseau's opinions about the potentially nefarious effects of particular performances than I am with his understanding of what performance entails, and specifically, musical performance. To put it simply, it is not a question of what the audience thinks or feels at the close of a choral concert, but rather of imagining everyone as a potential participant in the choral performance.[24] Like a sing-along at a ballpark or a performance of Handel's *Messiah* in which the audience participates, using Rousseau's music theory to understand his political theory requires reorienting our understanding of aesthetic production toward those instances in which the wall between performer and audience is effaced. If music theory has political implications of this type, they are not related to reception, but rather to performance as a political act, breaking down the kinds of distinctions that we saw in chapter 1. The implications of musical theory for political theory relate to concerns that bridge the theory-practice gap.

The General Will

The general will of *Du contrat social* indeed poses one of the more difficult theory-practice problems in Rousseau's corpus. It stands as a kind of pivot point at the center of a theory that wants to be both idealistic and practical at the same time. Rousseau maintains that unanimity in deliberations signals the appearance of the general will. "Plus le concert regne dans les assemblées, c'est-à-dire plus les avis approchent de l'unanimité, plus aussi la volonté générale est dominante" (3:439) [The more that concert reigns in assemblies, that is to say, the more opinions approach unanimity, the more the general will is dominant], indicating the confluence of theory and practice under these circumstances. Although he carefully distinguishes between the will of all and the general will (3:371)—underscoring the influence of self-interest in the case of the former and the general interest in the case of the latter—he nonetheless tends to equate the general will with unanimity. His pronouncements about the desirability for a small state with homogeneous interests, where everyone knows everyone else, and where there is conformity in matters of public opinion (3:388–91, 394, 404), reinforce the notion that the ideal state rarely if ever has to deal with differences of opinion. These practical considerations that favor homogeneity and uniformity enable the realization of the ideal within the real, but at the cost of dissension. What is more difficult to imagine, given Rousseau's various formulations, is how the general will is to be formed in cases in which unanimity of opinion does not determine deliberations. Continuing in the same passage cited above concerning unanimity, Rousseau writes, "mais les longs débats, les dissentions [sic], le tumulte, annoncent l'ascendant des intérêts particuliers et le déclin de l'Etat" [but long debates, dissension, tumult, announce the ascendancy of particular interests and the decline of the state]. Rousseau views the appearance of dissenting opinions as evidence of the breakdown of the general will and, therefore, a return to private interests. This formulation opens a gap between theory and practice by reading dissent as the harbinger of self-interest. In other words, Rousseau has a difficult time conceptualizing ways in which dissent may be useful in generating the general will, rather than always detrimental to its determination.

But the possibility of legitimate conflict must be considered from within the theory of the social contract. Rousseau posits the opposition between particular and general, individual and state, in order to articulate the solution that is the social contract. Althusser's powerful reading of the discrepancies within the text brings this structure clearly to light.[25] If individual interests are to be reconciled with the general interest, Rousseau famously asserts, then the solution must be all or nothing: "l'aliénation totale de chaque associé avec tous ses droits à toute la communauté" (3:360) [the total alienation of each associate with all of his rights to the whole of the community]. With total alienation comes total perfect confluence of interests: "Les engagemens qui nous lient au corps social ne sont obligatoires que parce qu'ils sont mutuels, et leur nature est telle qu'en les remplissant on ne peut travailler pour autrui sans travailler aussi pour soi" (3:373) [The engagements that tie us to the social body are only obligatory because they are mutual, and their nature is such that in fulfilling them one cannot work for anyone else without also working for oneself]. Working for someone else within the social body amounts to working for oneself. There is a posited perfect correspondence between individual interest and group interest that is resolved in the notion of the general will, which is nothing other than the common good. But the assertion of the perfect confluence is belied by other passages of *Du contrat social* that clearly indicate potential conflict between individual interest and the general will.[26] The theory maintains the ideal of unanimity predicated on this perfect coincidence of individual and group interests, but also articulates inevitable points of tension.²⁷

In book 1, chapter 7, having just outlined the terms of the contract, Rousseau acknowledges that individuals may have interests that are not coincidental with those of the group: "En effet chaque individu peut comme homme avoir une volonté particuliere contraire ou dissemblable à la volonté générale qu'il a comme Citoyen. Son intérêt particulier peut lui parler tout autrement que l'intérêt commun" (3:363) [In effect, each individual can, as a man, have a particular will that is contrary to or dissimilar from the general will that he has as a citizen. His particular interest can speak to him completely differently than the common interest].

Most of the other formulations of this conflict are articulated in similar ways: All citizens of the state are internally divided between their own interests—as individuals or as members of particular social groups within the body politic—and the common interest of the entire social body. Because it is an internal division within each member of the body politic, it always threatens to subvert the smooth functioning of the community led by the general will.²⁸ Perhaps for this reason, Rousseau makes the infamous claim that individuals will sometimes need to be forced to follow the dictates of the general will: "Afin donc que le pacte social ne soit pas un vain formulaire, il renferme tacitement cet engagement qui seul peut donner de la force aux autres, que quiconque refusera d'obéir à la volonté générale y sera contraint par tout le corps: ce qui ne signifie autre chose sinon qu'on le forcera d'être libre (3:364) [In order therefore that the social pact not be a vain formula, it tacitly contains this engagement that can alone give force to all the others, that whoever refuses to obey the general will shall be constrained to do so by the entire body: which means nothing other than that he will be forced to be free].

Constraining individuals to act in accordance with the dictates of the common interest is necessitated by the need for absolute coincidence between individual and group interest. Because the potential conflict is framed as being internal to each individual, it always pits self-interest against group interest, private concerns against the public good. The only possible solution, given this understanding of the opposition, is to force people to act according to the common interest (hence the infamous formulation above), thereby reconciling the seeming internal conflict. According to this understanding, individuals who desire to act out of self-interest will be corrected to act out of group interest, ultimately making them realize the coincidence of their own private interest with the general good.

Although Rousseau posits the conflict between particular and general wills in terms of a potential internal division within each member of the social body, he also indirectly acknowledges that all persons do not always agree on all matters. The internal division formulation tends to mask the potential for legitimate differences of opinion in matters concerning the public good by making it seem as though all conflict is always a matter of overcoming self-interest in order to form the general will.[29] But what about cases in which individuals disagree about the common good in ways that do not engage private particular interests? Might not legitimate differences of opinion arise that are not conditioned by self-interested motives?

The more practical considerations in books 3 and 4 of *Social Contract* suggest possible procedural means for instantiating the general will. Rather than the absolute theoretical coincidence of individual and group interests, these sections seem to acknowledge that political practice needs to provide a framework in which differences may be worked out. Specifically with respect to the convening of assemblies and voting procedures, Rousseau concedes that unanimity may not always be possible (3:426–28, 440–41). This lack of unanimity does not alter the legitimacy of the deliberations of the assembly. Bearing this set of practical considerations in mind, I would like to return to Rousseau's music theory to seek other practical models for negotiating among legitimate differences of opinion to achieve an outcome consistent with the general will.

The General Will and Musical Practice

As we have seen in the theory-practice problem posed by the general will, resolving legitimate differences of opinion without imposing an absolute standard on the community requires procedural mechanisms for enabling the negotiation of multiple perspectives. Rousseau insists on constitutionally mandated periodic assemblies in which the entire citizenry would gather (3:426), underscoring the need for democratic deliberations. In the following section, I argue in favor of a musical analogy to provide some interesting possibilities for understanding the determination of the general will in these circumstances. Rather than read the general will as a fixed absolute imposed on the community, I suggest that the general will functions as a "relative absolute" within Rousseau's political theory, in much the same way that tuning functions for musical performance. Given Rousseau's personal experience as a harpsichord tuner, this analogy seems particularly apt.[30] As in politics, the gulf between music theory and practice can be a wide one. In the realm of tuning, the problem is made more acute by the mathematical conundrum that some kinds of tuning present. As my discussion will highlight, the tuning of keyboard instruments in the eighteenth century presented a particularly thorny area in which certain compromises needed to be made in order to enable performance.

Instruments must be tuned in order to make the sounds that they emit pleasing to our ears.[31] So, for example, before playing a stringed instrument, it is necessary to make sure that it is in tune with itself. That is to say, that the strings, when plucked or bowed, must emit sounds at the proper intervals for performance. The process of tuning is complicated by the addition of other instruments: instruments should be in tune with themselves and with one another in order for the piece of music performed in concert to sound "right" to our ears. In modern symphony orchestras, accordingly, it is often the practice, before the first piece of music is performed, to have the oboe play an A, so that the other members of the orchestra can tune their instruments to it.

Rousseau's entry in the *Dictionnaire de musique* for *entonner* (to intone or to begin to sing) highlights the importance of having a common standard for proper intonation:

> Entonner, *v. a.*: C'est dans l'exécution d'un Chant, former avec justesse les Sons et les Intervalles qui sont marquées. Ce qui ne peut guères se faire qu'à l'aide d'une *idée commune* à laquelle doivent se rapporter ces Sons et ces Intervalles; savoir, celle du Ton et du Mode où ils sont employés, d'où vient peut être le mot *Entonner*. (5:809, my emphasis)

> [Intone, v. a.: It is in the execution of song, to form with accuracy the sounds and the intervals that are indicated. This can hardly be done without the aid of a *common idea* to which the sounds and intervals must be in relation, namely, that of a tone or mode in which they are employed, from which derives perhaps the word *intone*.]

Whether it is for the voice or the orchestra, correct tuning and pitch require a common standard against which the tones and intervals can be measured.

Returning to my orchestral example, the oboe is chosen not because it always produces a perfect A equal to 440 Hz, but because of the difficulty of tuning double-reed instruments. In Rousseau's time, woodwinds were used in tuning for the same reasons:

> A l'égard des Flûtes, Hautbois, Bassons, et autres Instrumens à vent, ils ont leur Ton à-peu-près fixé, qu'on ne peut guères changer qu'en

changeant quelque pièce de l'Instrument. On peut encore les allonger un peu à l'emboiture des pièces, ce qui baisse le Ton de quelque chose; mais il doit nécessairement résulter des tons faux de ces variations, parce que la juste proportion est rompue entre la longueur totale de l'Instrument et les distances d'un trou à l'autre. (5:634)

[With regard to flutes, oboes, bassoons, and other wind instruments, they have a more or less fixed tone that can hardly be changed except by changing some piece of the instrument. One can lengthen them a little at the joints of the instruments, which lowers the tone somewhat; but false tones necessarily result from these changes, because the just proportion between the total length of the instrument and the distance from one hole to another is broken.]

The rest of the orchestra tunes to the oboe (or the woodwinds in the eighteenth century) because it has the least amount of flexibility in tuning. For the purposes of orchestral performance, the A that the oboe produces is the absolute standard against which the other instruments make the appropriate adjustments to get in tune. The oboe produces a *relative absolute*: relative with respect to perfect tuning—it is not necessarily A 440 Hz—but absolute with respect to the other instruments in the orchestra—they must tune to this common standard.

In Rousseau's article "Ton" in the *Dictionnaire*, a third definition emphasizes the approximate nature of the note against which the other instruments tune:

On donne encore le même nom à un Instrument qui sert à donner le *Ton* de l'Accord à tout un Orchestre. Cet Instrument, qui quelques-uns appellent aussi Choriste, est un sifflet, qui, au moyen d'une espêce de piston gradué, par lequel on allonge ou raccourcit le tuyau à volonté, donne toujours à-peu-près le même Son sous la même division. Mais cet à-peu-près, qui dépend des variations de l'air, empêche qu'on ne puisse s'assurer d'un Son fixe qui soit toujours exactement le même. Peut-être, depuis qu'il existe de la Musique, n'a-t-on jamais concerté deux fois sur le même *Ton*. (5:1123)

[We give the same name to an instrument that serves to give the tuning *tone* to the entire orchestra. This instrument, that some also call chorist, is a whistle that by means of a kind of a graduated piston, by which the tube can be lengthened or shortened at will, gives more or less the same sound under the same division. But this more or less, which depends on the variations of the air, prevents us from being able to be certain of a fixed sound that would always be exactly the same. Perhaps, since the beginning of the existence of music, we have never performed with the same tone twice.]

Functioning in much the same way as an oboe in a modern orchestra, the pitch pipe that Rousseau describes here cannot be counted on to produce a precisely accurate tone according to which the other instruments may be tuned. The approximate value of the pitch, stressed in Rousseau's repetition of "à-peu-près" [more or less], even leads him to speculate that musical sounds can never be exactly duplicated. Nonetheless, the sound emitted from the decidedly less than perfect instrument, like the oboe, must create a common standard for the orchestra.

I would argue that it is precisely this type of relative absolute that the general will represents within Rousseau's political theory, especially with respect to the resolution of legitimate differences of opinion. Both the oboe's A and the notion of the general will establish a normative standard for performance—either musical or democratic—without which performance could not exist. This common idea or normative standard creates the conditions for the possibility of musical performance or democratic procedure.[32] The tuning standard, as well as the ideal of the common good or public interest, are both absolute with respect to the conduct of the individuals involved in collective endeavor, but relative insofar as they are changeable with respect to context—at the next performance, the common standard may indeed be a different one. In the case of periodic democratic assemblies, the general will conceived as relative absolute could be invoked to remind participants in deliberations to consult notions of the common good without necessarily imposing a rigid standard.

To continue with the analogy, tuning entails the initial establishment of the A for the ensemble players, but does not end there. During the performance of each piece of music, ideally the musicians listen to themselves and one another and make minute adjustments to stay in tune with the other players. Numerous minute adjustments occur as the musicians continuously attempt to blend the sounds to create a seamless whole. These adjustments occur almost automatically, without the performers' needing to think about them.[33] Ideally, in Rousseau's democratic republic, the same kinds of adjustments ought to be taking place: people should come together to vote on a piece of legislation or decide on a common course of action, all the while bearing in mind the common interest or public good. The individual notions of the common interest should be adjusted as deliberations proceed. That is to say, ideally the individuals ought to listen to one another and check their own conception of the public interest against those expressed by others in the assembly. As with tuning and intonation, and the constant minute adjustments that musical performance requires, the democratic deliberations ideally entail constant adjustments based on listening to the voices of others.

During a concert, the orchestra will often retune after a piece has been performed. Taking into account all of the factors that affect the tuning of instruments—temperature and humidity, and the effects they have on the raw materials of which the instruments are made—it is necessary for the oboe to play another A and for the rest of the orchestra to make the appropriate adjustments. In the entry for *accorder*, Rousseau mentions these pitch changes that take place as wind instruments are played:

> On observe que les Instrumens dont on tire le Son par inspiration, comme la Flûte et le Hautbois, montent insensiblement quand on a joué quelque tems; . . . il faut, en *Accordant*, avoir égard à l'effet prochain, et forcer un peu le vent quand on donne ou reçoit le Ton sur ces Instrumens; car pour rester d'Accord durant le Concert, ils doivent être un peu trop bas en commençant. (5:635)

> [One observes that the instruments from which one draws sound by breathing, like the flute and oboe, go up imperceptibly when one has played a little while; . . . it is necessary, in tuning, to be mindful of the proximate effect, and force the air a little when one gives or receives the tone on these instruments; for in order to remain in tune during the concert, they must be a little too low to begin with.]

One cannot help but be struck by the felicitous coincidence of meaning in the phrase "pour rester d'Accord durant le Concert" [in order to remain in tune during the concert] between staying in tune and staying in agreement. In anticipation of the rise in pitch due to playing, Rousseau advocates that these instruments be tuned lower to begin with, if they want to stay in tune with the rest of the group throughout the performance.

Likewise, the political practice ought to follow the musical one: after debating an issue and taking a vote, the individuals should make the appropriate adjustments to their perception of the public good consistent with the explicit act of the body politic—an expression of the general will—that has just been completed. We might imagine that this entails a moment of reflection or a public reading of a motion or law that has just been passed. For those individuals who expressed views in opposition to a motion that ultimately carried, this might involve questioning their own motivations to determine whether or not they believe they spoke in their own self-interest or out of concern for the public good.

This is not to say that the minority opinion necessarily reflects private interest. In fact, Rousseau explicitly states that the general will is not the same thing as the will of all. "Il y a souvent bien de la différence entre la volonté de tous et la volonté générale; celle-ci ne regarde qu'à l'intérêt commun, l'autre regarde à l'intérêt privé, et n'est qu'une somme de volontés particulieres" (3:371) [There is often a significant difference between the will of all and the general will; the latter only regards common interest, the other regards private interest and is nothing but the sum of particular wills]. Thus it would be appropriate for all members of the collective to "retune," as it were, whether having been on the side of the majority or the minority, and readjust their notions of the collective interest so as to try to avoid acting out of self-interest.

In addition to questions of tuning, musicians also make other adjustments while performing a piece of music. The tempo of the piece, although established at the outset by the conductor or leader of the group, varies as the music progresses. Often marked in the score, or improvised during a performance, are sections of *rallentando* where the music intentionally slows, or *accelerando* where the music speeds up. There are also dynamic changes, crescendos and decrescendos, when the ensemble gets progressively louder or softer for sections of the music. These changes depend at times on a preestablished and rehearsed interpretation of the piece of music, and at other times on the spontaneity of the group of performers. In both cases, they require the synchronization that comes from listening attentively and responding while performing. I would suggest that these kinds of changes should also be reflected in democratic practice. Akin to toning down one's rhetoric or increasing the intensity of argumentation in response to others, listening to and responding accordingly to the other members of the group is as essential a part of democratic procedure, as is voting. Indeed, it is listening and responding in this way that creates the conditions for the group to exist as a collective.

As with music, what this ultimately means in political life is that each individual will subordinate his or her own interests to the greater good of the group. In so doing, Rousseau argues, the individual will ultimately be acting out of self-interest. As I cited above: "Les engagemens qui nous lient au corps social ne sont obligatoires que parce qu'ils sont mutuels, et leur nature est telle qu'en les remplissant on ne peut travailler pour autrui sans travailler aussi pour soi" (3:373) [The engagements that tie us to the social body are only obligatory because they are mutual, and their nature is such that in fulfilling them one cannot work for anyone else without also working for oneself]. In music, this entails a number of things; most succinctly, it means that each member of the ensemble will play in such a way as to maximize the beauty of the musical piece taken as a whole. This will require some instruments or voices to be silent at times, in order to allow other voices to be heard; it will require making concessions and compromises in one's individual part in order for the piece to work as a whole. Likewise, in political life, subordination to the higher goal of the common good might require individual sacrifices at times. Ultimately, however, what benefits the community benefits each of its members. In this way, the general will as a relative absolute establishes a moveable normative standard that enables the community to function as a collective and not merely as individuals.

Aesthetics and Morality: Singing Democracy

Finally, I would like to return to the question of singing to examine the relation between the musical analogy I have traced and the specifics of the human voice in Rousseau's thought. There are three ways in which the human voice distinguishes itself from other instruments that make it particularly well suited to express the democratic political ideal of the social contract.

First, and most obviously, everyone has a voice. Although not everyone is equally gifted as a singer, there is at least the potential for everyone to sing. Given Rousseau's concerns with disparities of wealth and their negative effects on democracy, it seems reasonable to assume that the fact that singing does not require money to purchase an instrument is relevant to the argument. Singing and choral music would seem to represent the most democratic of musical forms. Coupled with Rousseau's system for musical notation—enabling easier access both materially and educationally—vocal and choral music emerges as the simplest and most democratic form of aesthetic expression.

Second, the human voice has an infinite capacity for modulation. This second point requires some explanation of musical theory and the state of tuning and temperament in the eighteenth century. As I discussed in the preceding section, instruments require tuning. In order for the voice to be in tune with an instrument or with other voices, it is important to establish an initial tone in common—the *idée commune* in Rousseau's definition of *entonner*. The establishment of this point of reference enables the singer to stay in tune with the accompanying instrument(s). But beyond tuning, there is the question of key. While all orchestral instruments are capable of playing in all keys, for particular instruments some keys are easier than others. Instruments are individually tuned to and play in a particular key as a kind of default. The key of the instrument determines the relative ease or difficulty of executing a piece in one key as opposed to another. Even for the stringed instruments, certain keys are easier to play in than others, owing to the positioning of the hand for particular fingerings. Having a group of musicians play together on different instruments requires making the appropriate tuning and key adjustments so that they blend to produce a harmonious sound.

The question of tuning becomes even more complicated when we turn to instruments such as the harpsichord or organ, of which Rousseau, having worked as a tuner, would have been keenly aware. These instruments present special obstacles for tuning, related to the fact that they must sound all of the notes in a fixed way. That is to say, unlike the violin, for which minor adjustments can be made in the fingering to make the note sound right to our ears, each note on the harpsichord is produced in the same way every time a key is touched. Therefore, each string of the harpsichord must be tuned in such a way that it produces the correct interval with respect to the other strings in all keys. While this sounds relatively simple, the complexity of tuning keyboard instruments relates to a mathematical problem in music concerning the relationship between notes of the scale.

In Rousseau's article "Tempérament" for the *Dictionnaire de musique*, he explains the process by which notes are adjusted in the tuning of a harpsichord to produce pleasing intervals for all keys.

> Tempérament: Opération par laquelle, au moyen d'une légère alteration dans les Intervalles, faisant évanouir la différence de deux Sons voisins, on les confound en un, qui, sans choquer l'oreille, forme les Intervalles respectifs de l'un et de l'autre. Par cette opération l'on simplifie l'Echelle en diminuant le nombre des Sons nécessaires. Sans le *Tempérament*, au lieu de douze Sons seulement que contient l'Octave, il en faudroit plus de soixante pour moduler dans tous les Tons.
>
> Sur l'Orgue, sur le Clavecin, sur tout autre Instrument à Clavier, il n'y a, et il ne peut guère y avoir d'Intervalle parfaitement d'Accord que la seule Octave. (5:1106–7)

[Temperament: Operation by which, through means of a slight alteration in the intervals causing the difference between two neighboring sounds to disappear, one blends them into one, in such a way that, without shocking the ear, it forms the respective intervals of the one and the other. Through this operation, we simplify the scale by diminishing the number of necessary sounds. Without temperament, instead of the twelve sounds that the octave contains, more than sixty would be necessary in order to modulate in all the tones.

On the organ, on the harpsichord, on all other keyboard instruments, there are not and could hardly be an interval that was perfectly tuned, save the octave.]

The process of tempering a harpsichord necessitates minor adjustments between intervals to make them less than perfect (with the exception of the octave, as Rousseau points out), so that they are still pleasing to the ear, and yet allow the keyboard instruments to play in all keys. During the eighteenth century, mean-tone temperament and well temperament were more widely used than our current equal temperament system. I will discuss this controversy at length in the next chapter. But, without getting into too much technical detail, suffice it to say that both mean-tone and well temperament make specific adjustments between certain intervals that favor some keys while making others unusable. The current system of equal temperament, while proposed as early as the sixteenth century, was not widely adopted until the late eighteenth and early nineteenth centuries. Equal temperament sacrifices perfection, but it allows for playing in all keys.[34] Because of the widespread use of mean-tone and well temperament, the gulf between musical theory and practice is at its most acute in the realm of eighteenth-century keyboard tuning.

Thus, even with mean-tone or well temperament, a harpsichord can be well-suited to play in some keys, but ill-suited for others. There could potentially even be keys in which "wolf" tones would appear—howling intervals that would sound discordant to the ear. Rousseau's own formula for mean-tone temperament ameliorates tonal discrepancies in the sharp major keys, but worsens intervals in the flat keys, making playing in some keys almost unbearable.

The human voice, unlike orchestral instruments and especially keyboard instruments, has infinite flexibility for producing sounds and modulating them, thus avoiding the conundrum of sacrifice and compromise that keyboards present.[35] Rousseau's appreciation of this fact is evident in his definition for *chant* in the *Dictionnaire de musique*:

Chant, *s. m.*: Sorte de modification de la voix humaine, par laquelle on forme des Sons variés et appréciables. Observons que pour donner à cette définition toute l'universalité qu'elle doit avoir, il ne faut pas seulement entendre par *Sons appréciables*, ceux qu'on peut assigner par les Notes de notre Musique, et rendre par les touches de notre Clavier; mais tous ceux dont on peut trouver ou sentir l'Unisson et calculer les Intervalles de quelque manière que ce soit. (5:694)

[Song, *s. m.*: Kind of modification of the human voice, by which varied and appreciable sounds are formed. Let us observe that in order to give this definition all the universality that it must have, we must not understand *appreciable sounds* to mean only those to which we can assign notes in our music and render with the keys of our keyboard; but rather all those for which we can find or feel unison and calculate the intervals in whatever manner.]

Rousseau's use of the word *universality* underscores the ways in which the human voice exceeds the capabilities of other musical instruments. He suggests that there are an infinite number of sounds that the voice can produce that exceeds not only what keyboard instruments can produce, but also what we can represent through musical notation and even what we can calculate mathematically.

In this respect, the human voice has limitless potential. Although individual human voices have limitations—some are sopranos, some altos, some basses, and some cannot sing in tune at all—as an abstract concept, the human voice has seemingly infinite possibilities for producing sounds. In much the same way that individual humans in the state of nature, before the social contract, have limited capabilities and face numerous obstacles, after they join together, as a group, the body politic formed by the social contract has the potential for nearly godlike achievements. Although Rousseau often stresses human limitations, and perhaps nowhere as much as in the *Social Contract*—where he fears conspiracies, private interests, and all human vices that interfere with ideal forms of governance—he nonetheless expresses faith in human potential. The human faculty for perfectibility, although blamed for all of humanity's self-imposed woes, also posits the possibility for democratic and virtuous self-governance in concert.

Finally, the human voice, as we have seen above, elicits a moral response in the listener. For Rousseau, the voice is capable of making the listener aware of the presence of another sentient being producing beautiful sounds. More than speech, and more than other musical instruments, the human voice articulates an imitation of a cry of passion that moves the listener in a moral way. Characterizing this insistence on the voice as part of Rousseau's "sentimental aesthetic," Daniel K. L. Chua writes, "vocal music becomes the pure transmission of sentiment from soul to soul, linking the composer to the performer and ultimately to the listener. The authenticity of the experience lies in the recovery of an innate morality of feeling that is the ontological ground for human communication."[36] The moral feeling elicited through song is excited in the listener in much the same way that the perception of suffering causes humans to feel pity: both evoke an awareness of another sentient being. This moral feeling provides the basis for social life in Rousseau's thought, establishing the primary bond between individuals that will extend to create the bonds of community.

## Melody and the Fostering of Democratic Community

Music, like language, is a conventional sign system, organized according to formal laws that enable the production of meaningful sounds. For Rousseau, when music is able to imitate the human passions, it taps into moral feelings in the listener and moves the person to recognize the presence of another sentient being. In the article on *mélodie* for the *Dictionnaire de musique*, Rousseau relates melody to two different principles: harmony, which enables scales, chords, and generally pleasing intervals between notes, and accent, which gives music its expressive power:

> C'est l'accent des Langues qui détermine la *Mélodie* de chaque nation; c'est l'accent qui fait qu'on parle en chantant, et qu'on parle avec plus ou moins d'énergie, selon que la Langue a plus ou moins d'Accent. Celle dont l'Accent est plus marqué doit donner une *Mélodie* plus vive et plus passionnée; celle qui n'a que peu ou point d'Accent ne peut avoir qu'une *Mélodie* languissante et froide, sans caractère et sans expression. Voilà les vrais principes: tant qu'on en sortira et qu'on voudra parler du pouvoir de la Musique sur le cœur humain, on parlera sans s'entendre; on ne saura ce qu'on dira. (5:885)

> [It is the accent of languages that determines the *melody* of each nation; it is accent that determines that one speaks by singing and with more or less accent. The language whose accent is more marked gives a livelier and more passionate melody; the one that has little or no accent can only have a languishing and cold melody, without

character or expression. These are the true principles; as much as one departs from them and wants to speak of the power of music on the human heart, one speaks without understanding; one does not know what one says.]

While harmonious relationships between notes are clearly a necessary component of pleasing music, as we have seen in the preceding chapter, accent touches the listener.

In clear opposition to Rameau, Rousseau makes harmony a subcategory of melody, promoting melody and its accents as the essential feature of music that is capable of moving the passions.[37] In the article *Unité de mélodie*, Rousseau makes it even clearer that melody not only creates cohesion in a piece of music, but also sparks interest in the listener. Melodic unity provides formal cohesion in the sense that the piece may be perceived as a whole with relationships among the various parts, but also provides the listener with more than mere sensory pleasure:

> Il y a, dans la Musique, une *Unité* successive qui se rapporte au sujet, et par laquelle toutes les Parties, bien liées, composent un seul tout, dont on apperçoit l'ensemble et tous les rapports.
> 
> Mais il y a une autre *Unité* d'objet plus fine, plus simultanée, d'où naît, sans qu'on y songe, l'énergie de la Musique et la force de ses expressions. (5:1143)

[There is, in music, a successive *unity* that relates to the subject, and by which all the parts, well linked, compose a single whole, of which one may perceive the ensemble and all the relations.

But there is another, finer *unity* of object, more simultaneous, from which is born, without our thinking about it, music's energy and the force of its expressions.]

It is this sense of unity—the way in which it provides energy—that sets Rousseau's conception apart from music theory such as Rameau's, which privileges harmony and systematized relations.

As Rousseau develops the meaning of the expression "melodic unity," it emerges as the formal characteristic that enables music to communicate feeling and sentiment. As we have already seen in the discussion of the importance of form and mimesis in the *Essai*, music's ability to move the listener derives, not from the sounds themselves, but from the forms in which they are arranged. In "melodic unity," Rousseau distinguishes between harmonious relationships, that is, between sounds that are pleasing and melodious songs that speak to the heart:

> Or le plaisir de l'Harmonie n'est qu'un plaisir de pure sensation, et la jouissance des sens est toujours courte, la satiété et l'ennui la suivent de près: mais le plaisir de la Mélodie et du Chant, est *un plaisir d'intérêt et de sentiment qui parle au cœur*, et que l'Artiste peut toujours soutenir et renouveller à force de génie. (5:1143–44, my emphasis)

> [Now since the pleasure of harmony is only a pleasure of sensation and the enjoyment of the senses is always short, satiety and boredom follow close behind; but the pleasure of melody and of song is *a pleasure of interest and of feeling that speaks to the heart*, and that the artist can always sustain and renew by force of genius.]

Whereas the pleasure of harmony may be likened to the pleasure of eating or sexual satisfaction—and Rousseau's choice of the words "jouissance," "satiété" and "ennui" in this context evoke carnal pleasures—the pleasure derived from melody suggests an intellectual or moral pleasure. Rousseau asserts that while the sensual component of music—understood as both the sounds themselves and the harmonious relations between them—satisfies on a basic level, the formal quality of music—melody—produces satisfaction at a higher level. Parallel to the distinction above—between gestures that signify referentially and satisfy needs, and language and music that as signifying systems exceed mere referentially and communicate something more—harmony also seems to satisfy at a level akin to basic needs, whereas melody produces a type of satisfaction that brings higher-level cognition into play. If the sounds of music bring us a kind of physical pleasure that satisfies on a level akin to need, the structure of music produces a feeling of satisfaction or pleasure as it communicates what Rousseau calls "passion" through the form itself.

As we saw in the last chapter, by "passion" Rousseau does not mean physical pleasure, but rather the kind of emotional or metaphorical overlay that he describes in primitive language: words signify referentially but also retain an emotional residue. The cries and accents of speech communicate an excess of meaning. In music we can tap into not only the cries and accents of primitive speech, thereby communicating emotion in this way, but we can also use music's formal property, namely melody, to reinforce the communication of feelings. When we are moved by a piece of music, we find the sounds pleasing, but we feel something more: we understand a kind of moral communication through melody. We feel an intellectual pleasure listening to music because we understand a communication that speaks through emotions to reach an inner core of morality.[38]

Anticipating Kant's discussion of judgments of the beautiful in *The Critique of Judgment*, the perception of melodic unity, for Rousseau, brings with it an enduring and repeatable intellectual and moral pleasure derived from the perception of form. This pleasure elicited by the perception of form is recognition of the human capacity for morality.[39]

In order to create melodic unity, harmony must be subordinate to melody. Arguing against Rameau, Rousseau insists on the necessity of creating music that manages to communicate with one voice, despite the numerous voices that contribute to its production.

> La Musique doit donc nécessairement chanter pour toucher, pour plaire, pour soutenir l'intérêt et l'attention. Mais comment dans nos Systèmes d'Accords et d'Harmonie, la Musique s'y prendra-t-elle pour chanter? Si chaque Partie a son Chant propre, tous ces Chants, entendus à la fois, se détruiront mutuellement, et ne feront plus de Chant: si toutes les Parties font le même Chant, l'on n'aura plus d'Harmonie, et le Concert sera tout à l'Unisson. . . . L'Harmonie, qui devroit étouffer la Mélodie, l'anime, la renforce, la détermine: les diverses Parties, sans se confondre, concourent au même effet; et quoique chacune d'elles paroisse avoir son Chant propre, de toutes ces Parties réunis, on n'entend sortie qu'un seul et même Chant. C'est-là ce que j'appelle *Unité de Mélodie*. (5:1144)

[Music must thus necessarily sing in order to touch, to please, to sustain interest and attention. But how, in our systems of chords and harmony, can music go about singing? If each part has its proper song, all the songs, heard at the same time, will destroy one another and will no longer sing; if all the parts produce the same song, there will be no more harmony, and the concert will be in unison. . . . Harmony, which should smother melody, animates it, reinforces it, determines it: the diverse parts, without being merged, converge in the same effect; and despite the fact that each part seems to have its own song, from all these parts together, one only hears a singular and self-same song. That is what I call *unity of melody*.]

Ideally, music that exhibits melodic unity uses harmony to allow all the voices to be heard while at the same time enabling the piece to be perceived as a whole. Rather than drowning one another out, the separate voices create a single song.

Returning to the democratic community, the notions of melody and melodic unity provide further clarification of how the body politic might act as a single individual without abrogating the individual rights of members of the community. If something like melodic unity could operate in the democratic context, the individual voices would be respected and heard—each one has to play its individual part—while at the same time, the community as a whole would speak with a single voice.

Using the musical model to understand the political one enables a more nuanced understanding of group dynamics and the feelings that they elicit. The musical model for democracy enables an understanding of community that simultaneously allows for individual and communal expression. In contrast to dialogic models for democratic community, where individuals must remain silent while others speak, the musical model enables an understanding of simultaneous group action that is coordinated and has meaning. Functioning together as a group in this way allows for the simultaneous expression of individual parts and the emergence of a group form: the body functioning as a whole.

Musical performance, but most of all singing, then, fosters feelings of community. Listening to the human voice, with its limitless capacities for sound production and the continual reminder of our sense of belonging, tells us that we are not alone. We hear the imitation of passion in the song of another and are moved by the experience. In its most ideal form, spontaneous collective bursts into song ought to reinforce the social and moral bonds of the democratic community.[40]

If we can take the parallels between Rousseau's music theory and his social and political theory seriously and learn from them, and I believe that we can and should, music provides a model for practice that sacrifices perfection without losing sight of normative standards that can serve to orient practice. As a model for democratic community, the functioning of the musical ensemble provides a powerful tool for understanding the complexities of democratic group interaction subordinated to the greater good. In a singing democracy, all individual voices are heard *and* the voice of the community sings.

# 3

## Rameau and Rousseau on Absolute and Relative Value: The Theory/Practice Problem

Comment? Tous les intervalles de mon Clavecin sont altérés? . . . Fi, le vilain instrument; ne m'en parlez plus. . . . Je veux chanter.

—Anton Bemetzrieder, *Leçons de Clavecin*

The band of the night takes you to ethereal heights over dinner
And you wander the streets never reaching the heights that you seek

—Crowded House, "Chocolate Cake"

In the preceding chapter, I argued for an understanding of the general will as a relative absolute consistent with conceptions of normative group dynamics functioning in musical ensembles. Pitches are given to establish an absolute standard for tuning that can be revised according to conditions of practice and performance. As we saw using the tuning example, the general will can be understood to be absolute in the sense that all players are constrained to tune their instruments according to the tone given, but at the same time, adjustments to that pitch can be made as the instruments warm up. Likewise, I argued that in the democratic community, adjustments to the conception of the general will should be made in the process of democratic deliberation to enable a taking into account of legitimate differences of opinion. Thus the general will can be understood as a normative value that is both relative and absolute.

In this chapter, I propose to continue the exploration of the problem of absolute and relative value in the context of Rousseau's debates with Jean-Philippe Rameau, looking beyond the social and political domain to pose questions in epistemology, aesthetics, and metaphysics. At stake in the musical debate between Rousseau and Rameau are distinctly different understandings of the nature of philosophical or aesthetic systems, what is natural, and the ways in which values are derived.

## Opposing Camps: The Paradox of Temperament

The debates between Rameau and Rousseau span a wide array of musical topics—including the relative merits of harmony and melody, use of counterpoint, recitatives, and styles of accompaniment, to name just a few—and cover a fairly lengthy span of time, from Rousseau's *Lettre sur l'opéra italien et français* (1745, unpublished) through the articles penned for the *Encyclopédie* (1749), and finally, the *Dictionnaire de musique* (1767–68), published after Rameau's death.[1] The debates are often characterized as pitting Rameau's Cartesian physicomathematical harmonic system against Rousseau's reception-oriented, affect-driven theory of melody.[2] While Rameau's theory of the fundamental bass and sonorous body (*corps sonore*) grounds all music in a rational, empirically based system, Rousseau's insistence on the expressive capacity of melody, especially through the use of accent to communicate passion, offers a profound critique of Rameau's rationalism. At first glance, and based on these overgeneralizations of their positions, it would seem that Rameau would represent an absolutist point of view: all music can be derived from the mathematical relations among the vibrations that sounds set into play. Rousseau, on the other hand, would seem to be more of a relativist, at least in the subjective sense: music communicates passion and emotion from composer, through performer, to listener.[3] Before examining their positions in detail, I would like to offer a concrete example of an issue on which they take opposing sides (not unexpectedly), yet not the sides that we might imagine. I use this example in order to complicate from the outset what is at stake in the notion of absolute and relative value for both Rameau and Rousseau. The question concerns equal temperament.

As we saw in the preceding chapter, the tuning of keyboard instruments requires a degree of compromise. As I explained, each note is played in the exact same way when the plectrum or hammer causes the string to vibrate. The performer does not have the ability to shorten or lengthen the string inside the body of the instrument to adjust for key like a violin player might do with fingerings. The problem of tuning keyboard instruments arises because of the mathematical ratio produced by the sound waves of resonating notes. To take the example of tuning the octaves on the harpsichord as a starting point, Stuart Isacoff explains, "A *do* can be put in tune with every other *do*, for example; a *re* in tune with every other *re*. Each of these tones on the keyboard can be set to vibrate exactly twice as fast as the like-named partner below it." The problem arises when one attempts to play a piece of music with each note tuned perfectly to the octaves. Isacoff continues, "However, the musical tones that will produce those perfect 2:1 relationships across the keyboard are different from the ones needed to create perfect 3:2 relationships. So making all the *octaves* (the distance from *do* to *do*) 'pure' guarantees that all the *fifths* (the distance from *do* to *sol*, or *re* to *la*) can't be."[4] In other words, it is not possible to preserve all the "perfect" ratios that create harmonic intervals when tuning a keyboard instrument. As we saw in the previous chapter, various strategies were employed throughout the eighteenth century that entailed making minor adjustments to the ratios so that as many intervals as possible could be preserved.[5]

The idea of equal temperament essentially alters all the intervals equally: "the octave is divided into twelve completely uniform parts" (Isacoff, *Temperament*, 114–15). But this elegant solution is not as simple as it would seem. A problem arises in executing this tuning, because dividing the intervals that constitute a whole step on the scale leads to an irrational number: "a whole step—say, the distance from *do* to *re*—is produced by two strings in the ratio 9:8. This couldn't possibly be evenly divided, because the attempt would yield an irrational number" (115). The mathematical problem of creating equal parts was resolved in a variety of ways beginning in the sixteenth century.[6] But compromising some of the perfect relationships, especially thirds and fifths, was found to be disagreeable to a number of theoreticians, composers, and performers. For this reason, as I mentioned in the previous chapter, mean-tone and well temperament formulas persisted throughout the eighteenth century. Keyboard instruments were tuned in irregular ways that tended to preserve certain intervals (especially thirds) in certain keys while they sacrificed other intervals and other keys.

As an instance of value in music, it would seem that the solution of equal temperament for tuning keyboard instruments represents a thoroughgoing compromise: every interval on the keyboard is altered so that none is perfect. Mean-tone and well temperament formulas are also compromises, but to a lesser extent: the purity of particular intervals in certain keys is preserved while other intervals and keys are sacrificed. Returning to the characterization of Rameau's and Rousseau's respective positions on harmony and melody, it would seem likely that someone who adheres to a harmonic system based on the fundamental bass and the resonance of the sonorous body would be less inclined to support equal temperament and more inclined to favor mean-tone or well temperament, while an adherent of melody and a believer in the conventionality of music as an artificial sign system would favor equal temperament. The opposite, however, is true: Rameau after 1737 advocated for equal temperament, while Rousseau remained committed to mean-tone temperament. The partisan of the absolutist physicomathematical harmonic system favored thoroughgoing compromise, while the advocate of a relativist system based on melody did not accept the compromise represented by equal temperament.

While it is true that Rameau advocated in favor of mean-tone temperament in his 1726 *Nouveau système de musique théorique*, by 1737 he was convinced of the usefulness of equal temperament.[7] In *Génération harmonique*, he writes, "le Tempéramment est naturel, ou du moins nécessaire, & nous devons opérer en conséquence. Tout devant être fondé sur la succession fondamentale, comme on n'en peut plus douter, c'est donc sur cette succession même que nous devons établir notre Tempéramment" (94) [temperament is natural, or at least necessary, and we must operate accordingly. Everything necessarily being founded on the fundamental series, as one can no longer doubt, it is therefore on this same series that we must establish our temperament].[8] He goes on to argue that the minor adjustments made at every interval will be barely noticeable to the ear and that they will render all keys usable. He concludes the section on temperament with a statement about consistency that reveals what is at stake in the issue of equal temperament from the point of view of his harmonic theory: "Il est vrai que si c'est un défaut d'être toujours le même, notre Tempéramment le possede au suprême degré; car quelque Son qu'on y prenne pour principal, tout y est toujours en même proportion" (104) [It is true that if it is a fault to be always the same, our temperament possesses it to a supreme degree; for whatever sound that one may take as the principal (tonic), everything is always in the same proportion to it]. What matters most for Rameau, and justifies his advocacy of equal temperament, is that all intervals remain proportionate. Absolutism, understood in terms of preserving the "pure" ratios of octaves, thirds, and fifths, gives way to the pragmatics of playing in all keys and the consistency of a fully integrated, proportionately compromised system.[9] In the end, Rameau stays true to system theory and advocates for a compromise that will enable predictability, even if it means sacrificing perfect intervals throughout the entire range of the keyboard.

Rousseau, on the other hand, never fully accepts the compromise that equal temperament represents. As we saw in the last chapter, his own system of tuning relied on a mean-tone scheme that preserved the major sharp keys and sacrificed the flat keys (especially B flat and E-flat Major). In the

*Dictionnaire* under "Tempérament," he advocates for a mean-tone system that privileges practice over theory, arguing against Rameau that the compromises required in equal temperament will destroy the variety of tone available through mean-tone temperament. Denying Rameau's originality, he cites Couperin as having abandoned equal temperament long ago. "Cette méthode que nous propose aujourd'hui M. Rameau, avoit déjà été proposée et abandonnée par le fameux Couperin. On la trouve aussi tout au long dans le P. Mersenne, qui en fait Auteur un nommé Gallé, et qui a même pris la peine de calculer les onze moyennes proportionnelles dont M. Rameau nous donne la formule algébrique" (5:1111) [This method that M. Rameau proposes to us today, had already been proposed and abandoned by the famous Couperin. One finds it also throughout Father Mersenne, who attributes it to someone named Gallé, who even took the pains to calculate the eleven proportional means for which M. Rameau gives us the algebraic formula]. His objection to equal temperament amounts to an appeal to musicians' practice against theoretical formulations:

> Malgré l'air scientifique de cette formule, il ne paroît pas que la pratique qui en résulte ait été jusqu'ici goûtée des Musiciens ni des Facteurs. Les premiers ne peuvent se résoudre à se priver de l'énergique variété qu'ils trouvent dans les diverses affections des Tons qu'occasionne le *Tempérament* établi. M. Rameau leur dit en vain qu'ils se trompent, que la variété se trouve dans l'entrelacement des Modes ou dans les divers Degrés des Toniques, et nullement dans l'altération des Intervalles; le Musicien répond que l'un n'exclud pas l'autre, qu'il ne se tient pas convaincu par une assertion, et que les diverses affections des Tons ne sont nullement proportionnelles aux différens Degrés de leurs finales. (5:1111)

> [In spite of the scientific air of this formula, it does not appear that the practice that has resulted has been appreciated up until now by musicians or makers. The former cannot be resigned to deprive themselves of the energetic variety that they find in the different feelings of the tones that ordinary (or common) temperament occasions. M. Rameau tells them in vain that they are wrong, that the variety is found in the modulation of modes and in the different degrees of the tonics, and not at all in the alteration of the intervals; the musician responds that the one does not exclude the other, that he does not stand convinced by an assertion, and that the different feelings of

the tones are not at all proportional to the different degrees of their finales.]

He goes on to excoriate Rameau with evidence from harpsichord makers: he reports that the artisans cannot understand how, given such a tuning formula, "l'oreille cessera d'en être offensée" (5:1111) [the ear will cease to be offended by it].[10] Rousseau's argument against Rameau's stand on equal temperament employs the weapons of emotion and effect on the listener through practice against predictability and consistency (although there is an attention to practice here as well). Rousseau appeals to the range of feeling that mean-tone temperament can evoke and the feelings of the practitioners, both musicians and keyboard makers, about the sounds that they produce, to oppose the rational compromise of Rameau's mathematically oriented system. In the end, Rameau favors the predictability of system while Rousseau defends the emotion associated with practice—each understanding the desired outcome in practice with a slightly different valence. While Rameau's privileging of predictability enables smooth modulation in and among keys and complex harmonic schemes to be performed, thereby stressing the necessity of consistency in practice, Rousseau's attention to affect sacrifices the ability to perform certain types of music in favor of being able to strike specific pitches or tones for a desired emotional effect.[11]

Rameau, System Theory, and Absolutism

The debate between Rameau and Rousseau over music theory amounts to a difference that Ernst Cassirer describes in *The Philosophy of the Enlightenment* as one between the *esprit de système* and the *esprit systématique*.[12] Cassirer distinguishes the thought of the seventeenth century, characterized by "the love of system for its own sake" (8), from that of the eighteenth century, which, for Cassirer, favors a kind of rational empiricism rather than a slavish adherence to a priori systems. Cassirer argues that the attention to facts yields a marriage between rational systematicity and a new ability to allow for flexibility that he calls the *esprit systématique*. Summarizing the eighteenth-century perspective, he writes,

> One should not seek order, law, and "reason" as a rule that may be grasped and expressed prior to the phenomenon, as their *a priori*; one should rather discover such regularity in the phenomena themselves, as the form of their immanent connection. Nor should one attempt

to anticipate from the outset such "reason" in the form of a closed system; one should rather permit this reason to unfold gradually, with ever increasing clarity and perfection, as knowledge of the facts progresses. (9)

Cassirer cites d'Alembert's *Discours préliminaire* of the *Encyclopédie* as evidence of the turn away from the *esprit de système* in favor of a new form of system that will enable attention to facts.

Cassirer's citation of the *Discours préliminaire* as exemplary with respect to the new *esprit systématique* is not without a certain degree of irony, given the debate between Rameau and Rousseau. For, in the *Discours*, d'Alembert cites Rameau's work as achieving a degree of perfection that makes it ideally suited for inclusion in the *Encyclopédie*:

> M. Rameau, en poussant la pratique de son Art à un si haut degré de perfection, est devenu tout ensemble le modele & l'objet de la jalousie d'un grand nombre d'Artistes, qui le décrient en s'efforçant de l'imiter. Mais ce qui le distingue plus particulierement, c'est d'avoir refléchi avec beaucoup de succès sur la théorie de ce même Art; d'avoir sû trouver dans la Basse fondamentale le principe de l'harmonie & de la mélodie; d'avoir réduit par ce moyen à des lois plus certaines & plus simples, une science livrée avant lui à des regles arbitraires, ou dictées par une expérience aveugle.[13]

> [M. Rameau, in pushing the practice of his art to such a high degree of perfection, has become both the model for and the object of the jealousy of a great number of artists, who decry him at the same time that they strive to imitate him. But what distinguishes him most especially is having reflected with a great deal of success on the theory of the same art, of having known how to find in the fundamental bass the principle of harmony and melody, of having reduced through this means to simpler and more certain rules a science that before him was given over to arbitrary rules or ones dictated by blind experience.]

In d'Alembert's brief account in the *Discours*, Rameau provides the perfect bridge between science and art, a new form of rule-governed aesthetics that valorizes principles familiar to math and science: simple and certain rules of explanation.[14] Although the final line in the citation above does indicate a turn away from experience (*une expérience aveugle*) in its pejorative characterization, the mention of Rameau by name in the *Discours* suggests a position consistent with the basic tenets of the *Encyclopédie* project.

Thus d'Alembert's praise of Rameau's work in the *Discours*, as well as Cassirer's of the *Encyclopédie*, might lead one to believe that Rameau's work is consistent with the epistemological assumptions that lean away from a priori-based systems to privilege experience.

Thomas Christensen argues persuasively that the development of Rameau's thought over time is marked by the influence of scientific discourses of the day. Christensen, agreeing with d'Alembert's assessment in the *Discours*, also views Rameau's Cartesianism as tempered by empiricism.[15] While he recognizes tensions and ambivalences in his articulations, Christensen ultimately maintains that Rameau privileges experience over reason: "In Rameau's judicial system, experience seems to be the ultimate court of appeal, not reason" (33). Christensen's case for a dialectical tension in Rameau's work between theory and practice is quite compelling, and especially for its ability to explain Rameau's desire to account for empirical experience in music practice. And yet, in the context of eighteenth-century thought, the desire for complete and totalizing systematicity that Rameau's project represents nonetheless leans in the direction of older theory. In other words, while attempting to reconcile Cartesianism and Lockean-style empiricism, Rameau's theoretical contributions tend to fall back on modes of explanation and analysis that privilege theory and system over practice, at least insofar as they may be contrasted with Rousseau's approach, as I will develop a little later on.

Clearly, Rameau's early work provides a textbook example of what Cassirer characterizes as the older *esprit de système*. Citing Descartes' *Abrégé de la musique* and correcting as he goes, Rameau wishes to create a more disciplined and perfect Cartesian system for music. Rameau writes in the "Préface" to the *Traité de l'harmonie*, in Cartesian language, "En un mot, *les lumières de la raison dissipant ainsi les doutes où l'expérience peut nous plonger* à tout moment, seront de surs garants du succès qu'on pourra se promettre dans cet Art" [In a word, *the light of reason dissipating in this way the doubt into which experience can plunge us* at any moment, will be the sure guarantee of the success that we can promise ourselves in this art].[16] He concludes the "Préface" by making it clear that the system is more important than experience, privileging theory over practice for its explanatory power: "Il ne suffit donc pas de sentir les effets d'une Science ou d'un Art, il faut de plus les concevoir de façon qu'on puisse les rendre intelligibles; & c'est à quoi je me suis principalement appliqué dans le corps de cet Ouvrage" (3) [Therefore it does not suffice to feel the effects of a science or of an art, it is necessary in addition to conceive of them in such a way that one may render them intelligible, and that is what I have applied myself to principally in the body of this work].

While theory is privileged, it is nonetheless derived from experience. The relation between the two is evident from the opening pages of *Génération harmonique*, where Rameau lays out a series of twelve propositions concerning the generation of sounds in the physical environment and their relationship to one another, followed by a series of seven experiments designed to confirm the propositions concerning the generation of sounds (1–20). In the conclusions, Rameau highlights the importance of commensurability in the transmission of sound vibration in the physical environment. As sounds are generated, harmonic resonances are created at specific intervals above the sounded tone. He maintains that sounds are audible insofar as these harmonic resonances are present (27–28). These intervals derived from harmonic resonance form the "natural" building blocks of music, generated from the physical properties inherent in the production of sound. Rameau summarizes:

> Reconnoissons donc désormais l'Harmonie comme un effet naturel qui résulte de la resonance de chaque Corps sonore en particulier, c'est de là qu'elle tire son origine: le Son apprétiable n'est pas unique de sa nature, il est Harmonieux, & son Harmonie donne cette proportion 1 1/3 1/5, qui se reproduit dans celle-ci 1, 3, 5, par la puissance réciproque des Vibrations plus lentes & plus promptes les unes sur les autres. (28–29)

> [Therefore let us henceforth recognize harmony as a natural effect that results from the resonance of each individual sounding body,[17] it is from there that it derives its origin: the appreciable sound is not single in its nature, it is harmonious, and its harmony gives this proportion: 1, 1/3, 1/5, which is reproduced in 1, 3, 5, by the reciprocal power of slower and faster vibrations against one another.]

Because each sound gives rise to a series of harmonic resonances at specific intervals, for Rameau all harmony derives from this "natural" effect. The octave, major third, and fifth represent the basis from which all harmonic intervals can be derived. Indeed, no single pitch that is ever sounded is really a single tone; rather, it contains within it the harmonic intervals that its sounding generates (30).

Despite the support of the seven experiments in the opening pages of the *Génération*, Rameau quickly makes it clear that experience is not the object of his study. Music is "une Science Phisico-mathématique" [a physicomathematical science] and, while physics generates the harmonic sequence 1, 3, 5, mathematics does all the rest. Rameau insists:

> Quant à l'objet Mathématique, qui consiste dans les rapports qu'ont entr'eux les Sons en proportion Harmonique, on peut le tourner de toutes les façons, le combiner, le renverser, supposer les parties du tout détachées les unes des autres, les supposer successives, les comparer entr'elles, en chercher les differences, &c. pour en faire usage selon les cas. Cet objet Mathématique, qui prend sa source dans la proportion Harmonique, va devenir désormais notre seul & unique guide, sans y oublier sa réproduction dans 1. 3. 5, [sic] qui sont en proportion Arithmétique. (31)

> [As for the mathematical object, which consists in the harmonic proportion of the relationships that the sounds have among themselves, one may turn it in all directions, combine it, reverse it, suppose all the parts of the whole detached from one another, suppose them to be successive, compare them among themselves, find the differences among them, etc., in order to make use of them according to the context, as the case may be. This mathematical object, which takes its origin in harmonic proportion, will become henceforth our sole and unique guide, without forgetting its reproduction in 1, 3, 5, which are in arithmetic proportion.]

While physics explains the terms of the system—the signs—mathematics, and specifically arithmetic, takes over the explanatory function for the rest of the theory. Rameau turns away from experience and empirical data and toward the a priori system of mathematics to derive the bulk of his harmonic theory.[18]

As a sign system, Rameau's theory of harmony bears a striking resemblance to the systems of the classical age described by Michel Foucault in *The Order of Things*.[19] For Foucault, the sign systems of the classical *episteme*

> introduced into knowledge probability, analysis, and combination, and the justified arbitrariness of the system. It was the sign system that gave rise simultaneously to the search for origins and calculability; to the constitution of tables that would fix the possible compositions, and to the restitution of a genesis on the basis of the simplest

elements; it was the sign system that linked all knowledge to a language, and sought to replace all languages with a system of artificial symbols and operations of a logical nature. (63)

While Foucault does not distinguish between the sign systems of the seventeenth and eighteenth centuries, and, specifically, not between the *esprit de système* and the *esprit systématique* noted by Cassirer, the description above from the *Order of Things* owes a greater debt to the *mathesis* of the *Logique de Port Royal* than it does to the *taxinomia* characteristic of the *Encyclopédie*.[20] In other words, the type of closed sign system that enables probability, analysis, and combination is disrupted by the unpredictability and, ultimately, arbitrariness of empirical data. Rameau's harmonic system is perceived to straddle the fence—at least at the opening of the eighteenth century—between an a priori system and an empirical system. The grounding of the system in the physical properties of sound enables a claim to "naturalness" and empirical data, while the architecture of the theory, built on mathematical relations, enables truth claims resting on a kind of mathematical certainty. In this respect, it is no wonder that d'Alembert cites Rameau in the *Discours préliminaire* of the *Encyclopédie* as exemplary, for his work does seemingly bridge the methodological gap.[21]

But in the theoretically oriented works, the grounding in empirical data quickly takes a back seat to mathematics, as we saw in the citation above from the *Génération*.[22] Rameau's primary aim, once the basic building blocks of the system have been grounded in physical, empirical reality, is to extrapolate from those signs to construct a theory that is virtually self-enclosed and free-standing. One example of the will to turn away from physical reality is Rameau's further reduction of the major triad (1, 3, 5) to the more basic third. In effect, Rameau argues (in an effort to be pedagogically clear, it must be noted) that all intervals in music—consonant and dissonant—may be reduced to the basic third.[23]

> Pour se rendre les choses plus famileres, l'on peut regarder à present les *Tierces* comme l'unique objet de tous les accords: En effet, pour former *l'accord parfait*, il faut ajoûter une *Tierce* à l'autre, & pour former tous les *accords dissonans*, il faut ajoûter trois ou quatre *Tierces* les unes aux autres; la difference de ces accords dissonans ne provenant que de la differente situation de ces *Tierces;* c'est pourquoy nous devons leur attribuer toute la force de l'Harmonie, en la reduisant à ses premiers degrez. (*Traité de l'harmonie*, 29–30)

[In order to make things more familiar, one can at present regard *thirds* as the unique object of all chords: In effect, in order to form the perfect chord, it is necessary to add a *third* to another, and in order to form all the *dissonant chords*, it is necessary to add three or four *thirds* one to another; the difference in these dissonant chords coming only from the different position of these *thirds*; this is why we must attribute to them all the force of harmony, in reducing it to its first degrees.]

Rameau's system is built around the proposition that all harmonic relations are reducible to the third. Even the major triad (1, 3, 5) is simply two thirds added together. In effect, Rameau is asserting that the major third is the building block of all music and the degree zero of all harmonic relations and chord structure.[24] Furthermore, Rameau's most famous insight holds that the order of the tones does not matter. The first to systematize the concept of chordal inversion, Rameau maintains that the root of a chord does not need to be played in the bass position. As Christensen elegantly articulates the proposition of the fundamental bass, "The transformation of a *bassus* into the *basse fondamentale* entailed a profound reconceptualization in which the lowest note of the *accord parfait* was to be heard not only as the *foundation* of the harmony, but also as the generative *source*—what we today call a chord root. Only in this way could all spacings or inversions of the triad be related back to its original position."[25]

The basic idea is that all chords are constructed out of harmonic relationships that can be added on to, subtracted from, inverted—in sum, subjected to all the mathematical operations of arithmetic—in order to produce all other harmonic intervals: changing the order of presentation changes nothing about the essential relationships. While Rameau obviously recognizes the importance of the octave and the fifth in harmonic relations, his theory nonetheless relies on the interval of the third to reduce all music to its most basic principle. The theory of the fundamental bass ensures that basic chords are recognized through all their possible articulated inversions.

Going one step further, the relations of the fundamental bass not only generate chords, they also generate sequences of notes to be played or progressions. As David E. Cohen explains, the fundamental bass serves as an explanatory model for music that conforms to Rameau's principles as well as music that does not:

> The fundamental bass does not simply announce the acoustical generator of each chord; it also represents the harmonic logic by which

chords relate to and succeed one another. It thus constitutes an *interpretation* of the musical surface in terms of Rameau's theoretical principles. Now among these principles is the stipulation that the fundamental bass progresses properly by harmonic intervals, that is, thirds and fifths (or their inversions). Progression by step is therefore somewhat problematical for Rameau. His typical solution, at least for progressions by ascending step, is to regard them as being, in effect, elliptical expressions of a more correct progression, consisting of a descending third followed by an ascending perfect fourth, which is "understood" [*sous-entendu*] by the listener.[26]

Cohen argues that Rameau's theory asserts our "intuitive perception" of "naturally derived principles" that enable us to perceive order in music.[27]

Thus Rameau's harmonic theory represents a system based on combination, addition, subtraction, and inversion, derived from the tones generated when any particular pitch is sounded. The rules of the system are fixed and grounded in the physical fact of overtones, partials, and harmonics. However, once inside the system, there is a great freedom of movement, assuming that the rules have been sufficiently mastered. Composition or the sequencing of particular chords also follows the rules grounded in the intervals.[28] Before turning to Rousseau's theory of music, it is important to note that within this closed, highly reductionist mathematical system, Rameau's freedom of movement is astonishing.[29] This is a point to which I will return, but for the moment, suffice it to say that despite the reduction of all harmonic relations to the basic third, this simple tool will enable Rameau to go virtually anywhere in his system, providing both the theoretical and practical grounding for limitless flexibility and movement.

Rousseau, Practice, and Relativism

Whereas Rameau's harmonic theory presents a rigorous, largely closed system with fixed rules derived from acoustics (the monochord and theory of the *corps sonore*), Rousseau's work in music, as we have already seen, never approaches systematicity. The work in music beginning with the *Projet concernant de nouveaux signes* and ending with the *Dictionnaire* not only does not present a harmonic system, but it is also internally inconsistent, and at times even contradictory. Nonetheless, despite the lack of system, and perhaps because of it, it is abundantly clear that Rameau is an ever-present interlocutor. Rousseau sets up many of his theoretical positions in dialogue with and in opposition to positions held by Rameau.

To begin with the basics, Rousseau rejects the fundamental notion that there is anything "natural" in Rameau's system. He maintains that the so-called experiments in the opening of the *Génération* do not prove any of the propositions that Rameau claims. Rousseau writes in the *Dictionnaire* in the article "Harmonie,"

> Je dois pourtant déclarer que ce Systême, quelque ingénieux qu'il soit, n'est rien moins que fondé sur la Nature, comme il le répète sans cesse; qu'il n'est établi que sur les analogies et des convenances qu'un homme inventif peut renverser demain par d'autres plus naturelles; qu'enfin, des expériences dont il le déduit, l'une est reconnue fausse, et l'autre ne fournit point les conséquences qu'il en tire. (5:846)

> [I must, however, declare that this system, ingenious as it may be, is anything but founded on nature, as he constantly repeats; that it is established based only on analogies and conformities that an inventive man can reverse tomorrow with other more natural ones; and that, finally, of the experiments from which he deduces it, one is recognized as false and the other does not provide the consequences that he derives from it.]

Rousseau's pointed attack kicks the support out from under the most basic claim of Rameau's system: that his harmonic theory is derived from nature based on the overtone and partial series.[30] Rather than the physical, empirical determinism that grounds Rameau's system, Rousseau instead asserts the arbitrariness of Rameau's system, maintaining that there are potentially infinite harmonic series to be discovered and claimed as the basis of composition theory. He denies that any specific pitch only creates the harmonics of the major triad (1, 3, 5) and maintains that the overtones are countless:

> D'ailleurs, le corps sonore ne donne pas seulement, outre le Son principal, les Sons qui composent avec lui l'Accord parfait, mais une infinité d'autre Sons, formés par toutes les aliquotes du corps sonore, lesquels n'entrent point dans cet Accord parfait. Pourquoi les premiers sont-ils consonnans, et pourquoi les autres ne le sont-ils pas, puisqu'ils sont tous également donnés par la Nature? (5:848-49)[31]

> [Besides, the sounding body does not only give, beyond the principal sound, the sounds that compose with it the perfect chord [major

triad], but also an infinity of other sounds, formed by all the aliquots of the sounding body, that do not enter into the perfect chord. Why are these first sounds consonant, and why are the others not, since they are all equally given by nature?]

Rousseau thus accuses Rameau of having grounded his system on an arbitrary choice guided by expediency: deriving harmonic theory from what he claims is the natural occurrence of the major triad in the physics of sound. Rather than an empirically grounded system, Rousseau perceives an a priori system whose first principles are determined not by the natural resonance of the major triad, but rather by the taste for the major triad determined by the history of Western music.

Using an "anthropological" argument against Rameau, Rousseau attacks the *mathesis* of the a priori system with what Foucault would characterize as *genesis* and *taxinomia*:[32]

> Quand on songe que, de tous les peuples de la terre, qui tous ont une Musique et un Chant, les Européens sont les seuls qui aient une *Harmonie*, des Accords, et qui trouvent ce mélange agréable; quand on songe que le monde a duré tant de siècles, sans que, de toutes les Nations qui ont cultivé les beaux Arts, aucune ait connu cette *Harmonie*. (5:851)

> [When we imagine that, of all the peoples of the world, who all have music and song, Europeans are the only ones who have harmony, chords, and who find this mixture agreeable; when we think that the world has lasted many centuries without any of all the nations who have cultivated the fine arts having known this *harmony*.]

Given the variety of music around the world and across time, how can one privilege Western music and claim that it is natural? The major triad, for Rousseau, is a convention of Western music that conditions our Western perceptions of all music and, indeed, all signs. The choice of it as the basis of a harmonic system is arbitrary, and it is an act bordering on hubris or, at the very least, ethnocentrism, to try to ground that choice in nature.

If the ground of the system is arbitrary, then certainly the system to which it gives rise is equally arbitrary. Rousseau perceives Rameau's harmonic system to be not only without foundation, but also useless in enabling or explaining the creation of music. In this respect, Rousseau's critique takes another step away from the theoretical system toward experience to privilege performance and reception over the mathematical beauty of an internally consistent system. In the article "Harmonie" in the *Dictionnaire*, he argues that even if we were to accept the proposition that all notes generate a harmonic sequence containing the octave, third, and fifth, such a "natural" sequence would not dictate how the notes should be combined to construct pleasing melodies:

> Le principe physique de la résonance nous offre les Accords isolés et solitaires; il n'en établit pas la succession. Une succession régulière est pourtant nécessaire. Un Dictionnaire de mots choisis n'est pas une harangue, ni un recueil de bons Accords une Pièce de Musique: il faut un sens, il faut de la liaison dans la Musique ainsi que dans le langage; il faut que quelque chose de ce qui précède se transmette à ce qui suit, pour que le tout fasse un ensemble et puisse être appelé véritablement un. (5:847)

> [The physical principle of resonance offers us isolated and solitary chords; it does not establish their succession. A regular succession is nonetheless necessary. A dictionary of chosen words is not a harangue, nor is a collection of good chords a piece of music: a meaning is necessary, connection is needed in music as it is in language; it is necessary that something of what precedes be transmitted to what follows, so that the whole creates an ensemble and may be truly called one.]

Echoing the argument concerning "unité de mélodie" discussed in the previous chapter, the argument about composition maintains the central importance of *liaison*, the stringing together of sequences of notes that together create not only the overall cohesion of a piece of music, but also the meaning to be communicated. While harmonic overtone series may determine our taste for certain combinations of notes sounded in chords, it does not offer any insight, at least for Rousseau, into why certain sequences of notes form phrases and ultimately parts of a larger piece of music.

Rousseau specifically attacks Rameau on the issue of rhythm, insisting that a sequence of notes says nothing without temporal indications of duration and meter.[33] In the textual fragment that has come to be known as "L'origine de la mélodie,"[34] Rousseau highlights the virtual quality of Rameau's conception of music by insisting on the importance of measure and note values for any piece of music:

Revenons un instant à la mesure. Qu'est-ce qu'une suite de notes indéterminées quant à la durée? des sons isolés et dépourvus de tout effet commun, qu'on entend séparement les uns des autres, et qui, bien qu'engendrés par une succession harmonique n'offrent aucun ensemble à l'oreille et attendent pour former une phrase et dire quelque chose, la liaison que la mesure leur donne. Qu'on présente au Musicien une suite de notes de valeur indéterminée, il en va faire cinquante melodies entiérement différentes, seulement par les diverses maniéres de les scander, d'en combiner et varier les mouvements; preuve invincible que c'est à la mesure qu'il appartient de déterminer toute mélodie. (5:337)

[Let us return for a moment to meter. What is a series of notes that are indeterminate with respect to duration? Isolated sounds deprived of any common effect that one hears separately, the ones apart from the others, and that, although generated by a harmonic sequence, does not offer any ensemble to the ear and waits for the liaison that meter gives them to form a phrase and say something. Present a musician with a series of notes of indeterminate value and he will make fifty entirely different melodies from them, solely through the different ways of scanning them, of combining them, and of varying their movements; irrefutable proof that it belongs to meter to determine all melody.]

Setting aside for a moment the privileging of melody over harmony, Rousseau's insistence on the infinite variety contained within the possibilities for performance of a sequence of notes related to time and meter demonstrates that his conception of music considers practice and performance over harmonic relations and mathematics. Creating a sequence of notes is not enough: music requires structure that binds the notes together through rhythm to create phrasing and, ultimately, formal coherence within the piece.

Rousseau's insistence on rhythm—a topic not often broached by Rameau[35]—underscores his more practice-oriented understanding of music. The insistence on practice, and the downplaying of the importance of theory, shifts the focus of attention from the formal mathematical properties of the system toward the performance and, especially, the reception of musical works.[36] For Rousseau, what is paramount is the effect that music has on the listener. As we have seen in the preceding chapters, and as I will discuss in detail in relation to folk music in the following chapter, music has the ability to move the passions and communicate through melody. What is significant in the debate with Rameau is that harmony, and especially music composed in order to highlight complex harmonic relations, does not have the same capacity to move the listener according to Rousseau.

In place of the empirically derived elements of Rameau's harmonic system, Rousseau introduces the radical notion that sign systems are conventional and arbitrary. Signs are not derived from nature but rather created by human beings to facilitate communication. While signs can be motivated to some extent, they are nonetheless ultimately arbitrary. As we saw in the preceding chapter in the discussion of the *Essai sur l'origine des langues*, the first languages were figurative, supplementing the referential capacity of gestures with the addition of emotion.[37] Indeed, according to Rousseau, it was the need to communicate emotion that necessitated the creation of music and language. Therefore, composition (the selection of sequences of notes, their rhythm, meter, phrasing, etc.) must be guided by emotion in order to communicate passion and feeling. Because the signs are arbitrary, there are no sure guides for composition other than listening to the heart and attempting to communicate passion to other human beings. Contra Rameau, acoustics and mathematics cannot provide the basis for meaningful musical communication. Melody (and not harmony) must be created from genuine feeling.

Rousseau's insistence on practice and reception contrasts sharply with Rameau's privileging of the abstract mathematical system on the question of temperament. As we saw at the opening of this chapter, while Rameau advocates for equal temperament, Rousseau continues to defend mean-tone and well temperament formulas because of what he believes is the force of the purer intervals. Most striking in this polemic from the standpoint of the theory/practice debate is Rameau's pushing aside of auditory experience in favor of maintaining the integrity of the entire system. Rameau writes in *Génération harmonique*, in defense of equal temperament,

> Qu'importe, après cela, que les Tierces, les Sixtes, les Tons, les Demi-tons soient plus ou moins altérés, l'Oreille y fait peu d'attention, dès qu'elle y est soutenue par son guide: tous ces intervales ne sont que passagers; au lieu que les fondamentaux existent continuellement, et font toujours sous-entendre avec eux la perfection qui manque à ce qu'on entend: ils font plus encore, ils donnent aux intervales telle qualité qui leur convient, la changent même, comme le prouve la Troisiéme Proposition. (96)

[What does it matter, after that, that the thirds, sixths, the tones, half tones be more or less altered, the ear pays little attention to it, as soon as it is supported by its guide: all these intervals are only momentary; whereas the fundamentals exist continuously, and always allow to be heard with them the perfection that lacks in what we hear: they even do more, they give to the intervals the quality that is appropriate to them, even change it, as the third proposition proves.]

Rameau maintains that our ears will "correct" what we hear, that the guide of the fundamental bass will enable us to adjust the intervals in our heads so that we may perceive the perfection that is lacking in the actual performance. Thus, in this respect, music as an aesthetic object remains a virtual object of perception: the performance gestures toward and evokes the perfect music that plays in our heads.[38]

As we have already seen, Rousseau invokes the experience of musicians and harpsichord makers against Rameau's arguments in favor of equal temperament. Responding to Rameau's claim that our ears will become accustomed to the new temperament with time, Rousseau retorts in "Harmonie" that the trained listener will have a difficult time getting used to the "beating" [battements] that the tuning causes: "Il paroît donc que s'accoutumer à cette manière d'Accord n'est pas, pour une Oreille exercée et sensible, une habitude aisée à prendre" (5:1112) [It seems that becoming accustomed to this type of tuning, for a trained and sensitive ear, is not an easy habit to acquire]. Oddly enough, shifting the terrain to Rameau's mathematical argument, he goes on to cite the simplicity of the mathematical relations as the cause of our pleasure in hearing perfect fifths: "Au reste, je ne puis m'empêcher de rappeller ici ce que j'ai dit au mot CONSONNANCE, sur la raison du plaisir que les Consonnances font à l'oreille, tirée de la simplicité des rapports" (ibid.) [Moreover, I cannot prevent myself from recalling here what I said under the word "consonance," on the reason for the pleasure that consonances produce in the ear, derived from the simplicity of the relations].

Rousseau's recourse to the judgment of the trained ear in response to Rameau's insistence on the integrity of the system is emblematic of the theory/practice divide between them. While Rameau embodies an *esprit de système* that blends theory and empirical practice, Rousseau represents an *esprit systématique* that is not overly wedded to systematicity. Nonetheless, the force of experience in performance and reception dictates aesthetic judgments for Rousseau.

## Absolute, Relative, Determined, Arbitrary: The Metaphysical Stakes in Music Theory

As we have seen, Rameau's harmonic system contains signs (intervals) determined by empirical facts. From Rameau's perspective, his theory is grounded in nature: the naturally occurring harmonic series present in every note dictate the terms of the system. All the moves within the system—once the terms have been established—are regulated by the rules of arithmetic. As in a mathematical proof or probability table, the laws governing musical composition are the fixed rules that enable great freedom of movement and creativity from within the system. On the other side, Rousseau maintains that the terms of the system are arbitrary: human beings select particular tones from an infinite series of possibilities in order to construct sequences and phrases that are meaningful. Much like language, Rousseau asserts that the choices and constructions of composers must be guided by something beyond a knowledge of harmony. While he recognizes the necessity of knowing how to fill in chords, develop a chord progression, etc., he also maintains that composition goes beyond these skills. Using the familiar comparison to language, in the article "Composition" in the *Dictionnaire* he asserts that "avec les seules règles de l'Harmonie on n'est pas plus près de savoir la *Composition*, qu'on ne l'est d'être un Orateur avec celles de la Grammaire" (5:720) [with only the rules of harmony one is no closer to knowing composition than one is to being an orator with the rules of grammar]. He goes on to assert that the composer must have something inside himself to consult: "Toutes ces choses ne sont encore que des préparatifs à la *Composition*: mais il faut trouver en soi-même la source des beaux Chants" (ibid.) [All of these things are only the preparations for composition: but it is necessary to find in oneself the source of beautiful songs].

To characterize succinctly the dispute at the level of harmonic system, Rameau's fixed system is derived from empirical data. While infinite possibilities of combination exist within the system, the terms of the system itself are fixed. Certain moves are simply out of bounds, determined by the physical properties of sound.[39] From Rousseau's standpoint, the rules of harmony exist, but without reference to a fixed point outside of the system. The terms of the system (notes), as well as the rules of the system (harmonic theory), are both conventions that have some reference to an outside reality related to acoustics and performance practice, but ultimately cannot be fixed in any permanent way. As the anthropological and historical arguments demonstrate, different forms of music with different sounds, scales, intervals, tempi, etc. are not only imaginable but have also been discovered in different parts of the world. The variety of world music only demonstrates the arbitrariness of the Western harmonic system.[40]

On the face of it, it would seem that Rameau's closed fixed system represents a more absolutist approach to music theory, while Rousseau's denial of empirical grounding and his appeal to convention represents a more relativist view. But as we saw when examining the question of temperament, these positions are not as clear-cut as they would first seem. Rameau is willing to sacrifice the purity of intervals on keyboard instruments—the very foundation of his theory—in order to preserve absolute freedom of mobility throughout the entire circle of keys. But before we go too far in identifying an element of relativism in Rameau's sanctioning of equal temperament, it is important to recognize that it may represent an effort to stave off even more "arbitrariness" in the harmonic system. As Alexander Rehding argues, Rameau's advocacy of equal temperament may amount to a guard against the inclusion of microtones in his system, elements that would lead to even more "arbitrariness." Rehding writes, "For Rameau . . . the keyboard instrument stands for a barrier demarcating what our "ear" is capable of perceiving, or rather, a safeguard to protect what Rameau considered harmonically inadmissible."[41] On the other hand, Rousseau, as willing as he is to acknowledge the arbitrariness in the selection of tones to structure a harmonic system, is unwilling to bend or compromise on the tuning of particular intervals. On the same question of microtones, Rousseau is more willing to accept not only their existence but also, more important, their potential effect on the listener. Thus, on the question of temperament, the absolutist (Rameau) is a relativist when it comes to practice (although he may fear more "arbitrariness" without the compromise), and the relativist (Rousseau) is an absolutist when it comes to performance.

Before turning to the metaphysical stakes in the dispute between Rameau and Rousseau, I would like to examine one more musical debate to illustrate the subtlety of the two positions. This debate concerns an exchange about a monologue from Lully's opera *Armide*.[42] Rameau cites the monologue "Enfin il est en ma puissance" in his *Nouveau système de musique théorique* as a perfect example of the rules of modulation that his treatise sets forth.[43] Some twenty-seven years later, the year after the eruption of the *querelle des bouffons*, Rousseau pens the *Lettre sur la musique française*, specifically taking aim at the Lully monologue praised by Rameau. In his criticism of the monologue, Rousseau rehearses his usual arguments against French opera and specifically recitative, claiming to judge the genre on its own terms. The basic line of criticism maintains that there is a serious disjuncture between music and text: while the monologue depicts an array of emotion and psychological depth and change, the music remains more or less static, unable to communicate the profound transformation that is occurring within the character on stage (5:322–23). While Rousseau criticizes many aspects of the monologue, the one point to which he returns—and to which Rameau will respond—concerns the lack of modulation.[44] The criticism, put in the simplest terms, maintains that while the lyrics communicate conflicting emotions, interior struggle, and ultimately profound transformation, the music does not adequately reflect the lyrical content. As Brian Hyer defines it, modulation for Rameau means "fitting both an accompaniment and a melodic part to the nuances of a poetic text." The criticism then amounts to an attack on "taste."[45] For Rousseau, some more marked type of change in the music (perhaps modulation from one key to another) would better "represent" this psychological change in the character. Instead, according to Rousseau, Lully chooses to indicate change with silence or rest, but inevitably returns with the same key palette, missing an opportunity to express emotional turmoil through tonal movement in the music:

> Voyons, maintenant, comment le Musicien a exprimé cette marche secrette du cœur d'Armide. Il a bien vu qu'il falloit mettre un intervalle entre ces deux vers et les précédens, et il a fait un silence qu'il n'a rempli de rien, dans un moment où Armide avoit tant de choses à sentir, et par conséquent l'orchestre à exprimer. Après cette pause il recommence exactement dans le même ton, sur le même accord, sur la même note par où il vient de finir, passe successivement par tous les sons de l'accord durant une mesure entière, et quitte enfin avec peine le ton autour duquel il vient de tourner si mal à propos. (5:324)

> [Let us now see how the musician expressed this secret progress in Armide's heart. He rightly saw that it was necessary to put an interval between these two verses and the preceding ones, and he creates a rest that he filled with nothing, at a moment when Armide was feeling so many things and, as a result, that the orchestra could have expressed. After this pause he begins again in exactly the same key, on the same chord, on the same note where he just finished, passes successively through all the notes of the chord during an entire measure, and finally leaves with difficulty the key in which he just moved so inopportunely.]

Rousseau's test of good music throughout the analysis amounts to the following: if you take away the lyrics and listen to the music alone, are you able to understand the meaning that is being conveyed? In the case of the Lully monologue, Rousseau reads the lack of tonal movement as a failure to represent the gamut of emotion expressed in the lyrics and, therefore, as a musical failure.[46] Quite pointedly, since Rameau had cited this particular piece of music as an excellent example of modulation, Rousseau goes after Rameau's conception of modulation to offer a stinging critique. Where Rameau sees a beautiful application of the rules of harmony, which I will discuss in detail below, Rousseau sees only a kind of rigid adherence to academic standards of composition that work against the expressive ability of the music (5:322).

Rousseau's standard of judgment applies a number of principles to Lully's monologue. In concluding the discussion, Rousseau gives a summary of the faults he finds with the piece that reveal the principles underlying his judgment:

> Pour résumer en peu de mots mon sentiment sur le célèbre monologue, je dis que si on l'envisage comme du chant, on n'y trouve ni mesure, ni caractére, ni mélodie: si l'on veut que ce soit du récitatif, on n'y trouve ni naturel ni expression; quelque nom qu'on veuille lui donner, on le trouve rempli de sons filés, de trilles et autres ornemens du chant bien plus ridicules encore dans une pareille situation qu'ils ne sont communement dans la Musique Française. La modulation en est réguliere, mais puérile par cela même, scholastique, sans énergie, sans affection sensible. (5:327)

> [To sum up in a few words my sentiment on this famous monologue, I say that if one imagines it as song, one finds neither meter, nor character, nor melody; if one desires it to be recitative, one finds neither naturalness nor expressiveness; whatever name one desires to give to it, one finds it full of strung-together notes, of trills and other vocal ornaments that are even more ridiculous in such a situation than they usually are in French music. The modulation is regular, but puerile for this very reason, pedantic, without energy, and without any perceptible feeling.]

Putting aside the generic question of whether the piece should be judged according to the standards of song or recitative,[47] it is clear that Rousseau's judgment relies on a fixed reference point of emotional expression to judge the work. In spite of his relativism with respect to musical signs in his disagreements with Rameau (as we saw above), in his analysis of Lully he adheres to a system in which certain types of modulation (in either the older or newer sense of the term) represent emotional conflict better than others. In his estimation of the piece, Lully has failed to represent the emotions accurately, charging him, in essence, with a lack of musical verisimilitude.[48]

The charge finds fault on at least three accounts. The first, as we have already seen, is that Lully fails to mark the range of emotion in the scene with either appropriate melodic movement or changes in key. The second is that Lully's regularity runs counter to the psychological transformation being represented. Rousseau suggests that Lully could have used "les réticences, les interruptions, les transitions intellectuelles que le Poëte offroit au Musicien" [the moments of reticence, the interruptions, the intellectual transitions that the poet offered to the musician] as a guide for the musical development, but instead maintained a boring regularity by adhering to the strict rules governing harmonic modulation. Finally, Rousseau maintains that filling in all of the chords and harmony actually detracts from the power of the music. In this final argument, Rousseau turns Rameau's harmonic theory against Lully to argue that if particular intervals have emotional effects, then the composer must take care not to dilute the effect of the intervals by filling in all the chording and voices. Citing Rameau for his own purposes, Rousseau asserts, "que chaque consonance a son caractére particulier, c'est-à-dire, une maniere d'affecter l'ame qui lui est propre; que l'effet de la tierce n'est point le même que celui de la quinte, ni l'effet de la quarte le même que celui de la sixte" (5:312) [that each consonance has its own particular character, that is to say, its way of affecting the soul that is proper to it; that the effect of the third is not the same as that of the fifth, nor the effect of the fourth the same as that of the sixth].[49] If the desired effect is to stimulate the audience to feel a particular emotion based on the quality of a fifth, then, according to Rousseau, adding a major third to create a major triad might actually weaken and not strengthen the effect of the music: "je vois clairement que deux consonances ajoutées l'une à l'autre mal à propos, quoique selon les regles des accords, pourront, même en augmentant l'harmonie, affoiblir mutuellement leur effet, le combattre, ou le partager" (5:313) [I see clearly that two consonances added one to the other inopportunely, even if according to the rules of chording, can, even while augmenting the harmony, weaken, fight against, or divide its effect]. While Rousseau never specifically levels this criticism at Lully, it seems clear that the lack of energy and emotion that he finds in the *Armide* monologue has everything to do with a form of harmony that is overly systematized to the detriment of the expression of emotion.

The turning of Rameau's argument against him reveals the point at which Rousseau shifts from being a relativist to having a fixed point of reference. Although his "system" is not based on harmonic relations in the way that Rameau's is, nonetheless intervals have meaning derived from the effects that they produce in the listener. Preserving that emotional charge, making the appropriate connections between the emotional force of intervals and the lyric content of scenes, is what makes good music for Rousseau.[50] The critique of lack of verisimilitude goes to the heart of the system: Rousseau perceives in Lully a strict adherence to a self-contained system like Rameau's, whereas he desires a reference point for the system anchored in the subjective experience of sound. The standard of verisimilitude reveals the limits of Rousseau's relativism in music.

Taking up the gauntlet thrown down by Rousseau in the *Lettre*, the following year Rameau responds to Rousseau's analysis of *Armide* in his *Observations sur notre instinct pour la musique, et sur son principe*. As the title of the work indicates, Rameau defends a notion of instinctual (natural) enjoyment of music based on harmony, not melody. For the listener who abandons him or herself to the music, the experience awakens feelings that are lost on the listener (here Rousseau) who is preoccupied with musical technicalities (iii–viii). Answering directly Rousseau's charge about the lack of modulation in the Lully monologue, Rameau states emphatically that Rousseau got it wrong: "Qui croiroit, dit Monsieur Rousseau, que le Musicien a laissé toute cette agitation dans le même ton, et cetera. Qui croiroit qu'après une affirmation aussi absolue on eût pû se tromper? Non-seulement toute cette agitation n'est pas dans le même Ton, mais il y change par du Chromatique sous-entendu à chaque demi-hémistiche (96–97) [Who would believe, says Monsieur Rousseau, that the musician left all this agitation in the same key, etc. Who would believe that after such an absolute affirmation one could possibly be wrong? Not only is all this agitation not in the same key, but there is also an implied chromatic change in each half hemistich].

Rameau goes on to argue that not only is there near-perfect chromatic modulation in the Lully piece that Rousseau fails to recognize, but, more pointedly, that it is also necessary to judge the piece based on listening, not just examining the score: "on dira peut-être qu'on ne voit aucun de ces Diézes ni Bémols dans le Chant, dans la Basse, nonplus que dans le Chiffre: aussi faut-il plus que des yeux pour juger en pareil cas" (98) [one will say perhaps that none of these sharps or flats is visible in the song, in the bass, or in the figuration: but maybe it is necessary in such cases to judge with more than the eyes]. Rameau seems to turn the table on Rousseau as Rousseau attempted to do with him: from Rameau's perspective, Rousseau has based his analysis on pure theory and not allowed himself to feel the emotion of the piece. If he had, he would have recognized the subtle emotion expressed through the suggested chromatic modulation in the harmony.[51]

Rather than the closed-system type of analysis that one would expect from Rameau, he delivers a subtle reading of the Lully monologue that hinges on the recognition of an implied chromatic development (characteristic of his harmonic theory) in tune with the emotions of the piece. While the analysis certainly owes a great deal to his complex and complete understanding of the rules of harmony, it nonetheless makes reference to both performance and reception, arguing that it is the harmony, and not the melody, that moves both singer and listener.

> Aussi lorsque le Chanteur reconnoît, par les paroles, qu'il doit marquer du trouble à je frémis, sa voix l'exprime comme d'elle-même: et sans penser à la cause qui le fait agir, sans la soupçonner même, il se trouve entraîné à cette expression par le fonds d'Harmonie qui la lui inspire; l'Auditeur, de son côté, se trouve ému: qu'il n'en cherche donc pas la raison, puisqu'il peut s'y tromper, ou du moins qu'il la reconnoisse dans le Bémol exprimé ou sous-entendu, qu'améne le fonds d'Harmonie par une espèce de Chromatique en descendant: qu'il reconnoisse pareillement que le sentiment de fureur qu'il éprouve, en entendant Vengeons-nous, vient de deux nouveaux Diézes, dont l'un forme le Chromatique en montant avec la Soudominante ut qui le précede immédiatement, ce même Diéze descendant ensuite à son Bémol pour exprimer je soupire. (102–4)

> [Furthermore, when the singer recognizes from the lyrics that she must show agitation at "je frémis," her voice expresses it as if by itself: and without thinking about the cause that makes her act, without even suspecting it, she finds herself led to this expression by the basis of the harmony that inspires it in her; the listener, on his side, finds himself moved: let him not look for the reason, since he can be wrong about it, or at least let him recognize it in the expressed or implied flat that conveys the basis of the harmony through a kind of descending chromatic. Let him likewise recognize that the feeling of fury that he feels, in hearing "vengeons-nous," comes from two new

sharps, the first of which forms the ascending chromatic with the subdominant C that immediately precedes it, this same sharp afterward descending next to its flat to express "je soupire."]

The technical analysis of Lully's chromatism hinges on the effects of the harmony on both the performer and the listener. Against Rousseau, Rameau argues that Lully's subtlety lies in his simple suggestion of the movement of emotion. Charging Rousseau indirectly with a lack of feeling, limited talent, and of "forcing nature," Rameau suggests that the failure to appreciate the music comes from being preoccupied with melody and, therefore, ignoring the effects of harmony (105–6).[52] Ironically, Rameau marshals the force of performance and reception to defend Lully against charges of lack of feeling, by countering that it must be the listener who is at fault.

Rousseau's mistakes in the analysis of Lully allow Rameau an opening to defend his conception of the predominance of harmony from recent attacks by Rousseau.[53] But the mistakes also point out the blind spot in Rousseau's understanding of Rameau's conception of music. Unable to perceive the implied chromatic development in the monologue, he sees only static, academic composition. Rameau, on the other hand, hears a great deal of movement and subtlety in the piece. From the perspective of his all-encompassing closed harmonic system, Rameau appreciates Lully's freedom of movement through the implied chromatic development. I would argue that the sophistication and subtlety of Rameau's system allow him an almost limitless freedom of movement, while Rousseau's attention to melody prevents him from hearing what Rameau hears.[54] Paradoxically, the closed system produces nearly limitless possibilities, while the relativism of conventions leads to an adherence to verisimilitude that closes down certain lines of compositional creativity.

In addition to the paradoxical shift with respect to absolutism and relativism, the debate over the Lully recitative also marks a change in positions with respect to performance and reception. Whereas many of Rameau's treatises, as we have seen, ultimately privilege theory over practice, here Rameau emphasizes listening over reading the music. And, in an attempt to score points against his chief musical rival and adversary, Rousseau attempts to argue with Rameau on Rameau's terms: he invokes harmonics and intervals in support of the claim that French music fails to express emotion. While it is clear that some of these strategies of argumentation are designed for polemical purposes, it is also true that the flip-flops must necessarily complicate our understanding of each side's perspective. Absolute and relative values, natural determination and conventional signs, exist on both sides, as do appeals to "nature," "emotion," and rule-governed composition.

One final point needs to be stressed in the debate about *Armide*. While Lully's musical accompaniment to Quinault's libretto is the nominal subject of the debate, it is important to note that the monologue "Enfin il est en ma puissance" concerns a scene in which the heroine feels compassion toward her intended victim. At a critical moment of the recitative, when Armide intends to kill Renaud in his sleep, she sings,

> Quel trouble me saisit? qui me fait hésiter?
> Qu'est-ce qu'en sa faveur la pitié me veut dire?
> Frappons! . . . Ciel! Qui peut m'arrêter?[55]

> [What confusion seizes me? What makes me hesitate?
> What is pity trying to say in his favor?
> Let's strike! . . . Heavens! What can stop me?]

Overcome with feelings of love for Renaud, she cannot follow through with the planned act of vengeance.

From the perspective of Rousseau's work, the appearance of the word "pitié" in the climactic scene is significant. In his analysis of this passage of the monologue in the *Lettre*, he acknowledges that Lully modulates (in the older sense) from the tonic to the dominant, but rejects the modulation on the grounds that it is insufficient to express the emotion of the scene: "il est bien question de tonique et de dominante dans un instant où toute liaison harmonique doit être interrompue, où tout doit peindre le désordre et l'agitation" (5:325) [it is indeed a question of tonic and dominant in a moment when all harmonic connection should be interrupted, when everything should depict disorder and agitation].[56] While the debate between Rameau and Rousseau is often understood from the musical standpoint of harmony versus melody, the appearance of pity in the scene in question suggests that, alongside the aesthetic criteria, other factors may be at work in Rousseau's judgment of Lully.[57] I would suggest that Armide's attempt to deny her own feelings of pity represents for Rousseau an "unnatural" act—an attempt to deny one of the most basic aspects of our human identity. The *Discours sur l'origine de l'inégalité* famously posits pity and the self-preservation instinct as two principles that exist in the state of nature, anterior to the development of reason.[58] For a character to wrestle with her conflicting desire for vengeance and her "natural" feeling of pity represents a kind of tragic struggle for Rousseau. In Rousseau's worldview, it would be on a par with seventeenth-century struggles between duty and amorous passion.[59] In the context of the Lully opera, no doubt the force and import of the epic struggle between "natural" pity and the desire for vengeance appear to Rousseau to be weakened and demeaned. From Rousseau's perspective, pity—the foundation for all human morality—cannot be lightly shaken. The battle that rages in Armide between her natural goodness and her corrupted social self is nothing less than the struggle between good and evil. The slight movement from the tonic to the dominant cannot begin to capture the epic emotion of this psychological struggle to suppress her natural morality. A careful examination of the lyric content of the scene reveals that the dispute goes beyond the harmony versus melody debate, and beyond the theory versus practice disagreement, suggesting a kind of moral imperative to express emotion through a musical vehicle that is appropriate to the scene. If Lully fails to express the anguish of Armide's attempt to deny natural pity, then he has committed not only an aesthetic faux pas of overly academic composition, but he has also failed to signal the depth of emotion inherent in the moral struggle of the scene.

Aesthetics, Epistemology, Metaphysics

The debate over the monologue in *Armide* lays out in full detail the scope of the disagreement between Rameau and Rousseau. As we have seen, the crux of the matter concerns a kind of musical verisimilitude demanded by Rousseau that finds the modulation inadequate to express the depth of passion present in the scene. Where Rameau sees subtle chromatic development, Rousseau misses and/or dismisses subtlety and demands a bolder statement. Rameau's *esprit de système* finds no fault with complex harmonic development that for him beautifully illustrates the capacity of harmonic systems. At the other extreme, Rousseau's demands for more emotional expression echo his understanding of the source of all musical impulses in the passions.

Rameau's conception of harmonic theory—and musical composition as a part of harmonic theory—in a sense privileges epistemology over aesthetics. While it is true that he has a fine appreciation for subtle and complex forms of musical expression, as is evident in the Lully analysis, it is also true that for Rameau harmony is first derived from the fundamental bass and then from the physical constraints of the sounding body (*corps sonore*). Rameau never loses sight of the fact that all notes, all sounding bodies, simultaneously produce their principle tone and the harmonic series of overtones and partials that they generate.[60] For his later theory, any assessment of a piece of music must be grounded in a deep understanding of the acoustic conditions for the possibility of forms of musical expression. The empirical fact of harmonics produces a system of rules of composition against which any piece of music ought to be judged. These are not arbitrary rules. For Rameau, these rules are grounded in "nature" and, as such, can never be circumvented.[61] The goal of the composer is to find ever new ways of combining, through addition, subtraction, and inversion, the notes that form "natural" harmonic relations in such a way as to move freely throughout the system.

While Rousseau is clear that the goal of musical composition is to express passion (and I will return to his position below), Rameau's position on the role or meaning of music is a little more difficult to tease out. His modified Cartesian approach to music maintains that the system is paramount. Truths within the system are derived from the empirical experience of the sounding body and the mathematical possibilities to which it gives rise. In a sense, art and science are inseparable in his system. As he writes in the preface to the *Traité de l'harmonie*,

> La Musique est une science qui doit avoir des regles certaines; ces regles doivent être tirées d'un principe évident, & ce principe ne peut gueres nous être connu sans le secours des Mathematiques: Aussi dois-je avoüer que, nonobstant toute l'experience que je pouvois m'être acquise dans la Musique, pour l'avoir pratiquée pendant une assez longue suite de temps, ce n'est cependant que par le secours des Mathematiques que mes idées se sont débroüillées, & que la lumiere y a succedé à une certaine obscurité, dont je ne m'appercevois pas auparavant. (unpaginated, iii)

> [Music is a science that must have certain rules; these rules must be derived from an evident principle, and this principle can hardly be known to us without the aid of mathematics: Moreover, I must admit that notwithstanding all the experience that I might have acquired in music, for having practiced it for a fairly long period of time, it is only with the aid of mathematics that my ideas were sorted out and that light followed a certain obscurity there, one that I had not perceived before.]

While mathematics enabled him to see the truth and system behind musical composition, this does not mean that there was no good music before him. He reserves for himself, in increasingly self-aggrandizing and arrogant terms over the course of his works, the role of having shed the light of reason on the mysteries of music. But he does acknowledge that others before him have written beautiful music that is consistent with his principles without the advantage of his insight. Lully is one such example. In his assessment of Lully's recitative, he credits Lully's instinct for having led the way to perfect composition:

> Qu'on y fasse réflèxion, après s'être bien mis au fait du fonds de l'Art, et l'on verra de quoi le seul Instinct est capable; car Lulli, conduit par le sentiment, et par le goût, n'avoit aucune connoissance de ce fonds, inconnu de son tems. En voyant ce que peut le seul Instinct, on voit en même tems la simplicité du principe qui le guide: deux Toniques dont l'une est soumise aux loix que l'autre lui impose, voilà tout ce qui est employé pour rendre une expression dans la plus grande perfection qu'on puisse désirer. (*Observations*, 76–77)

> [Let us reflect on it, after having made ourselves fully acquainted with the facts of the basis of the art, and we will see what instinct alone is capable of, for Lully, guided by feeling and by taste, had no knowledge of this basis, unknown in his time. In seeing what instinct alone is capable of, we see at the same time the simplicity of the principle that guides him: two tonics, of which one is submitted to the laws that the other imposes on it, that is all that is employed to render an expression in the highest perfection that we can desire.]

Instinct as the key that guides musical creativity reinforces the claims of grounding music in "nature." Understood as prerational, naturally occurring impulses, instinct guides the composer to write work in accordance with the laws of acoustics that are established by the "natural" laws of harmony.[62] In a kind of Cartesian perfect fit between human instinctual ability and the ordered world, music appears as an expression of this "natural harmony." Rameau says as much in the incomplete final manuscript known as "Vérités intéressantes," in which he expresses his most metaphysical claims about music in relation to mathematics, science, and theology.[63] While the fragmentary text only suggests the contours of the complete argument, the movement among music, mathematics, science, and theology is clear. Rameau claims that the sounding body represents a kind of "antecedent," it contains within it all the sounds that will be generated in the succeeding musical progression. The harmonic system derived from the sounding body establishes a kind of horizon of possible sounds and directions that enables and contextualizes all melody and all musical creativity. Directly parallel to mathematical antecedents, the sounding body also corresponds to God as the ultimate antecedent of all creation. Toward the end of the manuscript, Rameau indulges in a wild series of associations that draws out the connections among music, math, science, and theology:

> Quelles images. Peut on en conçevoir qui repondent mieux aux attributs dignes d'un Dieu Créateur? images qui nous parlent, qui se montrent aux yeux, et se font toucher au doigt. Dieu, cet Antécédent de toute éternité, contient tout dans son esprit, dans son intelligence, sans pouvoir etre contenu: et ce tout ne peut etre pour nous que la matiere, où cet Antécédent a choisit des *Moiens*, appellez *Causes secondes*, pour s'en reposer sur eux de l'etablisssement de cet univers, en leur cédant le droit (sans les abandonner cepend<sup>t</sup> puisqu'il est présent partout) de former de cette matiere, une infinité d'Etres innombrables, dont chacun puisse cooperer continuellement de l'un à l'autre à sa propagation, en se remplaçant successiment [*sic*], le tout dans un ordre si beau qu'on n'a pas su lui donner un autre titre que celui d'harmonie. (95–96)

> [What images. Can one conceive of any that responds better to the attributes worthy of God the Creator? images that speak to us, that show themselves to our eyes, and make themselves felt to the touch. God, that Antecedent of all eternity, contains everything in His spirit, in His intelligence, without being able to be contained: and this whole can only be material for us, where this antecedent chose the *means*, called *secondary causes*, in order to rest on them the establishment of this universe, in ceding the right to them (without however abandoning them since He is present everywhere) to form from this matter an infinity of innumerable beings, in which each one can cooperate continually with one another for their propagation, by replacing themselves successively, the whole in an order so beautiful that it has been given no other title than that of harmony.]

God, the first cause, creates the manifold of material creation, setting in motion a chain of causes and effects that aligns perfectly with the principles of mathematics, the sciences, and music. It is no wonder, claims Rameau, that we call this "harmony."

But if God the creator set this entire system in motion, what then is the role of the composer or musician? How and why does she or he create music? In "Vérités intéressantes," Rameau repeats his earlier claims about the role of instinct. In speaking about algebra, he writes, "une pareille invention doit faire admirer en même tems, et son auteur et l'instinct qui la lui a suggérée: je dis l'instinct, d'autant qu'il est *l'unique source de l'imagination*" (81, my emphasis) [such an invention must at the same time make us admire both its author and the instinct that suggested it to him: I say instinct, inasmuch as it is *the unique source of imagination*]. Instinct guides the musician, mathematician, and scientist to discover foundational truths about the harmony of the universe that God created. Making music is a matter of both following this "natural" instinct and following the scientific and mathematical principles discovered by Rameau. While feeling and taste have a role to play, they are clearly overshadowed by the unyielding force of a system backed by metaphysics. All imagination finds its source in natural instinct.

Anticipating Rousseau's position on these questions, it seems odd that Rameau offers no explanation of music as a kind of tribute to the deity that created a harmonious world. Perhaps desirous of keeping the focus on the mathematicoscientific basis of the system, and away from questions of metaphysics, the mere existence of harmony in nature seems to stand in for any explanation about why human beings make music. Even the final manuscript fragment begins in medias res, leaving us to ponder whether or not the finished text would have tackled the question.

Perhaps the question does belong more to the historical, anthropological type of account characteristic of Rousseau and the *esprit systématique*: philosophy tries to make sense of empirical data from the physical world through the creation of systems. The systems are not a priori, nor are they transcendent; they serve an explanatory function. In this respect, Rousseau's debates with Rameau highlight a further shift in thinking away from a Cartesian approach to music and toward a contextualized understanding of the development of aesthetic forms.

For Rousseau, human beings make music for a variety of reasons, but the core impulse remains the communication of passion and feeling. In "L'origine de la mélodie," he dismisses Rameau's metaphysical explanations as insufficient to ever account for the power of music over the emotions:

Ne pensons donc pas qu'avec des proportions et des chiffres on nous explique jamais l'empire que la Musique a sur les passions. Toutes ces explications ne sont que du galimathias et ne feront jamais que des incrèdules, parce que l'expérience les dément sans cesse, et qu'on ne peut leur découvrir aucune *espéce de* liaison avec la nature de l'homme. Le Principe et les régles ne sont que le matériel de l'art, *il faut une métaphysique plus fine pour en expliquer les grands effets.* (5:343, my emphasis)

[Let us not therefore think that the empire that music has over the passions is explained to us with proportions and numbers. All these explanation are only nonsense and will never produce anything except disbelievers, because experience constantly belies them and one cannot discover in them any *kind of* connection with the nature of man. The principle and the rules are only the material of the art, *a finer metaphysics is required in order to explain its great effects.*]

Rules and science, instinct and system, offer no satisfactory explanation of the emotional power of music. They can only explain proportional relations and why certain combinations of sounds are agreeable to our ears.

Recalling the discussion of the Lully scene, Rameau's system cannot offer grounds of critique other than adherence to abstract principles of mathematicomusical combination. Rameau is struck by the beauty and perfection of the implied chromatic development, while Rousseau perceives only lost opportunity for passionate expression. Moreover, as we saw, the presence of the struggle between Armide's desire for revenge and her natural feeling of pity evoked the harshest rebuke from Rousseau. If music draws its motivation from the communication of passion, then surely this kind of epic struggle ought to warrant a kind of musical expression that can communicate this passionate struggle to the audience.

Rousseau's criteria for judgment exceed the boundaries of the aesthetic established by Rameau. While Rameau judges based on his mathematico-scientific system, Rousseau demands a musical verisimilitude replete with dramatic pitch movement that will support the weight of the emotion being expressed. For Rousseau, it is not simply a matter of writing chord sequences and progressions according to the principles of harmonics, writing good music means tapping into the emotional source material, finding a form of melodic expression to communicate those emotions, and making the audience feel Armide's interior struggle.[64] As I have already suggested, the expression of pity in the scene is key to understanding the stakes of aesthetic judgment for Rousseau: Lully's recitative is not good music, not only because it lacks energy and passion, but also, more important, because it depicts a moral dilemma in the terms of a flat academic exercise. Aesthetic judgments are inextricably related to moral judgments.

If human beings are moved by the passions to communicate emotion through music, then music may be judged according to standards other than academic principles of harmonic composition. Reverting to his historical/anthropological accounts of the development of music to understand its true purpose, in "L'origine de la mélodie" Rousseau offers a vision parallel to the famous passage describing the birth of the community around the fountain in the *Essai sur l'origine des langues* (5:403–7). In this textual fragment, he imagines a primitive people singing of gods, heroes, and virtues:

> A peine les prémiéres étincelles de ce génie celeste *eurent-elles* embrasé les cœurs *que les peuples assemblés se mirent à chanter d'un ton sublime les Dieux* qu'engendroit leur imagination échauffée, les héros dont ils déploroient la perte, et les vertus que leurs vices naissans rendoient necessaires; tous leurs sentimens étoient des Transports, les rustiques sons d'une flute à trois trous suffisoient pour les mettre hors d'eux-mêmes; cette bouillante *ardeur* se transmetant à toute la personne anima les prémiers pas, le geste des assistans répondoit aux discours du Coryphée et marquoit *l'applaudissement* universel. *Jamais le vain bruit de l'harmonie* ne troubla ces divins concerts. Tout étoit héroïque et grand dans ces antiques fétes. (5:334)

> [The first sparks of this celestial genius *had barely* ignited hearts than *assembled people began to sing in a sublime tone of the gods* that their heated imagination engendered, of heroes whose loss they deplored, and of the virtues that their nascent vices made necessary; all their feelings were transports, the rustic sounds of a three-holed flute sufficed to put them beside themselves; this boiling *ardor*, transmitting itself to everyone animated the first steps, the gestures of the assembly responded to the speeches of the chorus leader and registered universal *applause*. *Never did the vain sound of harmony* disturb these divine concerts. All was heroic and grand in these ancient festivals.]

In terms of subject matter as well as form of expression, nothing could be more different from Rameau's account of musical creativity. Rousseau attributes the birth of song to the need for the community to express feeling together. While the form of expression is important, clearly the effects of the expression are even more important: the transmission of this transport or rapture throughout the entire assembled body.[65] Rousseau uses the word *personne* to refer to the assembled body, underscoring the sense in which the community forms a single entity.[66] While Rameau's solitary composer can follow the dictates of the system and his own imagination fueled by instinct, for Rousseau creativity is born of the communal expression of powerful moral feeling. The need to express the feeling is equally as important as the effect of that expression on the assembled body.

In this respect, Rousseau's judgment of the value of music represents a significant paradigm shift. Human beings sing to one another driven by a moral need to communicate feeling. Their creativity comes from the forms of expression that they are able to harness in order to both represent and evoke moral feeling. As we saw in chapter 1, rhythm and meter have a significant role to play in the transmission of feeling through music. While primitive peoples may have sung of, and even to, the gods, modern humans sing to one another.

Singing represents a moral imperative for Rousseau, one that both grounds and confirms the community, as we saw in the preceding chapter. But beyond the social and political implications for music, there are moral and metaphysical positions that counter Rameau's acoustically grounded, transcendent system. Karol Berger has argued that Rousseau occupies a pivotal position in the history of ideas. Reading Rousseau against Augustine, Berger identifies Rousseau's insistence on humanity's autonomy and freedom as a crucial step away from the necessity of divine intervention for salvation: "In Rousseau's world, man is no longer confronted with a transcendent realm representing a level of reality radically different from his own; instead, humanity and nature occupy one and the same level of reality. Because we are natural beings and a part of nature, our fall is a denial of ourselves, the result of disobedience toward our own nature. Further, because there is no transcendent realm—no outside—saving grace cannot come from outside. If we are to be saved, it can only be by our own efforts."[67]

Taking Berger's argument a step further, it would seem that if our own efforts are required for salvation, then music must be harnessed for moral effect. We now begin to see why the Lully scene appears "unnatural" to Rousseau. The struggle between pity and vengeance is a struggle of our own nature against itself. This ultimate moral conflict should find its musical correlate in a form of expression that moves the audience toward salvation by communicating rupture and distress in a forceful way. Instead,

Rousseau only hears the "unnatural" strains of a music dissociated from its true origins.

From Rousseau's perspective, composers and musicians have an obligation—and especially in the case of Lully being presented with such rich material from Quinault—to communicate moral struggle. In a sense, this moral imperative represents an "absolute" for Rousseau: the aesthetic standard of judgment depends on a moral judgment about the adequacy of the music to communicate feeling and passion. Missed opportunities, such as in the recitative from *Armide*, signal "bad" music, for they fail to communicate at the deepest level.

Rousseau's inability to see the implied chromatic modulation in the recitative becomes irrelevant when seen from this perspective. The implied chromatic modulation—whether there or not—could never adequately depict the anguish and distress necessary to move the audience. Subtlety of this type has little to no aesthetic value because it lacks the force required to instill music with sufficient moral worth. Rameau and Rousseau are locked in a *différend* with only the appearance of a common language between them to mediate the dispute. Both invoke technical musical analysis, a language of feeling, and the ultimate referent, nature, but for radically different aesthetic agendas. Rameau's aesthetic ideal, though founded in the empirical reality of harmonic resonance, asserts "absolute" standards within an a priori transcendent system. Rousseau's aesthetic ideal, founded in the "empirical" reality of historical/anthropological modes of explanation, also asserts "absolute" standards, but within a system that claims to be conventional and, therefore, arbitrary. Rameau, for his part, also partakes of the arbitrary. As we have seen, his defense of equal temperament recognizes the ear's ability to "correct" what it hears, paradoxically eschewing the mathematical perfection (interval ratios) he elsewhere defends. Rousseau, on the other hand, staunchly defends the power of perfect intervals, appealing to a seemingly absolute standard when it comes to the effect on the audience.

Ultimately, the difference between them may lie in the answer to the question why do people make music? For Rameau, the answer seems to be a modified Cartesian position: human beings are endowed with an instinct that makes their imaginations create according to the principles of a system that reflects the harmony of the universe. Musical creations are then perhaps just a divine extension into the human realm, a reflection of the qualities endowed in us by our creator that enable us to mirror back the order of creation. For Rousseau, as we have seen, human beings make music out of necessity. We need to communicate feeling to other human beings. We feel this as a psychological, but also, more important, as a moral imperative. And these creations, while conditioned by the physical properties of sound, are nonetheless driven by our own feelings. Creativity springs from the passions.[68]

As we saw in chapter 1, the passions are opposed to reason for Rousseau, residing in the body rather than the soul (*âme*). In the "Profession de foi du vicaire Savoyard," Rousseau has the vicar espouse a metaphysical position that opposes the will and matter (4:565–635).[69] Arguing in favor of a mind/body dualism, the vicar advocates looking to the heart rather than the mind for proof of faith (4:565–66, 569). Man's dual nature, thus, contains within it a perpetual conflict between body and soul, freedom and determinism:

> En méditant sur la nature de l'homme, j'y crus découvrir deux principes distincts, dont l'un l'élevoit à l'étude des vérités éternelles, à l'amour de la justice et du beau moral, aux régions du monde intellectuel dont la contemplation fait les délices du sage, et dont l'autre le ramenoit bassement en lui-même, l'asservissoit à l'empire des sens, aux passions qui sont leurs ministres, et contrarioit par elles tout ce que lui inspiroit le sentiment du prémier. En me sentant entraîné, combattu par ces deux mouvemens contraires, je me disois: non, l'homme n'est point un: je veux et je ne veux pas, je me sens à la fois esclave et libre; je vois le bien, je l'aime, et je fais le mal: je suis actif quand j'écoute la raison, passif quand mes passions m'entraînent; et mon pire tourment quand je succombe est de sentir que j'ai pu resister. (4:583)

> [In meditating on the nature of man, I believed that I discovered there two distinct principles, one of which elevated him to the study of eternal verities, to the love of justice and moral beauty, and to the regions of the intellectual world whose contemplation is the wise man's delight, and the other of which brought him back basely to himself, subjected him to the empire of the senses, to the passions that are their ministers, and by these means hindered everything that the feelings of the former inspired in him. Feeling myself carried away, struggling with these two contrary movements, I said to myself: no, man is not one. I want and I don't want; I feel myself enslaved and free at the same time; I see the good, I love it, and I do evil, I am active when I listen to reason, passive when my passions carry me

away; and my worst torment when I succumb is to feel that I could have resisted.]

From the perspective of music, the mind/body dualism sets up the conditions for aesthetic reception. While the passions are most often associated with vice and evil in the "Profession," as they are in the first and second *Discourses*, it would seem that music holds open the possibility to stir the passions in a moral way.[70] Bad music—the Lully recitative?—appeals to the senses and potentially enslaves us with a sirenlike call. Good music that is appropriately uplifting and morally directed might just work to overcome the dualism that makes human nature bifurcated in this way. Good music might just lead us to positive moral feelings and an overcoming of the dichotomy between passive and active, slavery and freedom. As we will see in the following chapter, particular types of music may be better suited to this kind of moral task than others, helping us to overcome narcissistic individualism and inspiring communal sentiment and the desire for political self-determination.

# 4

## Folk Music:
## Authenticity, Primitivism, and the Uses of Roots Music

Music is associated with happiness in the beginning of the *Confessions*. Rousseau describes his early childhood in elegiac, idealized terms, as a time when he had no wants or needs that went unmet. In the bosom of his extended family of father, nurse, aunt, friends, and neighbors, he paints a peaceful portrait of a contented and fulfilled childhood. Music plays a role in this happiness and is particularly associated with his aunt, to whom he attributes his passion for music in later life. Overwhelmingly, the associations with music in the opening of the *Confessions* are emotional and positive. When writing more than forty years later, the memory of a little song that his aunt would sing to him still brings tears to his eyes, even if he can no longer remember the entire song:

> Je suis persuadé que je lui [my aunt] dois le gout ou plustot la passion pour la musique, qui ne s'est bien développé en moi que longtems après. Elle savoit une quantité prodigieuse d'airs et de chansons qu'elle chantoit avec un filet de voix douce. La serenité d'ame de cette excellente fille éloignoit d'elle et de tout ce qui l'environnoit la rêverie et la tristesse. L'attrait que son chant avoit pour moi fut tel que non seulement plusieurs de ses chansons me sont toujours restées dans la mémoire, mais qu'il m'en revient même, aujourdhui que je l'ai perdue, qui, totalement oubliées depuis mon enfance, se retracent à mesure que je vieillis, avec un charme que je ne puis exprimer. Diroit-on que moi, vieux radoteur, rongé de soucis et de peines, je me surprends quelquefois à pleurer comme un enfant en marmottant ces petits airs d'une voix déjà cassée et tremblante? (I:11)

> [I am quite sure that it is to her [my aunt] that I owe my taste, or rather my passion, for music, though it did not develop in me till long afterward. She knew an enormous number of songs and tunes, which she sang in a thin voice that was very sweet. Such was the serenity of this excellent woman that it kept melancholy and sadness away, not only from her but also from anyone who came near her; and such delight did I take in her singing that not only have many of her songs remained in my memory but, even now that I have lost her, others that I had completely forgotten since my childhood also come back to me as I grow older, with a charm that I cannot express. It may seem incredible but, old dotard that I am, eaten with cares and infirmities, I still find myself weeping like a child as I hum her little airs in my broken, tremulous voice. (22)[1]]

Although he goes on to reproduce only a portion of the little song that she used to sing—no longer able to remember all the lyrics—the memory of the song and of his aunt singing it still choke him up: "Je cherche où est le charme attendrissant que mon coeur trouve à cette chanson: c'est un caprice auquel je ne comprends rien; mais il m'est de toute impossibilité de la chanter jusqu'à la fin sans être arrêté par mes larmes" (1:11–12) [I strive in vain to account for the strange effect that that song has on my heart, but I cannot explain why I am moved. All I know is that I am quite incapable of singing it to the end without breaking into tears (23)].

The early childhood association in memory between music, his aunt, and the happiness of childhood, and specifically Rousseau's attribution of this coincidence as the origin of his passion for music, create a powerful nexus of interlocking social and psychological factors that color his perception of music. The little song sung to him by his aunt has an emotional charge that overpowers even the adult Rousseau while writing the *Confessions*. In this chapter, I propose to explore the nexus of relations inscribed in this episode from the *Confessions* in order to look at the ways in which conceptions of folk music, primitive music, or even music passed down from earlier times are perceived and valorized for Rousseau. To put it another way, I will be asking what kind of hold this music had over him and why. What is valorized, not just in this particular tune, but also in forms of music that are presented as "authentic," "primitive," or, today, as "roots music" within the context of contemporary musical expression?

Being Moved by Music

As I discussed in chapter 1, the power of music to move individuals and to stir emotions is related in the *Essai sur l'origine des langues* to its birth out of the need to communicate passion. As I argued in that chapter, the power of music as an art form to move listeners is also tied to its temporal and rhythmic properties: listeners are guided through an experience of time whose pace is set by the tempo of the music. Although the example of the moving song from the opening of the *Confessions* no doubt shares the general quality that Rousseau ascribes to all music in this sense, it also moves him in a more specific and particular way. This little song stirs emotion because it is tied in memory to a person who is now lost, and a time and place that are also lost. The memory of the music—and especially singing the little song to himself—brings these feelings to the surface. The elegiac quality of the passage underscores the loss that occurred. Remembering the song means remembering a happier time and, along with it, remembering that that time is now irretrievably in the past.

In this specific instance, the memory of the song elicits a strong emotional reaction that signals a further emotional component of music as an art form. Beyond the general ability to move listeners because of its proximity to passion deriving from its origins, and beyond the ability to shape listeners' experience of time, Rousseau suggests that particular pieces of music carry affective charges related to their context in memory. This little song reminds Rousseau of his aunt and his early childhood, not unlike Proust's associations with the madeleine or contemporary couples who have a certain song ("our song") that they associate with their relationship.[2] Music is different from the visual arts in this respect, in that each individual is capable of committing the song or piece of music to memory and even singing it at any given moment to produce a flood of affective associations.[3] Today, one plays a CD deliberately to create a mood or hears a song on the radio that invokes a chain of associations.[4] For Rousseau, the choices are more limited—rehearse the song quietly in your head or hum the tune out loud. In either case, the willful bringing of memories and emotions to consciousness through the use of a particular piece of music distinguishes it from the visual arts. Whereas in the eighteenth century one would be obliged to look at a portrait to produce the same effect with a visual stimulus, one need only hum or sing a song to trigger an emotional response. Rousseau carries the piece (or most of it) in his head at all times, able to spark his emotions and memory more or less at will.

While this is certainly true of most of us—we all have certain songs that make us think of specific times and places and, therefore, carry an emotional charge—I would like to broaden the argument beyond each individual's personal associations to encompass a more general association of certain types of music with particular emotional charges. In the case of

Rousseau's aunt, while this particular song is linked to a specific person and memory, the kind of song that it is may be more broadly interpreted to represent a class of music with specific associations. In other words, while musical associations may work on a highly personal, subjective, and individual level, they also may function in ways that reflect cultural associations.

Music as Sign

Rousseau is clear that music, like language, is not natural. Man in the state of nature does not have language or music. In the article "Chant" of the *Dictionnaire de musique*, he states this unequivocally:

> Le *Chant* ne semble pas naturel à l'homme. Quoique les Sauvages de l'Amérique chantent, parce qu'ils parlent, le vrai Sauvage ne chanta jamais. . . . Les enfans crient, pleurent, et ne chantent point. Les premières expressions de la nature n'ont rien en eux de mélodieux ni de sonore, et ils apprennent à Chanter comme à parler, à notre exemple. (5:695)

> [*Song* does not seem natural to man. Even though American savages sing, because they speak, the true savage never sang. . . . Children scream, cry, and do not sing. The first expressions of nature have nothing melodious or sonorous about them, and they learn to sing, as they learn to speak, following our example.]

Likewise, in the *Discours sur l'origine de l'inégalité* and the *Essai sur l'origine des langues*, the simultaneous appearance of language and music requires at least a rudimentary form of social life. Indeed, as conventional sign systems, they cannot be natural for Rousseau.[5] In the *Discourse on the Origin of Inequality*, language is initiated by the child who needs to communicate with the mother, but is quickly lost, given the impermanence of even familial relations in the state of nature (3:147). In the stage of social development characterized by family groups, Rousseau imagines a primitive kind of language composed of inarticulate cries, gestures, and imitative sounds, but it is clearly not natural, being developmentally removed from the true state of nature (3:167). The *Essai sur l'origine des langues* also emphasizes the fact that language is not natural and arises from the desire to communicate feelings and ideas to fellow humans, "Sitot qu'un homme fut reconnu par un autre pour un Etre sentant, pensant et semblable à lui, le desir ou le besoin de lui communiquer ses sentimens et ses pensées lui en fit chercher les moyens" (5:375) [As soon as a man was recognized by another for a feeling, thinking being similar to himself, the desire or the need to communicate with him his feelings and his thoughts made him look for the means]. Such communication can only be possible with the advent of contact and social life not present in the state of nature.

In the *Essai*, Rousseau further insists on the simultaneous and indistinguishable appearance of music and language. Because, for Rousseau, simple needs may be communicated through gesture, and the potential conflict over needs would have made early humans flee one another, only the communication of emotion and passion required the invention of language. In the *Essai* he argues that

> l'origine des langues n'est point düe aux prémiers besoins des hommes; il seroit absurde que de la cause qui les écarte vient le moyen qui les unit. D'où peut donc venir cette origine? Des besoins moraux, des passions. Toutes les passions rapprochent les hommes que la nécessité de chercher à vivre force à se fuir. Ce n'est ni la faim, ni la soif, mais l'amour[,] la haine[,] la pitié[,] la colère qui leur ont arraché les prémiéres voix. Les fruits ne se dérobent point à nos mains, on peut s'en nourrir sans parler, on poursuit en silence la proye dont on veut se repaitre; mais pour émouvoir un jeune cœur, pour repousser un aggresseur injuste la nature dicte des accens, des cris, des plaintes: voila les plus anciens mots inventés, et voila pourquoi les prémiéres langues furent chantantes et passionnées avant d'être simple et méthodiques. (5:380–81)

[the origin of languages is not due to the first needs of men; it would be absurd that from the cause of their separation would come the means of uniting them. Where then could this origin come from? From moral needs, from the passions. All the passions bring men together that the necessity of finding the means to survive forced to flee. It is not hunger, nor thirst, but love, hate, pity, anger that tore out the first voices. Fruits do not hide from our hands, one can nourish oneself without speaking, one can pursue in silence the prey that one wishes to feed on; but to move a young heart, to repel an unjust aggressor, nature dictates accents, cries, moans: these are the most ancient words invented, and this is why the first languages were singing and passionate before being simple and methodical.]

Early language characterized by accent and passion, thus, was largely indistinguishable from song. As language and music developed in such a way as to distinguish themselves from each other, only music preserved the close ties to emotion because of the use of accent.

Thus, for Rousseau, musical signs retain a greater affective force than do linguistic ones because of their potential to preserve accent. They are able to move the listener through accent, tone, and rhythm, making them closer to their origin in the passions. Music is then a privileged sign system for Rousseau because, although subject to the same types of degeneration in terms of the conveyance of meaning as linguistic signs—and clearly French music represents a degenerate form of music—it tends to retain more of its ability to move the listener than language does.

A telling example of this ability appears in the *Dictionnaire de musique*, under the entry "Musique." Rousseau indulges his national pride in a tangent on an old Swiss song, or more precisely, a herdsman's call. In a section of his discussion of the varieties of accent in the music of different peoples, in which he refers his reader to transcriptions of music from a number of countries in the plates, he mentions that he included the famous Swiss air, "Ranz des vaches," in his sample.[6] The mention of the Swiss material in the transcriptions sparks a brief discussion of the purported effects this song was capable of producing in the Swiss:

> J'ai ajoûté dans la même Planche le célèbre *Rans-des-Vaches*, cet Air si chéri des Suisses qu'il fut défendu sous peine de mort de jouer dans leurs Troupes, parce qu'il faisoit fondre en larmes, déserter ou mourir ceux qui l'entendoient, tant il excitoit en eux l'ardent desir de revoir leur pays. On chercheroit en vain dans cet Air les accens énergiques capables de produire de si étonnans effets. Ces effets, qui n'ont aucun lieu sur les étrangers, ne viennent que de l'habitude, des souvenirs, de mille circonstances qui, retracées par cet Air à ceux qui l'entendent, et leur rappellant leur pays, leurs anciens plaisirs, leur jeunesse, et toutes leurs façons de vivre, excitent en eux une douleur amère d'avoir perdu tout cela. La *Musique* alors n'agit point précisément comme *Musique*, mais comme signe mémoratif. (5:924)

> [I added in the same plate the famous "Ranz des vaches," that air so cherished by the Swiss that it was prohibited from being played to their troops under penalty of death because it made those who heard it melt into tears, desert or die, because it excited in them the ardent

desire to return to their country. The energetic accents capable of producing such surprising effects have been sought in vain in this air. These effects, that have no pull on foreigners, only come from habit, from memories, from a thousand circumstances that, retraced by this air for those that hear it, reminding them of their country, their former pleasures, their youth, and all their ways of life, excite in them a bitter pain at having lost all of that. *Music* then does not act precisely as *music*, but as memorative sign.]

Rousseau makes it clear that there is nothing intrinsic in the sounds themselves that moves the listener. Rather the strong psychological and emotional effects produced by the music come from the chain of associations that the music holds for the listener—reminding the listener of experiences in the past.[7] Significantly for its similarity to the passage from the *Confessions*, "Ranz des vaches" also, according to Rousseau's account, conjures a childhood and way of life that are now lost. As he concludes the discussion, Rousseau underscores the fact that this piece is no longer capable of eliciting the strong emotions it once did:

> Cet Air, quoique toujours le même, ne produit plus aujourd'hui les mêmes effets qu'il produisoit ci-devant sur les Suisses; parce qu'ayant perdu le goût de leur première simplicité, ils ne la regrettent plus quand on la leur rappelle. Tant il est vrai que ce n'est pas dans leur action physique qu'il faut chercher les plus grands effets des Sons sur le cœur humain. (5:924)

> [This air, despite being always the same, no longer produces today the same effects that it formerly produced on the Swiss; having lost the taste for their former simplicity, they no longer regret it when they are reminded of it. So much so that it is true that it is not in their physical action that one must look for the greatest effects of sounds on the human heart.]

Thus, strong emotional reactions to music, in this case by an entire nation, have nothing to do with the physical properties of the sound. Rather, songs are memorative signs. Perhaps this is what Rousseau means when he says that "La *musique* alors n'agit point précisément comme *musique*" [Music then does not act precisely as *music*], that music as it is normally understood is composed of sounds that create physical effects on the listener: the air vibrates and sounds are heard. The emotional effects of music go beyond the power of the physical properties of the sounds themselves.⁸ Music and specifically songs work to elicit memories of the past through strong cultural associations. In the case of "Ranz des vaches," Rousseau also laments the disappearance of the strong emotional reaction to the song among the Swiss. If it were merely a question of the physical properties of the sounds, then the emotional reaction could not be lost. But in the case of this song, Rousseau's read is that it has lost its appeal because of the type of simple life that it evokes—a simple life that no longer holds any sway among the Swiss.

If this song once moved a nation to the point that it had to be banned from being performed for troops with the threat of the death penalty (at least in Rousseau's account), then there are pieces of music that carry strong associations at the cultural level. I believe that it is no coincidence that the song evokes a simple past. As with his aunt's little song, Rousseau valorizes music that holds associations with a lost past most often associated with a simpler way of life. To put it succinctly, the memorial quality of music functions most often in the elegiac mode for Rousseau to evoke a lost historical past.⁹

Beyond the elegiac mode, it is significant that this cow call is placed alongside samples in the plates that have been collected from other cultures (fig. 1). Rousseau writes,

> Pour mettre le Lecteur à portée de juger des divers Accens musicaux des Peuples, j'ai transcrit aussi dans la Planche N un Air Chinois tiré du P. du Halde, un Air Persan tiré du Chevalier Chardin, et deux Chansons des Sauvages de l'Amérique tirées du P. Mersenne. (5:924)

> [In order to put the reader in the position to judge the diverse musical accents of peoples, I also transcribed in plate N a Chinese air taken from Father du Halde, a Persian air taken from Chevalier Chardin, and two songs of the American savages taken from Father Mersenne.]

The grouping of the material suggests a kind of similarity that Rousseau calls into question. "On trouvera dans tous ces morceaux une conformité de Modulation avec notre Musique, qui pourra faire admirer aux uns la bonté et l'universalité de nos règles, et peut-être rendre suspecte à d'autres l'intelligence ou la fidélité de ceux qui nous ont transmis ces Airs" (5:924) [One will find in all these pieces a conformity of modulation with our music, which could make some admire the goodness and universality of our rules, and perhaps render suspect for others the intelligence or fidelity of those who transmitted these airs to us]. Whether the similarity among the pieces reveals the universal validity of the Western harmonic system or the faulty transcriptions provided by Western listeners is less important for my argument here than the fact that Rousseau chooses to place the Swiss cow call in the group. The insertion of the Swiss material suggests an interesting categorization of music on the part of Rousseau according to its "source," in this case its popular source. These examples, including the Swiss one, are all from "the people."

The last statement may require a bit of qualification owing to the slippage in French and English between the terms "people" and "peoples," in other words, between "the people" understood as the lower classes and source of popular traditions and "peoples" understood as collective social groups from non-Western cultures.[10] Rousseau's inclusion of the Swiss example among the non-Western examples suggests his blurring of the significance of the distinction between Western and non-Western music. Indeed, in his grouping of the material, he seems to be suggesting that Swiss folk songs belong in the same category as Chinese, Persian, and American Indian music for the purposes of academic studies and, in so doing, anticipates the appearance of ethnomusicology.[11] At the same time, his questioning of the validity of the transcriptions and of the perceived similarity among the samples also raises doubts about this kind of categorization of music, and points up the difficulty of maintaining the position that there is a distinctive feature that separates Western and non-Western popular music in the period.

For my purposes here, I find it significant that the Swiss folk material appears with the other non-Western samples, despite Rousseau's caveat about the validity of the transcriptions. Rousseau asserts in the article and in plate N that this "type" of music shares certain features, or at least that we perceive that it does, no matter what the country of origin. Given the typology of cultures in the eighteenth century, and especially of Rousseau's understanding of cultural development that he builds from Montesquieu, it is safe to assume that placing the Swiss example alongside the other examples means that he assigns to it a more "primitive" quality than he does to other types of Western music.[12] That is to say, that Persian and Chinese, and most certainly American Indian cultures, are all more "primitive" in terms of their cultural development than Western European, and especially Swiss, culture. Their music, by extension, is also more primitive.[13] The grouping then suggests that this Swiss example is more primitive, more like the other samples, than, for example, a snippet from Rameau's *Les muses*

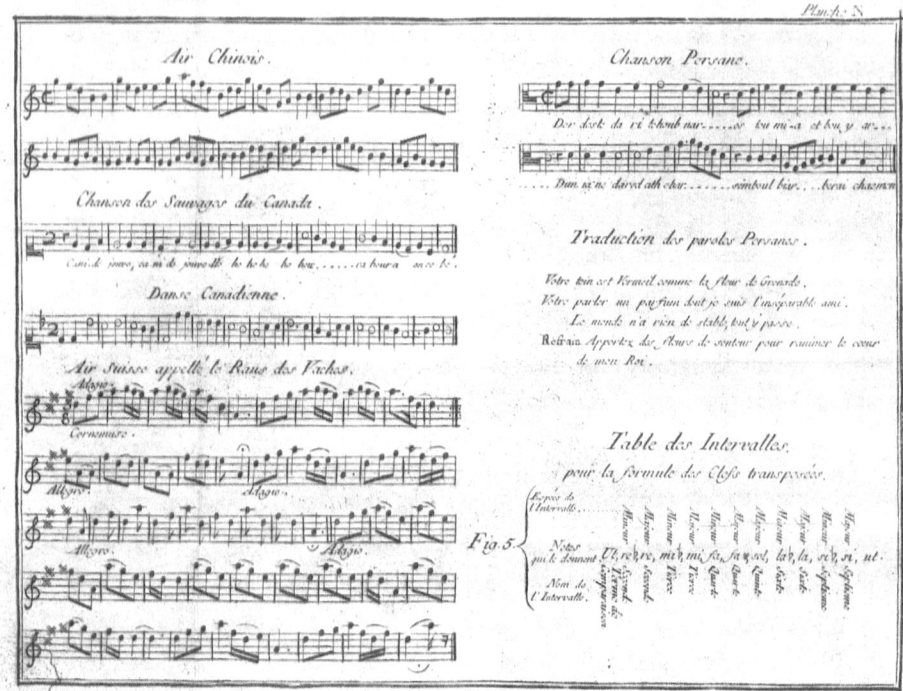

Figure 1  Plate N, Jean-Jacques Rousseau, *Dictionnaire de musique* (Paris: Chez la veuve Duchesne, 1768). Courtesy of the University of California Riverside Libraries, Special Collections and Archives.

*galantes*. Since Rousseau has already undermined to some extent the validity of finding musical reasons for this similarity, his own argument about their belonging together resides elsewhere. I believe that the grouping of the material relates, at least in part, to the more typical eighteenth-century conflation that occurs according to genetic logic between "primitive" cultures and earlier stages in European development. Genetic logic asserts the understandability of complex cultural and other formations through the analysis of the development of complex forms out of simpler ones. One need only cite the familiar arguments of the opening of the *Discourse on Inequality* as evidence of this methodological privilege in Rousseau: "comment l'homme viendra-t-il à bout de se voir tel que l'a formé la Nature, à travers tous les changemens que la succession des tems et des choses a dû produire dans sa constitution originelle, et de démêler ce qu'il tient de son propre fond d'avec ce que les circonstances et ses progres ont ajoûté ou changé à son Etat primitive?" (3:122) [how shall man be able to see himself, such as nature formed him, in spite of all the alterations that a long succession of years and events must have produced in his original constitution, and how shall he be able to distinguish what is of his own essence from what the circumstances he has been in and the progress he has made have added to, or changed in, his primitive condition?][14]

According to this way of thinking, more primitive cultures represent earlier versions of the way that we Europeans once were. It is also true that certain segments of European society may still retain traditions that reflect earlier modes of life.[15] Thus, the popular traditions that persist may conserve earlier modes of life and forms of cultural and artistic expression. The conflation that occurs within genetic logic enables those earlier European traditions to be equated with the practices of "primitive" cultures elsewhere. Following this mode of reasoning, European folk traditions are closer to the traditions of other non-Western cultures because they are more primitive than "contemporary" European high culture. In other words, Swiss folk music is closer to the music of non-Westerners than it is to elite forms of music, because they both in some sense reflect the simplicity of more primitive ways of life.

Musical Simplicity

Rousseau's inclusion of "Ranz des vaches" in the samples of the variety of musical accents among different peoples, and his highlighting of its affective charge, indicate several ways in which folk music moves listeners. Like the example from the *Confessions*, "Ranz des vaches" also carries an affective charge related to its ability to stir emotions related to memories of the past and, specifically, to an earlier and simpler time of life. This memorative quality, as Rousseau calls it in the *Dictionnaire*, relates to the elegiac mode of its reception. In addition to the elegiac mode of reception, the Swiss herdsman's song also belongs to a category of music associated with more primitive forms of culture. Its inclusion among the examples of non-Western music likens music from the lower classes—from "the people"—to music made by other primitive peoples around the globe.

As we have seen, Rousseau denies in the entry "Musique" in the *Dictionnaire* any physical property inherent in the sounds themselves that creates this powerful affective charge. I would like to argue that the music nonetheless has certain formal properties that are perceived by Rousseau as more primitive. I will argue that the cultural associations with certain formal properties of music are what condition the strong, albeit conventional, response.

Perhaps the most distinctive formal feature of the type of music that Rousseau identifies as capable of producing a strong emotional reaction is its lack of harmony. Rousseau gives a modern (as opposed to an ancient) definition of harmony as "une succession d'Accords selon les loix de la Modulation" (5:846) [a succession of chords according to the laws of modulation]. His discussion of modern harmony argues strongly against the positions of Rameau and Tartini, and, specifically, against the notion that harmony is natural. As we saw in the previous chapter, the absolute value of harmonic sequences cannot be derived from nature because they are part of a conventional and thus arbitrary sign system for Rousseau. For my purposes here, it is important to bear in mind that the perception of harmonic structures and their beauty is based on knowledge of a system: Those who know the system appreciate the beauty of counterpoint; those who do not, get lost in and/or cannot enjoy the complexity of the architecture:

> M. Rameau prétend cependant, que l'*Harmonie* est la source des plus grandes beautés de la Musique; mais ce sentiment est contredit par les faits et par la raison. Par les faits, puisque tous les grands effets de la Musique ont cessé, et qu'elle a perdu son énergie et sa force depuis l'invention du Contre-point: à quoi j'ajoûte que les beautés purement harmoniques sont des beautés savantes, qui ne transportent que des gens versés dans l'Art; au lieu que les véritables beautés de la Musique étant de la Nature, sont et doivent être également sensibles à tous les hommes savans et ignorans. (5:851)

> [Mr. Rameau maintains however that *harmony* is the source of the greatest beauty of music; but this feeling is contradicted by facts and by reason. By facts, because all the great effects of music have ceased, and it has lost its energy and force since the invention of counterpoint: to which I would add that purely harmonic beauty is learned beauty that only transports people who are versed in the art, whereas the true beauty of music being in nature, it is and should be equally appreciable by ignorant and learned men.]

Rousseau's claims are multiple here: The beauty of music derives from force and energy. Modern European music is not beautiful because it has no force or energy. The lack of energy is due to counterpoint. And, finally, if music is truly beautiful, it can be appreciated by everyone, including the untutored. This discussion of the lack of force in counterpoint serves as a perfect foil to the force of "Ranz des vaches" and the song that his aunt used to sing him: it is melody that provides the power, force, and beauty of music that is capable of stirring the emotions. Against Rameau and Tartini, Rousseau advocates for the relative naturalness of melody, here understood as the power to activate the emotions.

For Rousseau, the Western harmonic system is more of an aberration in the history of world music, produced more by the effects of cold northern climates on harsh voices under the influence of barbarians than by the culmination of the art.[16] His diatribe against European music points out that the only naturally occurring chord is unison:[17]

> Quand on songe que, de tous les peuples de la terre, qui ont tous une Musique et un Chant, les Européens sont les seuls qui aient une *Harmonie*, des Accords, et qui trouvent ce mélange agréable; quand on songe que le monde a duré tant de siècles, sans que, de toutes les Nations qui ont cultivé les beaux Arts, aucune ait connu cette *Harmonie*; qu'aucun être dans la Nature ne produit d'autre Accord que l'Unisson, ni d'autre Musique que la Mélodie. (5:850–51)[18]

> [When one thinks that, of all the people of the earth, who all have music and song, Europeans are the only ones who have *harmony*, chords, and who find this mix agreeable; when one thinks that the earth has lasted so many centuries, and of all the nations that have cultivated the fine arts without a single one having known this *harmony*, that not one being in nature produces a chord other than unison nor other music than melody.]

Monophonic song is valorized over the contrapuntal harmonies of European elite music for its proximity to nature and, therefore, its ability to excite the emotions and passions of the listener.

Not surprisingly, all of the examples in plate N share a lack of harmony: these moving songs are all simple monophonic melodies without harmonic development. But are they natural? As we have already seen, they are not natural in the sense that music does not exist in the state of nature. Nor are they natural in the sense that their ability to move the listener resides in some intrinsic quality in the sound. Especially in the case of "Ranz des vaches," but presumably in the other non-Western examples as well, the ability of the music to move the listener stems from cultural associations and memory more than the physical or natural properties of the sounds. The lack of harmony makes them closer to nature than the contrapuntal developments of European art music, but only sounds occurring in nature, such as bird songs, can be appropriately termed "natural." Thus, "naturalness" in music represents a continuum with sounds being more or less natural. Unison simple melodies are more natural than complex, contrapuntal harmonies and therefore have a greater potential to touch the emotions of their listeners.[19]

Beyond the privileging of monophonic song in the examples in plate N, the samples also display other similarities that indicate parameters for determining Rousseau's criteria for "authentic" folk music. To begin with "Ranz des vaches," the piece is written in a pentatonic scale (five pitches on the Western scale). This is also true of the sample labeled "Danse canadienne" by Rousseau. With the exception of one passing note in a descending pattern, it is also true for the sample labeled "Chanson des sauvages du Canada."[20] The perception of pentatonic scales as primitive—or more primitive than Western diachronic scales—is consistent with eighteenth-century categorizations of music. Vanessa Agnew argues that the use of Scottish bagpipe music to facilitate contact between Europeans and non-Westerners on voyages of discovery, especially in the South Pacific, was envisioned as a bridge to what was perceived to be more primitive forms of culture.[21] Bringing bagpipes (because of their droning tones and pentatonic scale) or other "primitive" instruments on board to be able to serenade non-Westerners with a form of music that they might find more familiar than, say, European art music, or so the logic goes, might help cross-cultural relations through a form of musical expression that the cultures share.[22]

Eighteenth-century judgments about the pentatonic scale likely derive from its identification with Greek modes. In both the article on "Genre" in the *Encyclopédie* and the later version in the *Dictionnaire*, Rousseau discusses Aristoxenus as the source of an understanding of Greek scales. According to this theory, all possible scales in ancient Greek music are derived from the tetrachord and are driven by the exigencies of melodic line.[23] Rousseau maintains a distinction between Greek scales and modern European ones that highlights the Greek privileging of melody over the modern European privileging of harmony:

Nous avons comme les anciens le *genre* diatonique, le chromatique & l'enharmonique, mais sans aucunes subdivisions; & nous considérons ces *genres* sous des idées fort différentes de celles qu'ils en avoient. C'étoit pour eux autant de manieres particulieres de conduire le chant sur certaines cordes prescrites; pour nous ce sont autant de manieres de conduire le corps entier de l'harmonie, qui forcent les parties à marcher par les intervalles prescrits par ces *genres;* de sorte que le *genre* appartient encore plus à l'harmonie qui l'engendre, qu'à la mélodie qui le fait sentir.[24]

[We have, like the ancients, the diatonic, chromatic, and enharmonic *scales*, but without any subdivisions, and we consider these *scales* according to very different ideas than the ones that they had. For them it was so many particular ways of leading a song on certain prescribed chords; for us, it is so many ways of leading the entire body of harmony, which forces the parts to move by intervals prescribed by these *scales* in such a way that the *scale* belongs more to the harmony that engenders it than to the melody that makes it felt.]

Rousseau's explanation of the difference between the ancient and modern conceptions of scales underscores the ancient insistence on melody over the more modern insistence on the harmonic system. Consistent with the earlier pronouncements that we saw concerning melody and harmony, using melody as a foundation is perceived to be the older way of creating music.[25] In this respect, the pentatonic scale of the Greeks is closer to the melodic root of ancient music than are the more modern versions of scales based on diachronic harmonic systems. For Rousseau, modern European harmonic systems and scales would then be more complicated than the ancient Greek ones in the sense that the ancient scales are closer to melody and contain simpler intervals.

The pentatonic scale then becomes another element in the identification of "folk" music in the eighteenth-century imaginary.[26] The Swiss "Ranz des vaches" shares this scale structure with the North American examples, establishing a formal link between folk music in Europe and music around the globe. Beyond the pentatonic scale in some of the examples, the melodies themselves are fairly simple. They display no large pitch changes, but rather tend to use small intervals and curving melodic lines. The rhythms in all the examples reproduced in plate N are also simple: they contain no dotted rhythms, with the exception of "Ranz des vaches," and in that case only one. The tempos of the non-Western examples are difficult to discern except from the mode of notation.[27] Indeed, Jean-Benjamin de Laborde criticizes Rousseau's notation of the Chinese air as being transcribed with quarter notes and eighth notes, leaving the impression that it is a lighthearted dance, when, according to Laborde, it is actually a serious piece of music that should have been transcribed with whole notes and half notes.[28] Again, "Ranz des vaches" alone bears the tempo markings of "adagio" and "allegro," signaling a tempo change in the piece that might identify it as "more sophisticated" than the other examples. Overall, from the standpoint of rhythm, tempo, scale, melody, and harmony, these pieces share many similar formal properties.

Finally, given the significance of the Scottish bagpipes on trips to the South Pacific, it is important to note that "Ranz des vaches" is also traditionally performed on the bagpipes. Beyond the pentatonic scale of the bagpipes, the droning of the sound (significantly at the octave) may contribute one last formal property of music perceived to be "primitive" and "authentic" to the eighteenth-century European listener.[29]

The formal properties of folk music as represented in plate N of the *Dictionnaire* provide a guide to constructing a continuum of music from most primitive to most complex, with European folk traditions and non-Western music on one side and European contrapuntal harmony at the other extreme. While the tendency is to think of the more primitive kinds of music as more natural, the analysis of the samples in plate N suggests that there are specific formal properties that condition our perception of this type of music as "primitive." As we have seen, specific scales, intervals, tempos, rhythms, and monophonic melodies are common to the examples, and we are conditioned to perceive them as "simpler" and more "primitive." In truth, the common formal properties in Rousseau's plate enable us to assert the conventional quality of this perception. In other words, our acquaintance with the variety of world music enables us to make discerning judgments and to categorize music in the way that sets up the continuum. Rousseau's discussion of the variety of accent in music, and especially his inclusion of the Swiss example among the others, in fact asserts the constructed nature of our perception. Music isn't inherently primitive, or complex, or anything else. We perceive formal structures and label them according to a cultural conditioning that conventionalizes those structures. In other words, Rousseau asserts that the primitive and the authentic are just as constructed and conventional as the complex and elite.

## Using the Primitive: The Faux Folk

Rousseau's *Dictionnaire* seems to be suggesting that there are tropes of authenticity in music. If the "primitive" and "authentic" are conventions, but ones that evoke powerful emotional responses in listeners, then might these forms be used to elicit a strong listener reaction? And given the formal conventions identified, might it not be possible to use this sociocultural conditioning to create elite European art music capable of tapping the emotions that Rousseau claims are absent from the complex contrapuntal harmonies of contemporary composers by invoking the "primitive"?

*Le devin du village* represents precisely this strategy of tapping the emotion of "primitive" music within the context of European elite music. Rousseau's well-known account in the *Confessions* of his experience as a member of the audience at a performance in 1752 underscores the emotional response of the listeners:

> Dès la prémiére scene, qui véritablement est d'une naiveté touchante j'entendis s'élever dans les loges un murmure de surprise et d'applaudissement jusqu'alors inouï dans ce genre de piéces. La fermentation croissante alla bientôt au point d'être sensible dans toute l'assemblée, et, pour parler à la Montesquieu, d'augmenter son effet par son effet même. A la Scene des deux petites bonnes gens cet effet fut à son comble. On ne claque point devant le Roi; cela fit qu'on entendit tout; la piéce et l'auteur y gagnérent. J'entendois autour de moi un chuchotement de femmes qui me sembloient belles comme des anges, et qui s'entredisoient à demi-voix: cela est charmant, cela est ravissant; il n'y a pas un son là qui ne parle au cœur. Le plaisir de donner de l'émotion à tant d'aimables personnes m'émut moi-même jusqu'aux larmes, et je ne les pus contenir au prémier duo, en remarquant que je n'étois pas seul à pleurer. (1:378–79)

> [From the first scene, which is really touching in its simplicity, I heard a murmur of surprise and applause, hitherto unknown at plays of this sort, rising from the boxes. The mounting excitement soon reached such a pitch that it was noticeable right through the audience and, to use an expression of Montesquieu's, began to increase its effect by its effect. There is no clapping when the King is present; for that reason

every note was heard, to the great advantage of the piece and its author. Around me I heard a whispering of women who seemed to me as lovely as angels, and who said to one another under their breath: 'That is charming. That is delightful. There is not a note that does not speak straight to the heart.' The pleasure affecting so many pleasant people moved even me to tears, which I could not restrain during the first duet, when I noticed that I was not the only one who wept. (353)]

Because it is Rousseau's own account of the effects that his music has on the contemporary audience, we have to take it with a large grain of salt.[30] Nonetheless, what he reports obviously accentuates what he most valorizes: tears, especially from the women.[31] This emotional response validates his own emotional outpouring in response to the simple melodies. He gives himself permission to cry—no longer holding back the tears—when he perceives the audience crying around him. Moving an audience of "aimables personnes" to tears through his musical creation validates his own emotional outpouring and, indeed, feeds the emotion. Not only does he enjoy a good cry at the opera—his own opera—but he especially enjoys a cry in the company of others moved to tears by his work. The scene of the reception of the *Devin* in the *Confessions* echoes the response to his aunt's ditty in book 1, only this time the effect is willfully inflicted on a community of listeners come together to experience Rousseau's own composition.

What accounts for the emotional effect the music has on its listeners? No doubt, Rousseau would credit the novelty of his style, "elle étoit dans un genre absolument neuf auquel les oreilles n'étoient point accoutumées" (1:375) [it was in an absolutely new style, to which people's ears were unaccustomed" (350)], to explain the emotional response.[32] He would also cite the melodic unity of the music, which, as he explains in the entry in the *Dictionnaire*, is the principle of composition to which he adhered in writing the opera.[33] His introduction to the response by the audience in the passage cited above highlights the "naiveté touchante" [touching naïveté] of the opening scene, leading the reader to believe that the emotional response comes from the unexpected simplicity of the work, as well as its surprising charm.

The opening of the *Devin* features perhaps the best-known aria of the opera, "J'ai perdu mon serviteur," in which the tearful Colette sings of her lost love, Colin, and sets out to consult the soothsayer. Invoking the conventions of the pastoral, Rousseau uses this form in order to create the effect of simplicity. Perhaps to those in the audience, who were accustomed to mythological characters, the "merveilleux," and the buffoonery of light comic opera, the return to the pastoral might have seemed quaint and old-fashioned, or tired and insipid.[34] Indeed, as Louis Auld has argued, the pastoral setting was used in early seventeenth-century France, despite the fact that it already represented, in the seventeenth century, "hackneyed themes, characters, and situations."[35] Auld argues that the outdated material enabled the seventeenth-century audience to accept the complexity of the new form: "music sometimes unites most easily with the detritus of poetic evolution, with the tag ends and remnants of used up, outdated poetic styles" (72). He goes on to explain that in the case of opera, "In a work involving several arts, it may be desirable that some elements be subordinated to others from the outset. Opera audiences are often content that the music ride, as it were, on an unobtrusive verbal framework and a simple story of archifamiliar outline" (73). It seems fair to say that if the pastoral mode could be described as consisting of "a simple story of archifamiliar outline" already in the seventeenth century, then Rousseau's resurrection of it in 1752, if it seemed appealing to the audience, no doubt did so because of its old fashionedness.[36] The opening scene of the *Devin* establishes the conventions of pastoral representation that were at once familiar, because of their extensive use in the past, and popular, for their reappearance in the mid-eighteenth-century context. By choosing the pastoral mode for his opera, Rousseau deploys one of the most conventional genres for opera in order to access the emotion that he believes has long since been drained from operatic performance. Paradoxically, a somewhat outdated genre provides the possibility to create an emotional response conditioned by the conventionalized perception of simplicity and naïveté.

Thus, the "new" style is really just the "old" style, but made new again for a jaded audience of experienced operagoers. The opening pastoral scene probably did provide a striking contrast to the usual fare.[37] The opening melody line of "J'ai perdu mon serviteur," with its simple I, IV, V progression, moves through its melody by small intervals (principally arpeggios). The simple melody coupled with the simple libretto in French penned by Rousseau afforded the audience an opportunity to understand what was being sung and to recognize forms familiar from vaudeville and dances.[38]

Whether it was the familiarity of the genre or the simplicity and vague familiarity of the music, the audience responded emotionally. As he narrates the reception of his opera, the emotional effect is contagious: a kind of fermentation takes hold of the audience so that the effect intensifies as it is experienced by increasing numbers of listeners: "La fermentation croissante alla bientôt au point d'être sensible dans toute l'assemblée, et, pour parler à la Montesquieu, d'augmenter son effet par son effet même" [The mounting excitement soon reached such a pitch that it was noticeable right through the audience and, to use an expression of Montesquieu's, began to increase its effect by its effect].[39] The emotional response leads to the desired physical response: tears as the emotion culminates. Rousseau describes the reaction that takes hold of the entire audience as a kind of transport:

> J'ai vû des Piéces exciter de plus vifs transports d'admiration, mais jamais une ivresse aussi pleine aussi douce aussi touchante regner dans tout un spectacle, et surtout à la cour un jour de prémiére representation. (1:379)

> [I have seen plays excite more lively transports of admiration, but I have never known so complete, so sweet, and so touching an enthusiasm pervade a whole theater, especially at a first performance before the court. (353)]

Rousseau pats himself on the back for having accomplished the feat of simultaneously tapping the emotions of the entire audience. The success is augmented by the fact that the performance occurs at court—the opera debuted at the Château de Fontainebleau—the locus of jaded emotions, amour propre, and the distance characteristic of an elite audience unaccustomed to this type of experience of "true" emotion.

But behind the congratulatory gestures for having provoked authentic emotion in an audience unaccustomed to feeling it at the opera lies the joy in having moved the women in the audience. The sexual element of the physical response is not lost on Rousseau. Just prior to the passage cited above, he describes his triumph in erotic terms:

> Je suis pourtant sûr qu'en ce moment la volupté du sexe y entroit beaucoup plus que la vanité d'auteur, et surement s'il n'y eut eu là que des hommes, je n'aurois pas été dévoré, comme je l'étois sans cesse du desir de recueillir de mes levres les delicieuses larmes que je faisois couler. (ibid.)

> [And yet I am sure that sexual passion counted for more at that moment than the vanity of an author; if there had been only men

present I am positive that I should not have been devoured, as I continuously was, by the desire to catch with my lips the delicious tears I had evoked.]

While he is clearly pleased to move the entire audience, he is particularly focused on the erotic element of the women's tears and his own response to them. Wanting to kiss the tears of the entire female audience suggests a level of emotional manipulation that goes beyond the desire to have an audience tap a wellspring of emotion long forgotten. While it is perhaps possible to argue that moving the audience to tears through the use of folk music in European high-art music might, in some sense, be in their interest—it may enable them to feel emotions they have forgotten, recall poignant memories, reconnect with a lost past, shed the cynical attitudes toward art learned in aristocratic life, etc.—it is more difficult to defend this kind of emotional manipulation in the service of sexual passion. If the desire is, at least in part, to make the women in the audience shed delicious tears for the composer's own sexual gratification, then the *Devin* becomes an elaborate seduction scheme to "émouvoir les coeurs" in the worst possible sense: a very elaborate ruse to gain sexual satisfaction.[40] Rousseau's own self-deception about the emotional charge of the opera and his participation in the emotional response spares him from the worst charges—that he is no better than Valmont in *Les liaisons dangereuses*, playing with the Présidente de Tourvel's virtuous emotions in order to seduce her. Nonetheless, the ultimate effect is nearly identical. Both manipulate female emotional response to gain personal satisfaction.

Rousseau is no libertine and I would not wish to suggest that he is. However, the emotional manipulation at the heart of the effect of the *Devin* raises a serious moral question: under what conditions and for what purposes is it appropriate to deliberately stir a passionate emotional response in an audience? If the purpose is to seduce the women in the audience, then it seems clear that the use of music to stir the passions is immoral. But when would such a manipulation be moral or virtuous? Could "authentic" folk music be put in the service of morality or political freedom in order to engineer social justice?

The Politics of Faux "Authenticity": Democracy?

The *vendanges* (wine harvest) letter in *Julie, ou la nouvelle Héloïse* offers one possible source for understanding the potential uses of music for social and political goals. In idealized, romantic terms, Saint-Preux narrates the happy scenes of harvesting the grapes and making wine at Clarens, underlining what he describes as the social equality implicit in agricultural work. Music enters the description at several key points to underscore the happiness that attends this type of physical labor. Through Saint-Preux's text, Rousseau insists on the emotional charge of even witnessing agricultural labor, and by extension, participating in it:

> Le travail de la campagne est agréable à considérer, et n'a rien d'assés pénible en lui-même pour émouvoir à compassion. L'objet de l'utilité publique et privée le rend intéressant; et puis, c'est la premiere vocation de l'homme, il rapelle à l'esprit une idée agréable, et au cœur tous les charmes de l'âge d'or. L'imagination ne reste point froide à l'aspect du labourage et des moissons. La simplicité de la vie pastorale et champêtre a toujours quelque chose qui touche. Qu'on regarde les prés couverts de gens qui fanent et chantent, et des troupeaux épars dans l'éloignement: insensiblement on se sent attendrir sans savoir pourquoi. Ainsi quelquefois encore la voix de la nature amolit nos cœurs farouches, et quoiqu'on l'entende avec un regret inutile, elle est si douce qu'on ne l'entend jamais sans plaisir. (2:603)

> [Work in the country is pleasing to watch and has nothing so painful in itself to move one to compassion. Its object in public and private utility makes it interesting; and then, it is man's first vocation, it brings to mind an agreeable idea and to the heart all of the charms of the golden age. The imagination does not remain cold at the sight of labor and harvests. The simplicity of pastoral country life always has something that touches us. Let anyone see prairies covered with people who toss hay and sing, and herds scattered in the distance: imperceptibly one feels touched without knowing why. In this way sometimes the voice of nature still softens our fierce hearts, and despite the fact that we hear it with useless regret, the voice is so soft and sweet that we never hear it without pleasure.]

Not unlike the description of the emotional reaction of the audience to the opening arias of the *Devin*, here Rousseau pens for Saint-Preux a moving experience before a pastoral scene of rural labor. The movement of the sentences in the passage elides the distance between the workers and nature herself: The singing among the laborers comes to stand in for the voice of nature that imperceptibly moves Saint-Preux. Just as it would happen at the opera, Saint-Preux is moved by the simplicity and naturalness of the scene before him.

The reference to the taming quality ("amolit nos cœurs farouches") of the voice of nature in the passage cited provides a clear contrast to the way in which Parisians experience the countryside. The opening of the letter asserts that Parisians bring Paris with them to the country, including "le jeu, la musique, la comédie" (2:602) [gambling, music, comedy], which prevents them from having an authentic experience of the pleasures that the countryside has to offer. The *vendanges* letter illustrates the proper way to benefit from the country: aesthetically, morally, and spiritually. The role of music in this experience is paramount, for music accompanies all the scenes narrated by Saint-Preux. I would argue that the music in these scenes is a crucial vehicle for the appropriate appreciation of the values of labor in the country and the political and social lessons that Rousseau wishes to impart.[41]

The wine harvest provides a moving spectacle of the joys of agricultural labor replete with the singing voices of women accompanied by rustic instruments: "le chant des vendangeuses dont ces côteaux retentissent; la marche continuelle de ceux qui portent la vendange au pressoir; le rauque son des instrumens rustiques qui les anime au travail; l'aimable et touchant tableau d'une allégresse générale qui semble en ce moment étendu sur la face de la terre" (2:604) [the song of the women harvesters with which the hills ring; the continual march of those who carry the harvest to the press; the raucous sound of the rustic instruments that animates them to work; the lovely and touching picture of general cheerfulness that seems in this moment to be spread over the entire surface of the earth]. Rousseau repeats the insistence on women's voices in this context—not unlike his emotional response to his aunt's voice in the *Confessions*—suggesting a link between the specifically female voice and "authentic" folk music.[42] In the article "Voix" in the *Dictionnaire*, he states a distinct preference for women's voices over men's and children's because of both their range and timbre.[43] In these harvest scenes, the women provide both solo and unison chorus voices with an affective function: Saint-Preux is specifically moved by the women's voices singing while they work:

> Après le souper on veille encore une heure ou deux en teillant du chanvre; chacun dit sa chanson tour à tour. Quelquefois les vendangeuses chantent en chœur toutes ensemble, ou bien alternativement à voix seule et en refrain. La plupart de ces chansons sont de vieilles romances dont les airs ne sont pas piquans; mais ils ont je ne sais quoi

d'antique et de doux qui touche à la longue. Les paroles sont simples, naïves, souvent tristes; elles plaisent pourtant. (2:609)

[After supper we stay awake another hour or two scutching hemp; each one sings his or her song in turn. Sometimes the women harvesters sing in chorus all together, or sometimes alternately in solo voice and refrain. Most of these songs are old ballads whose airs are not piquant; but they have a "je ne sais quoi" of oldness and sweetness that touches with time. The lyrics are simple, naïve, often sad; yet they please.]

Despite the simple and naïve lyrics of the old ballads—as was the case in the scene of the reception of the *Devin*—the erotic charge is also present. In this case, Saint-Preux, Julie, and Claire are all reminded of the amorous escapades of their youth. But here, the music serves to chasten the now mature former lovers and remind Saint-Preux of his current status and moral obligations.[44]

Rousseau concludes the musings on music in the letter with a return to the insistence on the superiority of simple melody and unison singing over the "educated" taste for harmony. The discussion brings together several aspects of the *vendanges* scene: the women's voices, the simplicity of the work, as well as a feeling of peace and contentment.

Je trouve à ces veillées une sorte de charme que je ne puis vous expliquer, et qui n'est pourtant fort sensible. Cette réunion des différens états, la simplicité de cette occupation, l'idée de délassement, d'accord, de tranquillité, le sentiment de paix qu'elle porte à l'âme, a quelque chose d'attendrissant qui dispose à trouver ces chansons plus intéressantes. Ce concert des voix de femmes n'est pas non plus sans douceur. Pour moi, je suis convaincu que de toutes les harmonies, il n'y en a point d'aussi agréable que le chant à l'unisson, et que s'il nous faut des accords, c'est parce que nous avons le goût dépravé. (2:609–10)

[I find in these social evenings a kind of charm that I cannot explain to you, and that is nonetheless very palpable. This meeting of different estates, the simplicity of this occupation, the idea of relaxation, of accord, of tranquility, the feeling of peace that it brings to the soul, has something touching that disposes one to find the songs more interesting. This concert of female voices is not without sweetness.

For myself, I am convinced that of all harmonies, there is none so agreeable as song in unison, and that if we need chords, it is because we have depraved taste.]

While the soothing feeling of the women's voices is associated with the peaceful simplicity of the evening work scene, the mention of the "réunion des différens états" [meeting of different estates] suggests a social harmony in parallel with the simple unison of the chorus of women. Like the sounds that blend together to produce beautiful music, the classes mix in a scene of natural harmony.

Yet the mention of different estates contrasts with other passages of the letter that insist on the "equality" inherent in agricultural labor. Indeed the narration of the *vendanges* letter oddly moves between an insistence on equality and the clear articulation of a social hierarchy. Saint-Preux delineates the division of duties:

> Mad<sup>e</sup> de Wolmar s'est charge de la récolte, le choix des ouvriers, l'ordre et la distribution du travail la regardent. Mad<sup>e</sup> d'Orbe préside aux festins de vendange, et au salaire des journaliers selon la police établie, dont les lois ne s'enfreignent jamais ici. Mon inspection, à moi, est de faire observer au pressoir les directions de Julie dont la tête ne supporte pas la vapeur des cuves. (2:604–5)

> [Madame de Wolmar is charged with the vintaging, the choice of workers, the order and distribution of work are her affair. Madame d'Orbe presides over the feasts of the wine harvest and the salary of the day laborers according to the established policy, whose laws are never broken here. My own inspection is to make certain that Julie's directions are followed in the press because her head cannot bear the vapors of the vats.]

Four paragraphs later, he exclaims the equality of the working group:

> Vous ne sauriez concevoir avec quel zele, avec quelle gaité tout cela se fait. On chante, on rit toute la journée, et le travail n'en va que mieux. Tout vit dans la plus grande familiarité; *tout le monde est égal*, et personne ne s'oublie. (2:607, my emphasis)

> [You cannot conceive with what zeal, with what gaiety all this is done. We sing, we laugh all day, and work only goes better because

of it. Everyone lives in the greatest familiarity; *everyone is equal* and no one forgets himself.]

The final line underscores the tension between equality and hierarchy.[45] Is everyone equal or does everyone remember only too well who and what he or she is? The following lines again assert the differences, only to try to efface them: "Les Dames sont sans airs, les paysannes sont décentes, les hommes badins et non grossiers. C'est à qui trouvera les meilleures chansons, à qui fera les meilleurs contes, à qui dira les meilleurs traits" (ibid.) [The ladies are without airs, the peasant women are decent, the men playful and not crude. It is about who will find the best songs, who will tell the best tales, who will say the best witticisms]. In the carnivalesque period of the wine harvest, Rousseau asserts that a simple and salutary equality reigns that enables the classes to mingle and understand one another.[46]

How are we to interpret the contradictory assertions about hierarchy and equality? Everyone is equal, yet everyone performs a specifically differentiated task that reinforces a social hierarchy. Julie and Claire, and to some extent Saint-Preux, as he stands in for Julie at the press, all serve in management positions: hiring, distributing work and salaries, and policing and enforcing the law. It would seem that the period of the wine harvest affords the elites (here Julie and her extended household) an opportunity to mingle with the workers and experience the pleasures of agricultural work. Part of the joy of agricultural labor, as Rousseau narrates it, is the pleasure of folk singing. But as we have seen from the analysis of the *Dictionnaire* and the *Confessions*, the perception and recognition of folk music depends on formal properties that may be created by composers and singers who may or may not be originally from the "folk." By extension of the same argument, it would seem that equality in this scene of the wine harvest is created in a way similar to the way that "faux folk" music is created: Julie, Claire, and Saint-Preux use the occasion of the yearly wine harvest to mingle with the laboring classes, share their work (from the position of overseers), and participate in the aesthetic creations that accompany that work. They intermingle with and share the work, listen to and enjoy the singing, and benefit from the peace, tranquility, and emotional transport that accompany the romanticized view of traditional forms of labor. In other words, just as folk music may be created to move a Parisian audience (*Le devin du village*), Rousseau suggests that a kind of equality may be created through the orchestration of communal agricultural labor. More important for my argument here, one of the conditions for the social engineering of equality through agricultural labor would seem to be the presence of music.

Music serves a number of different functions in the *vendanges* scene in *Julie*. The singing of the workers provides a sign that they are happy in their work: "Qu'on regarde les prés couverts de gens qui fanent et chantent." "Après le souper on veille encore une heure ou deux en teillant du chanvre; chacun dit sa chanson tour à tour." "Vous ne sauriez concevoir avec quel zele, avec quelle gaité tout cela se fait. On chante, on rit toute la journée, et le travail n'en va que mieux." [Let anyone see prairies covered with people who toss hay and sing. After supper we stay awake another hour or two scutching hemp; each one sings his or her song in turn. You cannot conceive with what zeal, with what gaiety all this is done. We sing, we laugh all day, and work only goes better because of it.] The singing accompaniment to work provides a kind of testimony to the workers' joy for the observers from another class.

The form of music indicates the "authenticity" of the experience: In the scene after supper, the women sing *romances* or ballads. "La plupart de ces chansons sont de vieilles romances dont les airs ne sont pas piquans; mais ils ont je ne sais quoi d'antique et de doux qui touche à la longue" [Most of these songs are old ballads whose airs are not piquant; but they have a "je ne sais quoi" of oldness and sweetness that touches with time.] Echoing the description from *Julie*, in the *Dictionnaire* entry for "Romance," Rousseau specifies, "Comme la *Romance* doit étre écrite d'un style simple, touchant, et d'un goût un peu antique, l'Air doit répondre au caractère des paroles; point d'ornemens, rien de maniéré, une mélodie douce, naturelle, champêtre, et qui produise son effet par elle-même, indépendamment de la manière de la Chanter" (5:1028). [As the *Romance* must be written in a touching and simple style and with a bit of old-fashioned taste, the Air must respond to the character of the lyrics; no ornaments, nothing mannered, a sweet, natural, rustic melody, and that produces its effect by itself, independently of the manner in which it is sung.] The lack of ornamentation and the natural style of singing associated with this type of sentimental song signal its relation to ancient forms and the lower classes. The ballad, particularly in the eighteenth century, harks back to ancient roots and primitive culture.[47] In this way, its formal properties reveal its "authenticity" as a folk form of expression.

Rousseau's own attachment to and, indeed, contribution to the genre for the eighteenth century is most evident in his adoption of the form in *Le devin du village* for "Dans ma cabane obscure," as well as his posthumously published collection of romances entitled *Consolations des misères de ma vie*.[48] No less an authority than *The Grove Dictionary of Music* cites Rousseau's "Dans ma cabane obscure" as an example of the genre, identifying its formal properties with class origins: "The strophic form, recurring three-bar phrases, thin texture and narrow range reflect the naive, natural state of the young peasant."[49] Thus, the romance's specific formal properties are both associated with older forms and consciously constructed within the context of art music. Their presence signals to the audience that the singer belongs to a particular class, and as the Grove definition indicates, the properties of the song form are associated with the singer. In other words, the "simple, naïve" form of the ballad reflects back on the person singing it to vouch for his or her innocent and guileless state.

In the context of *Julie*, the fact that Rousseau has the women sing ballads further underscores their "authenticity." Ruth Perry has suggested in the context of Scotland that women are "closer to the oral tradition within which ballads and songs were transmitted in the eighteenth century than were their menfolk."[50] Perry points to gendered forms of labor in Scotland similar to Rousseau's depiction in *Julie*, in which women gather together to wash, spin, sew, and knit (not unlike the scutching of hemp after supper), and talk and sing as they work. The ballads that they sing represent an oral tradition passed from mother to daughter while they work together. Thus, women represent a kind of living archive of musical forms: the songs that they sing while working have been passed down as part of an oral tradition and may trace back several generations. The singing of ballads specifically by women in the *vendanges* scene in *Julie* further signals the "authenticity" of this musical accompaniment to the eighteenth-century audience who associates folk music with lower-class women performing repetitive domestic labor.

The fact that the women sing both as soloists and in unison, "Quelquefois les vendangeuses chantent en chœur toutes ensemble, ou bien alternativement à voix seule et en refrain" [Sometimes the women harvesters sing in chorus all together, or sometimes alternately in solo voice and refrain], further emphasizes the equality and sorority of the community. Individual voices are heard, but the group also sings as an indivisible body—the unison marking the lack of harmony that would indicate both "inauthentic" art music and a kind of hierarchy within the group of voices. Instead, the women form a cohesive, undifferentiated whole whose mode of performance also underscores its "authenticity" as folk music.

Thus, these ballads, performed while the women labor, are anchored in specific classes and specific communities. Their performance communicates these class and communal origins in much the same way that Rousseau's aunt's song and "Ranz des vaches" signal their origins. Their "authenticity," constructed out of the cultural associations of the eighteenth-century public, helps to legitimize and validate the social engineering project that they accompany. Folk music in these scenes serves as a kind of soundtrack to engineered agrarian equality. In other words, folk music as aesthetic expression is designed—paradoxically—both to support the assertion of the authenticity of these scenes and to divert our attention from its constructedness.

The Soundtrack of Engineered Democracy

Returning to the question I raised earlier about the conditions under which it might be morally permissible to use music to manipulate an audience, the wine harvest scene in *Julie* suggests that certain forms of music accompany what Rousseau identifies as healthy forms of agricultural labor: a collective endeavor that fosters equality and, potentially, democracy. The associations with certain types of folk music, including the ballads sung by laboring-class women, reinforce Rousseau's message about the pleasures of certain kinds of labor. In order to persuade an educated eighteenth-century public distanced from agricultural labor of its virtues and pleasures, might not the beauty of the aesthetic expression associated with it be used to entice them to partake? In other words, if the Parisian public could be seduced by the pastoral simplicity of *Le devin du village*, might it not also be motivated to try its attendant lifestyle?[51] Could the operagoers be persuaded by the strains of "Dans ma cabane obscure" and "J'ai perdu mon serviteur" or one of Rousseau's collected ballads in the *Consolations* to try their hand at tilling, planting, and harvesting? And perhaps the simplicity of the music itself and the emotional outpouring that it taps might help move a public structured by strict hierarchy to be more positively disposed to more egalitarian social and political structures. The aesthetic form may itself help to soften a public to the delights of a simple life of rural equality and, eventually, democracy, or at least perhaps so Rousseau hopes.

    The use of the aesthetic realm to assist in social engineering may not be as far-fetched as it first appears. The *Lettre à d'Alembert* already argues for a converse effect for the theater. The establishment of a theater in Geneva will only destroy the manners and morals of a democratic people. For Rousseau, the aesthetic realm can have a negative influence on social and political formations. So why not use the aesthetic realm to positive effect, as Rousseau suggests at the end of the *Lettre*, citing the example of Spartan public festivals (5:123–24)?

    The texts on Poland and Corsica raise the question of social engineering directly as Rousseau attempts to condition these peoples for political formations oriented toward more equality and self-determination. In the case of the *Projet de constitution pour la Corse*, the effort to impose an agrarian social order in order to minimize economic inequalities and orient the national sensibility in a direction more conducive to democracy might well benefit from the type of idealization and glorification of the agrarian lifestyle that folk music provides. Providing a soundtrack of folk music to the social engineering project might just orient the Corsicans in the appropriate direction, softening their hearts and minds and reforming their morals to the pleasures of egalitarian agrarian culture.[52] For Poland, the project is complicated by the presence of an aristocracy not enamored of relinquishing privileges it has held for some time. While Rousseau does not propose a democratic republican model for Poland, he does suggest changes in the aesthetic domain designed to bolster Poland's political independence. Specifically, he counsels the Poles to forgo the usual forms of court entertainment that undermine the spirit of community:

> Il faut abolir, même à la Cour, à cause de l'exemple, les amusemens ordinaires des cours, le jeu, les théatres, comédies, opera; tout ce qui effemine les hommes, tout ce qui les distrait, les isole, leur fait oublier leur patrie et leur devoir; tout ce qui les fait trouver bien partout pourvu qu'ils s'amusent. (3:962)
>
> [It is necessary to abolish, even at court, because of the example, the ordinary amusements of courts, gaming, theater, comedies, opera; everything that makes men effeminate, everything that distract them, isolates them, makes them forget their country and their duty, everything that makes them feel good wherever they are, provided that they are amused.]

The effort to instill a sense of national identity aimed at preserving Polish political independence emphasizes "masculine" virtues of self-determination in anticipation of possible future military conflict with neighboring countries seeking to expand their territory.[53] The tendency toward aristocratic effeminacy must be countered by a change in court culture designed to bolster the nascent national spirit: "il faut inventer des jeux, des fêtes, des solemnités qui soient si propres à cette Cour-là qu'on ne les retrouve dans aucune autre" (3:962–63) [games, festivals, and solemnities must be invented that will be so appropriate to this court that they will not be found in any other].

While Rousseau never mentions folk music specifically in these texts, the social engineering projects could no doubt be supplemented by music written specifically to tap the wellspring of emotion that would foster a return to agrarian life in Corsica and stimulate national pride in Poland. Perhaps *Le devin du village* or one of the *romances* from the *Consolations* could be used to inspire a national moral consciousness, a return to rural roots, and an appreciation for simpler ways of life. Whether such a project could succeed or not, the potential use of music to reform morals and perhaps social and political life remains an open question. Rousseau's understanding of our emotional attachment to music enables an articulation of the use of aesthetic expression to mold moral and social life.

# 5

## Rousseau and Aesthetic Modernity: Music's Power of Redemption

Better known for his critiques of the project of Enlightenment and for the rhetorical barbs he aimed at the *philosophes*, Jean-Jacques Rousseau is not normally considered to be a defender of progress or a champion of social change. While *Confessions* (1770) is often invoked as the first modern autobiography, and *Social Contract* (1762) is widely considered to usher in an era of modern political theory, most of his assessments of humankind's development dwell on the negative effects of the movement of civilization.

Beginning with his tirade against the corrupting effects of the arts and sciences in the *Discours sur les sciences et les arts* (1750), written in response to the Dijon Academy's question, "If the reestablishment of the sciences and the arts has contributed to the purification of manners and morals," Rousseau's faith in the ability for enlightenment or aesthetic experience to overcome the fragmentation and alienation of modern eighteenth-century life is shaken, to say the least. Indeed, laying the blame for society's ills squarely on the shoulders of the "enlightened" arts and sciences seemingly leaves no room for Rousseau to use them for society's redemption. It is the arts and sciences throughout history that have led to the division of labor, increasing social dependence, the downfall of the ancient democratic republics, and the lack of satisfaction generally in public life.

Never one to flinch at self-contradiction, Rousseau is also the composer of operas, the author of plays and novels, and certainly an influential force in, if not the creator of, a certain romantic aesthetic. In his own creative work, as well as in his numerous theoretical writings on music, Rousseau articulates a role for aesthetic experience within modern life that would help to overcome the fragmentation and alienation that he so keenly experienced. In spite of his condemnations of the arts in the *First Discourse*, Rousseau holds open the possibility that aesthetic experience—and specifically musical performance—contains the potential to bridge the fragmentation of modern existence. In this final chapter, I argue that Rousseau's choice of music as privileged aesthetic object enables him to articulate an aesthetic based on experience that anticipates later developments in romanticism and modernism. Indeed, Rousseau's focus on music opens up the possibility of insight into aesthetic experience that goes beyond other formulations of the period, most often conceived with painting or the novel in mind. Most important, by locating the possibility of redemption within aesthetic experience couched in terms of musical performance, Rousseau articulates a modern role for the work of art that looks forward to nineteenth- and twentieth-century aesthetic theory, from the German Romantics through the Frankfurt School. Finally, in his articulation of an aesthetics that reserves a redemptive role for music, Rousseau may be read, retrospectively and ironically, as a defender of modernity against postmodern critique. His proffering of music as a remedy for the encroachment of modern life locates the cure within the illness itself, prefiguring solutions of a later modernism. In the unfolding of "an aesthetic modernity," Rousseau's understanding of music reasserts for us the ongoing urgency of the Enlightenment project.

Defining Aesthetic Modernity

In order to situate Rousseau's contribution to aesthetic theory, it will be necessary to trace a brief history of developments in aesthetics related to the emergence of modernity. Beginning in the seventeenth century, progress in the sciences, and specifically Cartesian rationalism, with its insistence on truth and reason grounded in logical a priori propositions, redefined the basis for knowledge. From the standpoint of the sciences, nature is viewed with respect to stable standards for the determination of truthful propositions. As we saw in chapter 3, Rameau's aesthetic is representative of the view that nature provides rules that may be applied to works of art. These same conceptions and concerns are echoed in classical aesthetic theory, where stable rules guarantee the content of art oriented toward the exposition of eternal truths. As Ernst Cassirer asserts with respect to the Cartesian influence in seventeenth-century aesthetic theory, "Art, likewise is to be measured and tested by the rules of reason, for only such examination can show whether or not it contains something genuine, lasting and essential."[1]

Thus, nature, through the lens of the sciences and the arts, is viewed as governed by stable, knowable, rational laws that should also condition aesthetic production and reception. Cassirer concludes, "The course of seventeenth and eighteenth century aesthetics was thus indicated once and for all. It is based on the idea that, as nature in all its manifestations is governed by certain principles, and as it is the highest task of the knowledge of nature to formulate these principles clearly and precisely, so also art, the rival of nature, is under the same obligation" (280).

The influence of Cartesian rationalism on scientific method marks a shift often identified with the emergence of modernity. From the perspective of science, this modernity is located in Cartesian radical doubt, the rise of experimentation, and the insistence on the necessity of repeatability. However, the aesthetic principles that accompany this shift toward a scientific modernity do not coincide with what one normally associates with a modernist aesthetic. Indeed, the insistence on stable truth and unifying principles accentuates formal considerations in aesthetics. In the realm of music, as we have seen in the case of Rameau, this type of aesthetic tends to reduce music as an aesthetic object to its mathematical principles and formal properties, focusing on its virtual existence rather than its performance. While Rameau's theory ties empirical data—the fundamental bass and the *corps sonore*—to the production of meaningful and beautiful sequences of notes and chords, his attempts to ground the system in mathematical relations ultimately lead to a privileging of the closed system. In other words, formal and mathematical relations are the ultimate arbiters of good taste.[2] Further developments in scientific modernity fuel the movement of aesthetic theory away from formal considerations and toward the possibility for critical analysis that could account for and appreciate musical practice, in the ways that I have suggested for Rousseau.

According to Cassirer's analysis of the development of Enlightenment thought, it is the emergence of empiricism and skepticism that enables the shift away from the privileging of logical judgment characteristic of Cartesian rationalism, and toward a scientific and aesthetic theory that allows for the intervention of the phenomenal world in both scientific and aesthetic judgments. In the realm of science, this opens the closed systems of the seventeenth century toward the more open-ended modes of thought of the eighteenth century. Rather than the "unity, uniformity, simplicity, and logical equality [that] seem to form the ultimate and highest goal of thought"[3] characteristic of the seventeenth century, philosophical and scientific thought of the eighteenth century attempts to account for multiplicity, variety, and change. The individual point of view becomes central to the Enlightenment project as the universal Cartesian subject cedes its place to the situated subject of Lockean empiricism, Leibinizian monadology, and Humean skepticism.

From the standpoint of aesthetics, this shift inaugurates a subjective turn, as logical judgments are no longer as highly prized as those judgments that are limited in scope, but as such necessarily valid, as in judgments of taste that rely on the subject's knowledge of its own perceptions.[4] The break with classical aesthetics that occurs during the eighteenth century enables the consideration of works of art from the standpoint of experience. For music, this means the beginning of a turn toward musical practice, performance, and reception. For Rousseau, as we saw in chapters 1 and 3, it is the attention to musical practice, informed in part by changes in aesthetic considerations, that enables him to formulate an aesthetic that is distinctly modern.

All aesthetic theories choose a privileged object that illustrates their principles. For the French classical aesthetic of the seventeenth century, the privileged objects are poetry and theater, illustrating the eternal and stable truths of classical formalism. For the eighteenth-century aesthetic, oriented toward subjective perception and feeling, the novel and genre painting play a pivotal role in illustrating the effects of the work of art on the perceiving subject.[5] In many respects, the choice of object is not only conditioned by the theoretical principles, but it also serves to reinforce and further delineate the aesthetic theory. Forming a dialectical circuit, aesthetic theory and privileged object mutually condition and reinforce each other.

In the case of Rousseau, who nowhere articulates an independent aesthetic theory, I would argue that the choice of object is paramount. Indeed, Rousseau's concentration on music enables the articulation of an aesthetic theory that breaks in dramatic ways with aesthetic theory of the period.[6] Because of both his exclusive attention to music and his failure to develop an independent aesthetic theory, Rousseau gains insight into aesthetic experience—understood in relation to musical practice—that prefigures nineteenth- and twentieth-century conceptions of the work of art. Rousseau's modernity in this respect, although clearly in some sense a product of the emergence of a certain scientific modernity, nonetheless also represents a radical break with the seventeenth-century classical aesthetic and even the more subject-centered aesthetic theory of Rousseau's contemporaries, pointing the way toward the conception of modernity and the aesthetic modernism of the mid-nineteenth through to the early twentieth century.[7]

## Rousseau's Modernity

Classing Rousseau among the moderns, or as a thinker who not only gives voice to a certain conception of modernity as a critic of the Enlightenment, but also shapes our understanding of the emergence of modernity, is least problematic from the standpoint of his social and political thought.[8] Rousseau's social and political theory diagnoses many of the ills of modern life, inaugurating, as I have argued elsewhere, philosophical critical theory.[9] Specifically with respect to the wedge he drives between nature and society, Rousseau's thought necessitates a reconceptualization of social life and puts into question the possibility for happiness, sparking debates that continue today.

Karol Berger argues that the sense of human history in Rousseau ushers in a new perspective that will be continued in the thought of Kant and Hegel. For Berger, who contrasts Rousseau with Augustine, the difference amounts to a theological, metaphysical, and political shift: "In Rousseau's world, man is no longer confronted with a transcendent realm representing a level of reality radically different from his own; instead, humanity and nature occupy one and the same level of reality. Because we are natural beings and a part of nature, our fall is a denial of ourselves, the result of disobedience toward our own nature. Further, because there is no transcendent realm—no outside—saving grace cannot come from outside. If we are to be saved, it can only be by our own efforts."[10] With mankind responsible for its own corrupted present state, the only hope for correction and, ultimately, redemption, lies, as Berger maintains, within.

In a similar vein, Hans Robert Jauss asserts that Rousseau's thought opens the door toward a new kind of historical thinking that positions man within a narrative of his own creation. Jauss writes: "The resulting question that is asked by Rousseau, a question that has been epoch-making for ensuing generations, is, as condensed from its many variations: how can man in the modern world, considering his second existence as *homme civil*, reappropriate his lost totality of the *homme naturel* and so recover his chance for happiness?"[11] This question, sparked by Rousseau's assessment of mankind's present state, introduces a distinctly modern attitude with respect both to the historical present and to the possible sources of redemption. Many critics, Jauss among them, consider the response to the question posed by Rousseau, and specifically the identification of works of art as a locus of potential happiness, to be a product of later thought, particularly romanticism, modernism, and the avant-garde movements. However, I believe that Rousseau already hints at such an answer to his own question in his understanding of music.

Although Rousseau himself inaugurated a certain conception of modernity conceived as historical consciousness, it is the philosophers of the twentieth century who have fully articulated the view glimpsed by Rousseau. In a now celebrated speech, given in Frankfurt upon receiving the city's Adorno prize, Jürgen Habermas argues in favor of conceiving of modernity as an "unfinished project."[12] Against the disillusionment of postmodernists, who would proclaim both the project of Enlightenment and modernity dead or, at the very least, not worth pursuing, Habermas defends the ideals of the Enlightenment and, specifically, the reintegration of the aesthetic and the life world. Paradoxically, although a defender of the Enlightenment, Habermas is not so far from Rousseau in seeking a remedy for the ills brought about by enlightenment and modernity from within the project of Enlightenment itself.

In the course of his argument, Habermas, citing Adorno on Baudelaire, conceives of modernity as a relation to the "new." Habermas isolates the present's relationship to the past as particularly significant for defining the modern. As Habermas sees it, the move away from the models of classical antiquity and toward independent standards of beauty defines modernity:

> With varying contents, the term *modernity* repeatedly expresses the consciousness of an era that relates itself to the past of classical antiquity in order to conceive itself as the result of a transition from the old to the new. This is not true merely of the Renaissance, with which the modern age [*Neuzeit*] begins *for us;* people also thought of themselves as "modern" at the time of Charlemagne, in the twelfth century, and during the Enlightenment—that is, whenever the consciousness of a new era in Europe developed through a renewed relationship to classical antiquity. In this process, *antiquitas*, antiquity, was considered a normative model to be imitated. . . . Only with the French Enlightenment's ideals of perfection and the notion, inspired by modern science, of the infinite progress of knowledge and an infinite advance toward social and moral betterment was the spell that the classical works of antiquity exerted on the spirit of those *early* moderns at each point gradually broken. (343)

Significantly, it is with the French Enlightenment that Habermas locates a break that inaugurates a new relationship with the past that will reconfigure conceptions of beauty for modernity. Consistent with Cassirer's understanding of the emergence of eighteenth-century aesthetics outlined above,

Habermas also stresses the open-ended quest—unbounded by rationalist classical ideals—for human progress as characteristic of the modern subjective turn.

Similarly, Luc Ferry's account of the development of aesthetics also highlights the shift occurring during the Enlightenment: "Among the *ancients* the work is conceived of as microcosm—which permits them to think that outside of it, in the macrocosm, an objective or, better, substantial criterion of the Beautiful exists—it is given meaning among the *moderns* through reference to subjectivity, to become for the *contemporaries*, the pure and simple expression of individuality."[13] A part of the shift that both Ferry and Habermas locate in the subjective turn that occurs during the Enlightenment relates to the conception of imitation. As Habermas recounts the development, classical aesthetics insists on eternal aesthetic standards having their roots in antiquity and grounded in rational truths. With the turn toward subjectivity, the concept of the beautiful itself becomes subjective, pushing aside the need for, and indeed the belief in, the imitation of absolute objective standards of beauty.[14] Rather than imitate classical models, or eternal singular truths, the new aesthetic of the eighteenth century relies on judgment and subjective experience of the natural world in order to produce artistic imitations. Mimesis of this new type emphasizes the subjective experience of the aesthetic object, in the effort required by both artist and audience to relate the work of art back to nature through judgment.

In the area of music, the debates concerning music's mimetic ability are more acute than those of the other arts. In effect, defenders of music during the eighteenth century struggle to maintain its status as an art, and not a science, by insisting on its potentials for imitation.[15] In part, this defense of music relates back to the earlier classical aesthetic, such as Rameau's, that would have viewed music's mathematical and formal qualities as indices of its ability to represent eternal and stable truths. For the newer, subjectively oriented aesthetic, music's rational and stable formal qualities pose an obstacle to the imitation of nature conceived as dynamic and changing. What is at stake in the arguments concerning mimesis in music is music's status as an art.[16]

Many critics have treated in detail Rousseau's debt to and departure from the various theories of imitation of his day.[17] While acknowledging Rousseau's debt to other theorists, and the historically specific reasons for his insistence on mimesis in music, it is important to highlight the ways in which, for Rousseau, mimesis relies on judgment—a subject to which I will return.[18] With respect to both painting and music, Rousseau articulates an aesthetic founded on a new type of mimesis. As we have seen in the preceding chapters, in the *Essai sur l'origine des langues*, he argues in favor of an aesthetic based on formal relations between both colors and sounds that produces an imitation that goes beyond the merely pleasing or agreeable. For Rousseau, art moves its audience through formal relations that imitate nature:

> Comme donc la peinture n'est pas l'art de combiner des couleurs d'une maniére agréable à la vüe, la musique n'est pas non plus l'art de combiner des sons d'une maniére agréable à l'oreille. S'il n'y avoit que cela, l'une et l'autre seroient au nombre des sciences naturelles et non pas des beaux arts. C'est l'imitation seule qui les élêve à ce rang. Or qu'est-ce qui fait de la peinture un art d'imitation? C'est le dessein. Qu'est-ce qui de la musique en fait un autre? C'est la mélodie. (5:414)

> [Just as painting is not the art of combining colors in an agreeable manner for the view, music is not the art of combining sounds in an agreeable manner for the ear. If it were only that, the one and the other would number among the natural sciences and not the arts. It is the imagination alone that elevates them to this rank. So what makes painting an art of imitation? It is design. What makes of music another one? It is melody.]

It is form—in its arrangement of colors and sounds—that distinguishes the work of art from science. Simple color and sound production belongs either to the realm of science or simple physical pleasure; formal design aimed at mimesis characterizes art for Rousseau. But the formal qualities of music, as we shall see, must be redefined in order to move away from the earlier conception of music so prized by the classical aesthetic as merely formal or mathematical.

Imitation of nature as a defining feature of art does not in and of itself mark a significant break that one could characterize as modern. The move away from classical aesthetics toward a dynamically conceived nature as the model for art, although significant for the reconceptualization of the understanding of the present, does not provide sufficient ground for a new understanding of the role of the work of art in the modern world.[19] Rousseau's emphasis on formal criteria for judging works of art as imitations of nature requires further elaboration of the function of these imitations in modern life.

Coupled with the shift in emphasis toward nature is a new attitude concerning the present. I would characterize the attitude as elegiac, expressing a feeling of irrecuperable loss with respect to the past.[20] Indeed, although the Enlightenment marks a break with antiquity, and stands on its own, as it were, in Rousseau's thought, the *present* of the Enlightenment stands abandoned, or at the very least in mournful solitude, with respect to all that has gone before.

The plaintive relation to the past is perhaps most evident in the *Discours sur les sciences et les arts* and *Discours sur l'origine de l'inégalité* (1755) and other works that sketch a time of origin and subsequent development of humanity that has led to man's perdition in the modern world.[21] The elegiac solitude of the *Rêveries du promeneur solitaire* (1777) and of *Rousseau juge de Jean-Jacques* (1772–1775), and to some extent the hermetic isolation of small family groups in *Julie, ou la nouvelle Héloïse* (1761) and *Emile, ou de l'éducation* (1761), also voices the alienation and lack of community that Rousseau perceives in modern life.[22] Most significantly for my purposes here, the *Essai sur l'origine des langues* gestures to a lost age in which singing, poetry, and speech were one: "les vers, les chants, la parole ont une origine commune" (5:410) [verses, songs, speech have a common origin], providing a kind of sonorous plenitude of energy and passion. In most of Rousseau's corpus, there is a general feeling, an overall pathos, of loss with respect to the past—an elegiac lament for an immediacy, fulfillment, plenitude, and, ultimately, a satisfaction that is lacking in the present. The character Pygmalion, in the opening lines of Rousseau's *scène lyrique*, expressing despair over his lost talent, epitomizes the plight of the modern artist, "Il n'y a point-là d'ame ni de vie; ce n'est que de la pierre. Je ne ferai jamais rien de tout cela. O mon génie, où es-tu? Mon talent qu'es-tu devenu? Tout mon feu s'est éteint, mon imagination s'est glacée, le marbre sort froid de mes mains" (5:1224) [There is no soul there nor life; it is only stone. I will never make anything of all that. O my genius, where are you? My talent, what have you become? All my fire is extinguished, my imagination is frozen, the marble leaves my hands cold].[23] Pygmalion the sculptor, Rousseau the modern writer, and by extension, all we moderns, have lost our fire and our imagination, and are haunted by a memory, or traces of the primordial fire left in works of art.

The elegiac mode of Rousseau's works implies a need for redemption. Pygmalion finds what he seeks in his own chef d'oeuvre, Galathée. As Shierry Weber has persuasively argued, Pygmalion finds intimacy and a "new" whole self in his fusion with Galathée, the work he has produced.[24] Likewise, Patrick Coleman reads *Pygmalion* as a commentary on Rousseau's anxiety in anticipating the reception of his own work—an anxiety that anticipates modernism.[25] The title of Rousseau's collection of romances, *Les consolations des misères de ma vie*, suggests that art, and specifically simple forms of music, may offer consolation in the face of life struggles. If the artist finds solace in his relationship with his own creation, is society to do the same? Can and do works of art provide what is missing in the modern world?

Returning to the historical argument concerning the emergence of modernity—which in many respects extends Rousseau's argument of the *First* and *Second Discourses*—for Weber and Habermas increased rationalization and separation of the domains of knowledge leads to the severing of ties between formerly united spheres of expression. This "differentiation of the values spheres," and splitting off of expert domains of knowledge, leaves art independent from either religious-metaphysical value or moral value.[26] Art, as an independent sphere, has its own experts—artists, collectors, connoisseurs, critics—and its own value: authentic aesthetic expression.[27] Many of these cultural changes were already palpable by the mid-eighteenth century.

But the differentiation and secularization of the spheres and the appearance of expert knowledge in the aesthetic domain does not go far enough in explaining the crisis in values expressed in Rousseau's elegiac mode. Clearly, cutting artistic expression loose from either religious-metaphysical or moral-practical expression does create difficulties for understanding the role of the work of art. But the crisis seems to go even deeper than the splitting off of the aesthetic domain. Well before the nineteenth century, Rousseau is not simply lamenting increased rationalization in the form of specialization and compartmentalization—either in life in general or in the aesthetic domain. Given the state of society, as Rousseau sees it, produced in large measure by the increase in knowledge generated by the Enlightenment, and, indeed, by society itself as it necessarily divorces man from nature, art must provide something to replace the displaced values. Increased secularization and expert knowledge has led to a crisis in meaning and value, not only for art but also for all domains of knowledge. For Rousseau, questions of legitimation lie at the heart of man's self-examination in a secularized modern world. The realm of art may offer a last bastion of hope for a secularized society grappling for meaning and value. At the very least, the elegiac mode laments the increased alienation and secularization in the modern world expressed through the means of literary art.[28]

Finally, the break with the past articulated in the elegiac mode, coupled with the need for redemption, invites a consideration of the future. The aesthetic expressions of modernity loosely grouped under the rubric "modernism" are characterized by a specific temporal attitude with respect to the present that cuts ties with both the past and the future. Looking to Baudelaire, Adorno and Habermas—and Foucault as well—define a modernist aesthetic as a certain relation to the "now." In Baudelaire's work they locate its modernity in "the ephemeral, the fleeting, the contingent."[29] In this relationship to the now, modernism celebrates the present, not by attempting to capture and freeze it, but rather, writes Habermas, in "the forward orientation, the anticipation of an undefined, contingent future, and the cult of the New." Habermas continues, "What is expressed in the new value accorded the transitory and the ephemeral and in the celebration of dynamism is the longing for an immaculate and unchanging present. Modernism, a self-negating moment, is 'nostalgia for true presence.' This says, Octavio Paz, 'is the secret theme of the best modernist writers.' "[30] Rather than try to recapture a lost past, or freeze a fleeting present, the modernist aesthetic celebrates the ephemeral.

Rousseau's political theory provides one locus for conceptualization of the eternal present. C. N. Dugan and Tracy B. Strong have argued that sovereignty exists only in the present moment for Rousseau; they tie his political and aesthetic theories together because of their emphasis on the present. In a fascinating incorporation of Rousseau's aesthetic thought into a reading of the ban on representation in democratic politics, Dugan and Strong assert that sovereignty and the general will exist in the immediate present only:

> To say that something exists in the present means (at least) that we have no way of encountering it except as what it is. To say that the general will is what it is is to say that the judgments of the general will cannot be references to analogous (but not identical) situations; each judgment expresses a claim that holds unambiguously for the exact circumstances and citizenry at hand.... This is why sovereignty cannot be represented. Representation gives a temporal dimension to sovereignty, something that could not but make it not what it is.[31]

In this respect, the emphasis on the present in Rousseau's thought brings together the political and the aesthetic as two instances of the same temporal phenomenon.

But perhaps the clearest and most forceful articulation in Rousseau's entire corpus of this type of relation to the present occurs in the Fifth Promenade of the *Rêveries du promeneur solitaire:*

> Mais s'il est un état où l'ame trouve une assiette assez solide pour s'y reposer tout entiére et rassembler là tout son être, sans avoir besoin de rappeler le passé ni d'enjamber sur l'avenir; où le tems ne soit rien pour elle, où le présent dure toujours sans neanmoins marquer sa durée et sans aucune trace de succession, sans aucun autre sentiment de privation ni de jouissance, de plaisir ni de peine, de desir ni de crainte que celui seul de notre existence, et que ce sentiment seul puisse la remplir tout entier[e]; tant que cet état dure celui qui s'y trouve peut s'appeler heureux, non d'un bonheur imparfait, pauvre et rélatif tel que celui qu'on trouve dans les plaisirs de la vie mais d'un bonheur suffisant, parfait et plein, qui ne laisse dans l'ame aucun vuide qu'elle sente le besoin de remplir. (1:1046)

> [But if there is a state where the soul can find a foundation solid enough to rest itself entirely and bring together there its whole being, without having to remember the past or connect to the future, where time would be nothing for it, where the present would last forever without nonetheless marking its duration and without any trace of succession, without any feeling of privation or of enjoyment, of pleasure or of pain, of desire or of fear other than that of our very existence, and that this feeling alone could fill it entirely; as long as this state lasts the one who finds himself there can call himself happy, not of an imperfect happiness, impoverished and relative such as the one that one finds in the pleasures of life, but a sufficient happiness, perfect, and whole, that leaves no void in the soul that needs to be filled.]

Using this description of the experience as a kind of template, we are driven to ask how this peace and tranquility, this plenitude and happiness, may be achieved in the modern world? What kinds of experiences, given the alienation, secularization, and compartmentalization produced by the Enlightenment, can evoke this feeling of "sufficient, perfect, and full happiness"? Can aesthetic experience provide the occasion for experiences of the eternal present?

The Musical Aesthetic

Modernism, as an aesthetic, responds to the needs of the modern world as articulated in the elegiac mode and expressed in the new attitude toward the present. Habermas's and Foucault's readings of Baudelaire relate the modernist aesthetic to a certain conception of modernity that identifies art as a possible response to and cure for the woes introduced by the Enlightenment project and continued in modernity. In both Habermas and Foucault, there is a tendency to elide the Enlightenment project, modernity, and modernism into one continuous developmental phenomenon. While I will try to keep these various strands separate, especially with respect to the differences between the eighteenth and nineteenth centuries, I would acknowledge that my reliance on Habermas's theorizations has led to some blurring of these nebulous boundaries. As we have seen, Rousseau's corpus exhibits many of the most significant traits associated with the nineteenth-century understanding of the term "modernity." The elegiac mode and especially the attitude toward the present echo the definition of modernity and modernism normally associated with Baudelaire.

There is, however, a significant difference between, on the one hand, voicing these attitudes toward modernity in works of art (such as novels, plays, and autobiographies) and other forms of writing and, on the other, articulating an aesthetic theory. Certainly this type of awareness of the present, especially expressed in laments over a lost plenitude in the past, characterizes many writings from many periods. What distinguishes aesthetic modernism as a definitive break is the theorization of a new aesthetic attitude centered on the subject as a response to the perception of the various aporia produced by the historical developments of the second half of the eighteenth century. Aesthetic modernity—both the artistic practice and its theoretical articulation—responds in a self-conscious way to the diagnosis of modernity's ills.

Although the articulation of a modernist view with respect to time is certainly clear in the passage from the Fifth Promenade of the *Rêveries* that I cited above, the *Rêveries* do not present an aesthetic theory. Setting aside the questions of composition and intended audience that the text of the *Rêveries* present—although related to modernist and postmodernist problematics—an autobiographical text does not offer aesthetic theorization on the order of Kant's *Critique of Judgment*. Moreover, although *Pygmalion* thematizes many of the central questions of aesthetic theory in its depiction of the artist in relation to his work, it does not articulate a fully developed aesthetic theory.

Rousseau's most fully developed aesthetic theory lies in the body of texts devoted to music. While the composition of these texts spans many years and genres, and therefore the texts do not offer an aesthetic system in the way that Baumgarten's and Kant's do, it is precisely Rousseau's specific attention to music—and his failure to articulate a fully theorized vision—that enables a coherent and audacious aesthetic theory to emerge. I contend that in this aesthetic theory, Rousseau makes art, and specifically music, respond to the needs generated by modern life.

Music plays the key role in Rousseau's aesthetic theory for a number of reasons. First, by way of negative argument, it is important to point out that none of the other arts—poetry, literature, painting, theater, or sculpture—can provide the type of solace and remedy for modernity's ills that music can. While this is true because of Rousseau's particular views of the other arts—which may relate to their privileged status as chosen object for other aesthetic theories—it is also specifically related to Rousseau's understanding of music as an art form. Rather than dwell on Rousseau's catalogue of complaints relating to the other arts, I turn to his specific characterization and understanding of music.

First, as we saw in chapter 1, Rousseau's conception of music, in its privileging of performance, is profoundly temporal.[32] In the *Essai sur l'origine des langues*, he specifically distinguishes music from painting as an auditory as opposed to a visual art form, anchored in time rather than space:

> Chaque sens a son champ qui lui est propre. Le champ de la musique est le tems, celui de la peinture est l'espace. Multiplier les sons entendus à la fois ou developer les couleurs l'une après l'autre, c'est changer leur économie, c'est mettre l'œil à la place de l'oreille, et l'oreille à la place de l'œil. (5:420)

> [Each sense has a field that properly belongs to it. The field of music is time, that of painting is space. To multiply the sounds heard at the same time or develop the colors one after another is to change their economy, it is to put the eye in the place of the ear and the ear in the place of the eye.]

As we saw in chapter 1, music's temporal form requires performance for its very existence. While painting and sculpture may be created and left behind for their audience, music, at least in the eighteenth century, is created only through performance in order for it to be perceived. While this argument may sound like a reiteration of the Derridean reading of the privileging of presence in Rousseau, rather, as I argued in the introduction, the privileged status of music has more to do with its existence in time, and the need for its perpetual (re)creation in performance, than it does with the need for musicians to be present in order for it to be experienced.³³ Music exists in a virtual form as notes written on a page, but it comes to life and exists in its "true" form, that is to say, as a temporal art form for Rousseau, only when it is performed. The performance of music privileges the existence in the here and now, the fleeting and ephemeral quality of music as an art form, which also cuts against the rational and purely formal conception of music as mathematical relations.³⁴ Put another way, music is inherently sequential. And while our experience of painting and sculpture may indeed be sequential as well, as our eyes pass over various parts of the work of art to take it in, all parts are nonetheless simultaneously present. Not so with music: the sequential and temporal nature of music means that one part succeeds another in time and that our experience of music is always ordered, sequential, and temporal.

To reframe Rousseau's position in relation to what I am calling the aesthetic of modernity, this means that music expresses through its very form one of the central tenets of a type of modernism: the ephemeral quality of the here and now. One might even go so far as to suggest that music, through its temporal form, expresses the elegiac theme of loss: at the conclusion of each performance, nothing remains but the memory of the sounds. "Les couleurs sont durables, les sons s'évanoüissent, et l'on n'a jamais de certitude que ceux qui renaissent soient les mêmes que ceux qui se sont éteints" (5:420) [Colors are durable, sounds evaporate, and there is never any certainty that those that are reborn are the same as those that have been extinguished]. The performance can never be exactly repeated.³⁵ Indeed, we can only return to the experience of the work of art in memory.

In addition to its temporal/sequential form, music also presents another formal attribute that aids its expression of an aesthetic characteristic of modernism: music is an inherently relational art. Rousseau writes:

> Chaque couleur est absolüe, indépendante, au lieu que chaque son n'est pour nous que relatif et ne se distingue que par comparaison. Un son n'a par lui-même aucun caractére absolu qui le fasse reconnoitre; il est grave ou aigu, fort ou doux par raport à un autre; en lui-même il n'est rien de tout cela. (5:420)

[Each color is absolute, independent, whereas each sound is only relative for us and only distinguishes itself through comparison. A sound has by itself no absolute character that makes it recognizable; it is low-pitched or sharp, strong or soft in relation to another, in and of itself it has none of all that.]

Whether one believes what Rousseau says about colors or not, it is his insight into the nature of musical sounds that is consequential. What Rousseau means is that, in contrast to colors, musical signs, like linguistic ones, are arbitrary: in and of themselves they have no particular value. Individual notes become recognizable and derive value from the signifying system in which they are embedded:

> Dans le sistême harmonique un son quelconque n'est rien non plus naturellement; il est ni tonique ni dominante, ni harmonique ni fundamental; parce que toutes ces propriétés ne sont que des rapports, et que le sistême entier pouvant varier du grave à l'aigu, chaque son change d'ordre et de place dans le sistême, selon que le sistême change de degré. (5:420)

> [In the harmonic system any sound is nothing naturally, it is neither tonic nor dominant, neither harmonic nor fundamental, because all these properties are only relationships and the entire system being able to move from low to high, each changes order and place in the system according to the change in degree of the system.]

Arguing in parallel and against the grain of Rameau's theory of the fundamental bass and *corps sonore*, Rousseau insists on the relational and relative nature of musical sounds.[36]

An art based on arbitrary signs that derive their meaning through relation has implications for aesthetic theory. In order to produce expressive and meaningful art, one must use formal attributes. In other words, for Rousseau, form and content are more intimately linked in music than in painting because of the nature of the musical sign. Moreover, in order for music to imitate nature, as we have seen above that it must, music must have recourse to form. In opposition to painting, which uses, according to Rousseau, a relatively stable medium (colors), music, in addition to its formal design elements, must use unstable content (sounds) arranged according to a harmonic system to imitate nature. While this might, at first glance, seem to place music at a disadvantage with respect to painting's ability to imitate nature, the opposite is true. Rousseau argues that music's reliance on an arbitrary sign system enables it to imitate nature better precisely because of its distance from nature. Paradoxically, the arbitrariness of the musical sign enables better mimesis because of aesthetic distance and formalism: "On voit par là que la peinture est plus près de la nature et que la musique tient plus à l'art humain" (5:421) [We see from this that painting is closer to nature and that music has more of human art]. And yet this revival of formalism does not return to a static conception of music's ability to communicate eternal truths consistent with a classical aesthetic. Rather, music's formal qualities actually distance it from nature because they represent a human element.

Rousseau holds that music announces itself better than painting as a "human art." Music's temporal performance quality, as well as its inherently relational character, aids it both in imitating nature and in communicating the human element operative in mimesis. As an art form, music seems better suited to mimetic expression of an aesthetic ideal found in nature because of its formal properties.

In the *Dictionnaire de musique*, Rousseau isolates movement within music, another of its formal properties, as a feature that enables its mimetic expressions to surpass those of painting. Related again to its sequential/temporal form, music communicates even rest through movement:

> La Peinture, qui n'offre point ses tableaux à l'imagination, mais au sens et à un seul sens, ne peint que les objets soumis à la vue. La Musique sembleroit avoir les mêmes bornes par rapport à l'ouïe; cependant elle peint tout, même les objets qui ne sont que visibles: par un prestige presque inconcevable, elle semble mettre l'œil dans l'oreille, et la plus grande merveille d'un Art qui n'agit que par le mouvement, est d'en pouvoir former jusqu'à l'image du repos. La nuit, le sommeil, la solitude et le silence entrent dans le nombre des grands tableaux de la Musique. (5:860–61)

> [Painting, which does not offer its scenes to the imagination but to the senses and to only one sense, only paints objects that are subject to view. Music would seem to have the same limits with respect to hearing, and yet it paints everything, even objects that are only visible: through an almost inconceivable marvel, it seems to put the eye in the ear, and the greatest marvel of an art that only acts through movement is to be able to form even the image of rest. Night, sleep, solitude, and silence enter into the great number of music's tableaux.]

As we saw in chapter 1, music's ability to imitate derives from the communication of movement that it entails. The musician uses movement, created through the relation of sounds, to evoke not the movement present in nature, but rather the movement created in the observer of nature. The musician evokes in the listener the same movements that nature itself would evoke:

> Que toute la Nature soit endormie, celui qui la contemple ne dort pas, et *l'art du Musicien consiste à substituer à l'image insensible de l'objet celle des mouvemens que sa presence excite dans le cœur du Contemplateur.* Non-seulement il agitera la Mer, animera la flamme d'un incendie, fera couler les ruisseaux, tomber la pluie et grossir les torrens; mais il peindra l'horreur d'un desert affreux, rembrunira les murs d'une prison souterraine, calmera la tempête, rendra l'air tranquille et serein, et répandra de l'Orchestre une fraîcheur nouvelle sur les boccages. *Il ne représentera pas directement ces choses, mais il excitera dans l'ame les mêmes mouvemens qu'on éprouve en les voyant.* (5:861, my emphasis)[37]

> [Let all of nature be asleep, he who contemplates it is not sleeping, and *the art of the musician consists in substituting for the imperceptible image of the object the movements that its presence excites in the heart of the one who contemplates.* Not only will he agitate the sea, animate the flame of fire, make the streams run, the rain fall, and the torrents swell; but he will also paint the horror of an awful desert, darken the walls of an underground prison, calm the tempest, make the air tranquil and serene, and will spread a new freshness over the groves from the orchestra. *He will not directly represent these things, but he will excite in the soul the same movements that one feels in seeing them.*]

Music indirectly represents nature by communicating human feelings associated with the experience of and reaction to nature. Rousseau's account of musical mimesis in the *Dictionnaire* stresses the turn toward subjective experience in privileging the reaction of the listener over the work of art itself or what it represents. Indeed, the work of art aims to re-create human reaction to nature rather than nature itself, focusing our attention on the subjective and experiential character of aesthetic judgments.

To take this argument even a step further, Claude Dauphin has argued that, within Rousseau's understanding of musical mimesis, there is a distinction between a form of imitation that music shares with other arts such as poetry and painting—although distinctly different, as we have seen—and another form of imitation peculiar to music.[38] This second form of mimesis, which Rousseau refers to as technical imitation, enables music to imitate itself:

> Imitation, dans son sens technique, est l'emploi d'un même Chant, ou d'un Chant semblable, dans plusieurs Parties qui le font entendre l'une après l'autre, à l'Unisson, à la Quinte, à la Quatre, à la Tierce, ou à quelqu'autre Intervalle que ce soit. *L'Imitation* est toujours bien prise, même en changeant plusieurs Notes; pourvu que ce même Chant se reconnoisse toujours et qu'on ne s'écarte point des loix d'une bonne Modulation. (5:861)
>
> [Imitation, in its technical meaning, is the use of a same song or of a similar song, in several parts that make it heard one after another in unison, at the fifth, at the fourth, at the third, or at whatever other interval that it might be. *Imitation* is always well done, even changing several notes; provided that the same song be always recognizable and that one does not depart from the rules of good modulation.]

While the first form of mimesis in music stresses the reaction of the subject, technical mimesis moves aesthetic expression even farther away from the necessity of "imitating nature" and toward an autonomous existence for music as a potentially self-referential art form. Although Rousseau never suggests that music should abandon the first type of mimesis, nonetheless, his recognition of technical mimesis in music moves him another step closer to a modernist aesthetic: a fully independent art capable of supplying its own frame of reference and value. Coupled with the understanding of musical mimesis as imitation of human movement, technical mimesis asserts the primacy of music for celebrating the human capacity to create art in the here and now.

A Kantian Turn—Toward a Subjective Aesthetic

In tracing the significant features of Rousseau's conception of music that lead him to privilege it as an art form over all others, the elements of a Kantian turn in this "musical aesthetic" become apparent. First and foremost, Rousseau traces a formalist aesthetic that depends on the perception not only of aesthetic form, but also, as we have just seen, on the appreciation of a kind of second-order, conditional mimesis: Music imitates the movements that the listener would experience, *if* he were before the spectacle of nature. As I quoted above, "l'art du Musicien consiste à substituer à l'image insensible de l'objet celle des mouvemens que sa presence excite dans le coeur du Contemplateur" (5:861) [the art of the musician consists in substituting for the imperceptible image of the object the movements that its presence excites in the heart of the one who contemplates]. Clearly, judgment is entailed on the parts of the composer and performer as they seek to elicit this movement in the heart of the listener. The relational and arbitrary character of the musical sign system also requires the use of judgment—by composer, musician, and listener alike. For, as Rousseau has argued, in and of themselves, musical notes communicate nothing. It is only through formal relations that sounds become meaningful in musical "communication." In his clearest articulation of the need for judgment in aesthetic perception specifically related to form, Rousseau writes in the article "Unité de mélodie":

> Tous les beaux Arts ont quelque *Unité* d'objet, source du plaisir qu'ils donnent à l'esprit: car l'attention partagée ne se repose nulle part, et quand deux objets nous occupent, c'est une preuve qu'aucun des deux ne nous satisfait. Il y a, dans la Musique, une *Unité* successive qui se rapporte au sujet, et par laquelle toutes les Parties, bien liées, composent un seul tout, dont on apperçoit l'ensemble et tous les rapports. (5:1143)

> [All the arts have some *unity* of object, source of the pleasure that they give to the mind: for divided attention rests nowhere, and when two objects occupy us, it is proven that neither one of them satisfies us. There is in music a successive *unity* that relates to the subject and through which all the well-linked parts form a single whole, of which we perceive the ensemble and all the relations.]

Melodic unity provides formal coherence that enables the perception of individual parts in a musical piece, while at the same time allows the perception of the piece as a whole.[39] Perceiving musical form, with the aid of melodic unity, implies an act of judgment: the listener must reassemble the various parts in order to "hear" the piece as a whole. Anticipating Kant, it is clear that Rousseau's understanding of music both highlights perception and at least implies judgment on the part of the subject.[40]

In these respects, Rousseau's conceptualization of our appreciation for music combines key elements of prior aesthetic theory in ways that anticipate Kant. The insistence on the perception of form reiterates the importance of form in classical aesthetics, but reconceives form in terms of relations and movements rather than static universal qualities. Likewise, the insistence on perception, which is central to the subjective turn in eighteenth-century aesthetics, is tempered by the insistence on form. For Kant, the perception of form is not sufficient to define aesthetic judgments. As is the case for Rousseau, for Kant too it is important to continue to distinguish between aesthetic and scientific judgments. To this end, Kant introduces the notion of disinterestedness, in part to distinguish aesthetic and "determining" judgment.

For Kant, all aesthetic judgments are by nature disinterested.[41] Kant argues that interest of any kind would color judgment by imposing a category of the understanding on the object, thereby rendering the judgment "determining" and no longer aesthetic. Indeed, Kant's understanding of aesthetic form as "purposiveness without a purpose" (55) necessitates that all aesthetic judgments be disinterested in this way. Rousseau's musical aesthetic, while not entirely consistent with Kant on this point, nonetheless goes a long way toward a conception of "disinterestedness." Already with his emphasis on the listener's perception of form, Rousseau makes a major step toward Kantian-style disinterestedness. Melodic unity as a formal attribute of the aesthetic object stresses a disinterested appreciation for musical works in the sense that music for Rousseau does not require or entail the imposition of a category or concept in order to perceive its form. Coupled with the second-order conditional mimesis, in which the musician imitates movements in the soul that could be elicited by nature, it is clear that aesthetic perception and the aesthetic object itself are highly abstract. The listener never believes him/herself to be "before nature," but rather experiences the same sorts of movements s/he might experience before nature. The second-order character of the representation entailed in music underscores nature's absence. Added to this is the ephemeral, temporal quality of musical performance, again stressing the fleetingness and "unseizability" of the musical work of art. This last attribute underscores music's odd form of material existence that belies "interest" of the type that Kant seeks to ban from aesthetic judgments.[42]

Finally, the emphasis on the aesthetic experience of music—rather than as music as an aesthetic object—also moves in a Kantian direction. Rousseau consistently returns to the theme of what the listener feels as s/he experiences a piece of music. Beyond the perception of form and the feelings elicited by nature, music is a profoundly human art. As John Scott has asserted, because music has a moral cause for Rousseau, music also has a moral effect: music, along with language, was born to communicate passion and not need.[43] For Rousseau, our interest in music is a moral and human interest. To continue with a passage that I cited above, "la peinture est plus près de la nature et . . . la musique tient plus à l'art humain. On sent aussi que l'une intéresse plus que l'autre précisément parce qu'elle rapproche plus l'homme de l'homme et nous donne toujours quelque idée de nos semblables" (5:421) [painting is closer to nature and music has more of human art. We feel also that one interests more than the other precisely because it brings man closer to man and always gives us some idea of those who are like us]. This interest in music suggests that we listen not only to be moved, but also because we recognize human feeling, passion, and, ultimately, morality behind the sounds.

While at first glance this interest in music appears to go against the Kantian proscription against interest in aesthetic judgments, on closer inspection it is clear that this type of interest does not entail the material existence of the aesthetic object.[44] The interest described by Rousseau relates to music's ability to capture and hold our attention as a meaningful and moving experience.[45] Indeed, I would argue further that the interest that Rousseau describes relates to what postmodern critics such as Jean-François Lyotard and Jean-Luc Nancy have perceived in the Kantian sublime: a moment when the subject accedes to an indirect experience of itself.[46] But in the case of Rousseau's conception of aesthetic judgment, the subject of musical aesthetic judgment does not experience itself in its own limitless potential, as Lyotard and Nancy argue in the case of Kant. Rather, for Rousseau the person listening to music and exercising aesthetic judgment glimpses human community. In other words, while Kant's conceptualization of aesthetic experience remains internal to the subject making aesthetic judgments (although there is the implication with the *sensus communis* of the potential agreement of the community on matters of taste), Rousseau's understanding entails the recognition of fellow human beings as an integral part of aesthetic judgments.[47] The work of music reminds the listener of other human beings in the world through the expression of emotion. If this is true, it makes Rousseau more modernist in his use of aesthetics than his celebrated successor, Kant, a point to which I will return.[48] In this respect, music helps to create the bonds of community through the exercise of judgment occasioned through aesthetic reception. When we listen to a piece of music and exercise judgment, we feel ourselves to be part of the larger community.

Musical Redemption

As a more human art form than painting, music offers a greater "shot at redemption" (to quote Paul Simon) than do other art forms.[49] Rousseau already recognizes a form of modernity in which increased alienation and secularization, as well as rationalization of the domains of knowledge, leads both to the splitting off of the aesthetic sphere and to the search for value within that sphere. Artistic production in the modern world offers what Habermas refers to as a *promesse de bonheur*, citing a line of criticism that runs from Schiller to Marcuse, and sees in works of art a promise of utopia.[50] This utopia, whether in the form of a promise of reconciliation or in the service of cultural critique, nonetheless represents a site of value and redemption for a world experiencing the pain of loss and separation. The project of modernity, a continuation of the Enlightenment project as Habermas defends it, continues to seek progress in the form of moral betterment and greater human happiness through the vehicle of artistic expression. The elegiac mode resurfaces as an articulation of hope for redemption in and through aesthetic expression itself. For Rousseau as well, in spite of his dire pronouncements in the *Discours sur les sciences et les arts*, hope for the future of humanity lies in some form of musical redemption.

Returning to my discussion of interest in aesthetic judgments, Rousseau believes that the performance of music creates interest in the listener, an interest that arises from a glimpse of human community through artistic form. As a quintessentially human art form, music requires the *presence* of both performer and listener. Rousseau returns to this theme time and time again, to insist that music communicates the existence of another sentient being in its very performance:

> Les sons announcent le movement, la voix annonce un être sensible; il n'y a que des corps animés qui chantent . . . la nature seule engendre peu de sons, et à moins qu'on n'admette l'harmonie des sphéres celestes, il faut des êtres vivans pour la produire. . . . La peinture est souvent morte et inanimée; elle vous peut transporter au fond d'un desert; mais sitôt que des signes vocaux frapent vôtre oreille, ils vous annoncent un être sensible à vous, ils sont, pour ainsi dire, les organes de l'ame, et s'ils vous peignent aussi la solitude ils vous disent que vous n'y étes pas seul. Les oiseaux sifflent, l'homme seul chante, et l'on ne peut entendre ni chant ni simphonie sans se dire à l'instant; un autre être sensible est ici. (5:420–21)

> [Sounds announce movement, the voice announces another sentient being; only animated bodies sing . . . nature alone engenders few sounds, and unless one admits the harmony of the celestial spheres, living beings are necessary in order to produce them. . . . Painting is

often dead and unanimated, it can transport you to the ends of a desert; but as soon as vocal signs hit your ear, they announce a sentient being to you, they are, so to speak, the organs of the soul, and if they paint solitude for you they also tell you that you are not alone. Birds whistle, only man sings, and one cannot hear a song or a symphony without immediately saying: another sentient being is here.]

Human beings are "interested" in music, according to Rousseau, because of the presence of another similar being that is communicated through it.[51]

This interest is clearly a moral interest: Music announces sentience, movement, passion, and life. In this communication of the presence of other beings like ourselves, music offers a glimpse at moral community. Like the early moments of contact between humans in the *Discours sur l'origine de l'inégalité* or *Essai sur l'origine des langues*, when natural man first experiences and, more important, recognizes beings like himself, listening to music stirs feelings of the potential for connection between like sentient beings.

Earlier, I suggested that the glimpse at community offered by music for Rousseau parallels the indirect experience the subject has of itself in the Kantian sublime. For Lyotard and Nancy, the uneasiness—what Kant dubs a "negative pleasure" (83)—engendered by the play of the imagination and reason in judgments of the sublime, marks a moment in Kant's thought when the transcendental subject perceives itself, if only through the violence of the experience. Kant writes, "We hence see also that true sublimity must be sought only in the mind of the [subject] judging, not in the natural object the judgment upon which occasions this state" (95).

For Kant's transcendental philosophy, the *Critique of Judgment*, and, specifically, judgments of the sublime, offer a window into the supreme blind spot of such a system: the subject itself. However, Kant's philosophical system does not share the elegiac mode and need for redemption that Rousseau's vision of humanity conditions. For Kant, the transcendental subject guarantees philosophical certainty as well as the future of humanity, again, grounded in the subject. Likewise, for the postmodernists Lyotard and Nancy, the Kantian subject's glimpse of itself typifies the self-referential circularity of unstable knowledge. Using the moment of the sublime to critique the Kantian transcendental subject, they diagnose the failure of both the Enlightenment project and modernity.

But the possible glimpse of fellow humanity that music provides in Rousseau offers neither the stability of Kantian aesthetic judgments nor the instability of postmodern self-referentiality. As we have seen, Rousseau shares the anxieties and fears about the future of later modernists and seeks a different source for redemptive experience from the musical aesthetic.

If the Kantian sublime offers a glimpse at the stabilizing base of a philosophical edifice, then Rousseau's musical aesthetic offers the same kind of window, but onto a very different future than Kant's. As we have seen, music elicits an interest in another sentient being, a feeling of moral recognition, through an essentially ephemeral aesthetic form. The performance of music reasserts the possibility of human community, against the ephemeral quality of the temporal nature of the performance, to incite us to listen to and appreciate other human beings. Rousseau's aesthetic of modernity offers moral redemption in a form of art that is inherently communal while at the same time fleeting. Musical performance enables repetition without exact duplication, avoiding the pitfall of a fully stable form. Rather, Rousseau's aesthetic answer to modernity posits a repeatable ephemeral phenomenon that offers a glimpse of shared humanity.

As a corrective to the alienation and increased separation and specialization in the modern world, music offers the hope of bridging these gaps and rebuilding communities. The emphasis on sentience as a significant feature for recognition in Rousseau runs counter to the rationalization and alienation of the modern world. And, against a Habermasian-style argument relying on rationality for communication, Rousseau argues for an aesthetic experience of feeling and belonging occasioned by the performance and reception of music. Listening to and recognizing the song of another sentient being—feeling interested in this way—means that links to other beings can be continuously re-created (although with differences), even in the face of modern fragmentation, destabilization, and the ephemeral quality of modern life. The answer to the problem of the fragmentation of community resides not in rational deliberation, but rather in shared moments of fellow feeling and consolation. Much like humans in Rousseau's state of nature, recognizing their fellow creatures (*semblables*) for the first time, the experience of listening to music enables us to reconnect with our fellow humanity and thus holds open the promise for meaningful collective experience and action.

# Conclusion:
# Rousseau Sings the Blues

> It's very difficult to explain the effect the first blues record I heard had on me, except to say that I recognized it immediately. It was as if I were being reintroduced to something that I already knew, maybe from another, earlier life. For me there is something primitively soothing about this music, and it went straight to my nervous system, making me feel ten feet tall. This was the feeling I had when I first heard the Sonny Terry and Brownie McGhee song on Uncle Mac, and the same thing happened when I first heard Big Bill Broonzy.
>
> — Eric Clapton, *Clapton: The Autobiography*

Of course Rousseau never heard the blues. The eighteenth-century Genevan was long gone when the form arose in the rural southern United States in the area near the Mississippi Delta between the 1880s and the 1920s. So why pose the question of what he would say about the blues? This speculation may just be a whim conditioned by two passions in my own life, but I believe that the thought experiment will prove useful in focusing on specific aspects of music in which Rousseau is strongly invested, and I aim to bring together the various strands of my argument concerning the relationship among politics, social theory, and aesthetics. I therefore ask my reader's indulgence as I embark on a somewhat fanciful examination of what Rousseau might have said about the blues by way of conclusion.

For those unfamiliar with the blues, let me briefly sketch the most significant features of the genre to enable a fuller understanding of my speculations about Rousseau's hypothetical engagement.[1] According to our best educated guess, the blues appeared in the post-Reconstruction era of the south, when conditions for African Americans reached an all-time low.[2] In the wake of emancipation, families and communities were broken up by the exigencies of the new social and economic reality. Many former slaves found work as itinerant manual laborers and sharecroppers. Prior to this period, African American music had been characterized by communal forms, primarily spirituals and work songs.[3] The disintegration of slave communities, diaspora, and economic hardship brought into being a new solo genre marked by the call and response structure of the earlier communal forms. First documented in the early 1900s, the blues emerged during a period of racist backlash and bleak economic conditions when individuals who had been separated from their former communities gave expression to a new aesthetic form.[4]

As a musical form, the blues is characterized by a number of loose formal constraints. That is to say, while it is a fixed-form genre, there is nonetheless a great deal of variation in the blues. The call and response structure may be one of the most stable aspects of the blues form. Likely derived from earlier call and response patterns in spirituals and work songs, the blues normally has a vocal line or "call," followed by a "response" played by an instrument. In the early blues, the response was often played by the guitar or harmonica. In addition to the call and response structure, the blues is also characterized by a fairly standard twelve-bar progression of chords (although other numbers of measures from eight to thirteen or more are possible) and an A, A', B lyric structure. The scale is usually pentatonic with "pitch areas" around the 3rd, 5th, and 7th, creating the famous "blue notes."[5] Within this fairly fixed form, a great deal of variation is possible, including significant room for improvisation both instrumentally and lyrically. Finally, the blues is usually characterized by lyrical content that highlights the isolation of the persona of the singer. As David Evans describes,

> Blues displays an intense concentration on the momentary feelings of the singer, or more accurately, the persona portrayed by the singer, i.e., the dramatized self. It incorporates and symbolizes a heightened sense of individualism, economic uncertainty, alienation from society, family, and community, and escape from problems through erotic activity, violence, gambling, drinking, and travel. Blues started as an "underground" and sometimes "underworld" or "outlaw" type of music, much despised by more respectable segments of society, who nevertheless often found it fascinating or titillating. It arose within an environment of massive racial oppression, which tended to intensify all these other qualities. Blues artists were not simply society's lower class but were part of a segregated low caste.[6]

Even from this brief characterization, it seems evident that for reasons of social justice alone Rousseau would have been drawn to the blues. A form of music associated with a disenfranchised, "segregated lower caste" would no doubt appeal to his sense of the need for increased social and political equality and justice. Music that gives voice to the alienation experienced by oppressed individuals provides an aesthetic outlet for society's ills as well as a form of articulation for the need for social change. I imagine that Rousseau would share the sentiments of Samuel Charters, the music historian most famously associated with introducing rural blues to a white audience via *The Country Blues* (1959).[7] In the preface to the 1975 edition, he wrote,

> *The Country Blues* was two things. It was a romanticization of certain aspects of black life in an effort to force the white society to reconsider some of its racial attitudes, and on the other hand it was a cry for help. I wanted hundreds of people to go out and interview the surviving blues artists. I wanted people to record them and document their lives, their environment, and their music—not only so that their story would be preserved but also so they'd get a little money and a little recognition in their last years. (xi–xii)

Charters's efforts met with great success: white America did take notice of the artists who were profiled in *The Country Blues*, as well as other artists, bringing them some money and recognition in their later years.[8] Rousseau would no doubt approve. Bringing recognition and some amount of redistributive justice through economic remuneration (perhaps not Rousseau's preferred mode) to deserving artists who struggled to survive would no doubt be lauded as a way of attempting to level the social playing field. That these artists would find recognition from the same group who formerly oppressed them seems like the kind of poetic justice that Rousseau would admire. So the political context of the blues: its birth in the post-Reconstruction rural south, the fact that it gives voice to a disenfranchised, oppressed, and alienated group, and the fact that those who study the genre see the gesture as political, as giving back what is deserved, would all appeal to the democratic, egalitarian impulses in Rousseau, the same impulses that fuel the desire for a simplified system of musical notation in the *Projet concernant de nouveaux signes pour la musique*.

While the political context and agenda of the blues bear a certain resemblance to some of Rousseau's passionate rhetoric in support of the downtrodden and disenfranchised, the blues as an aesthetic form proves even richer in what it can reveal about Rousseau's theoretical positions in a variety of areas. I now propose to review the central arguments of *Rousseau Among the Moderns* through the lens of a consideration of the blues. I will pose the question of what Rousseau might have said about the idiom, with specific attention to concrete phenomena that will rearticulate the main thrust of my thesis with special attention to this particular musical practice.

Performance and Community

Blues is a genre of music heavily weighted toward performance. Clearly in contrast to elite forms of music such as those performed by symphony musicians, or even in relation to jazz, rock and roll, country, or other popular genres, blues is more oriented toward live performance (rather than recording) for a number of reasons. First, the form, as I argued above, relies heavily on improvisation and variation, and in the post-Reconstruction south, on spontaneous composition through performance. In a sense, while "definitive versions" of particular songs now exist in recorded form, it could be argued that the essence of the blues is an ongoing conversation among blues players that relies on citation, improvisation, and variation to keep the conversation alive.[9] From one performance to the next, this conversation continues and evolves, placing the medium in a state of perpetual evolution. While this is also true in other genres, it seems less true of high-art music and other forms that lose less of their force through recording.

The blues come alive in performance for a number of reasons. In relation to the argument that I made in chapter 1, temporal considerations are paramount. Not only deciding the tempo of a particular song, but also the "groove," the feel of the song rhythmically, will differ from performance to performance. Each performer in the ensemble will make adjustments to produce a sound unique to that performance. The lead singer in particular will stress certain syllables, elongate words, shorten others, get ahead of the beat, fall behind the beat, in order to create the tension and release characteristic of the blues. This tension and release—a teasing game that is played with the audience—is key to the energy of the blues.[10]

These choices during live performance are part of what makes the blues the blues. While in other genres slight variations might be perceived by the audience as (unwelcome) "deviations" from expectations, such as when an aging band has to lower the key of a particular song to accommodate the dropping vocal range of the lead singer, these variations are integral to the blues. Audiences expect to be surprised and are conditioned by the genre to engage in this way. The audience hangs on to the movements of the vocalist and waits expectantly to hear the response from the instrumentalists, anxious to hear what they will do in the moment. This temporal immediacy responds to the type of engagement that Rousseau seems to privilege in some kinds of music. Rather than the dull, dragging monologues of French opera, I think he would like the sit-on-the-edge-of-your-seat feeling of listening to live blues.

In this respect, the blues is a form of music that highlights its temporal existence in important ways. Blues are generally not written out. Lyrics are available and guitar tablature has been worked out, but it is an essentially live music performed from memory. It responds in this way to Rousseau's call for music that privileges melody over harmony, live performance over written score. The music only really exists in the moment of its performance.

The singer helps to privilege the here and now in blues through the feeling of immediacy communicated through the performance. As the above quote from David Evans highlights, "Blues displays an intense concentration on the momentary feelings of the singer." He also argues that "no American popular song genre has displayed quite the degree of frankness and self-revelation as the blues does. Blues singers make themselves vulnerable as well as available to their audiences."[11] In this respect, the blues creates a bond between performer and audience that is conditioned by the risk assumed by the singer. The singer lays him/herself bare to the audience, initiating a bond of trust. I would argue, in keeping with Rousseau, that this psychological laying bare is achieved in part through temporal and rhythmic considerations. For example, the throaty, raspy, and highly percussive vocal style of the Delta blues creates a feeling of intensity and immediacy that draws the audience in.[12] Rousseau would hear the rhythmic choices of particular passions in these vocal performances, which create a bond of shared emotion between singer and audience. As the rhythm of the vocals intensifies, as the vocalist plays with anticipation and delay, the audience feels the emotions of the singer. In this respect, the pulse of the blues moves its audience to experience a common passion. The audience is moved physically (they can't help but tap their feet or move their bodies to the music), but also emotionally by the immediacy of the experience on display.

I believe that Rousseau would recognize the shared heartbeat of common association in the reaction of a blues audience. Blues audiences famously respond to performances. Indeed, the "call and response" structure of the blues extends beyond the formal qualities of each piece to their live performance: the artists call and the audience responds. Reminiscent of a church group shouting "amen," blues audiences call out to performers, becoming an integral part of the performance themselves. In this respect, the blues embodies the "act of association" so central to Rousseau's conception of the constitution of community. In live performance, a community of sorts is born. And while we can never know if the individual members of the community overcome private, particular interests to accede to common feelings, the emphasis on suffering, struggle, and perseverance in blues lyrics certainly points in a communal direction.

Although the blues is focused on the individual experience of the lead vocalist, the live performance of blues creates a bond that reaches beyond the singularity of individual experience to the broader community. Singers talk about bad luck, economic hardship, relationship problems, and other struggles in a way that suggests a bond with the audience. Indeed, these are singular experiences whose general parameters are shared by the majority of the community of listeners.[13] Listeners recognize feelings of depression, frustration, fear, but also hope, struggle, and the promise of a better future in the lyrics, but most especially in their live performance. It is the live performance of the lyrics that brings the sentiments to life. In much the same way that Rousseau views his unique and singular experience of life as worthy of representation in the *Confessions*,[14] the blues offers a bridge between individual experience and the feelings of a broader community that recognizes the truth in what is expressed. Like his collection of ballads, *Consolations des misères de ma vie*, the blues offer the possibility for performer and listener to connect through a medium that provides a measure of consolation for life's ills. I believe that Rousseau would valorize the overcoming of individual self-interest in blues and celebrate the awakening of a common feeling of struggle in the face of economic, social, and political adversity.

Singing Democracy

The blues is a decidedly vocal genre. While instrumental blues exist—Little Walter's "Juke" immediately comes to mind—the vast majority of blues songs are sung. That is to say, that the human voice carries a great deal of the burden of communicating the emotional message of the blues. Indeed, some would argue that the wailing blue notes of the guitar and harmonica imitate the infinite flexibility of the human voice. In this respect, I think Rousseau would be drawn to the genre, and not because the privileging of the vocals indicates an underlying narrative structure. On the contrary, blues lyrics usually provide only sketchy clues to the actual situation of the persona of the singer, leaving plenty of lacunae for the audience to fill.[15] This lack of precision in the lyrical content indicates another way in which the blues as a genre, although highly focused on the immediate situation of the singer, indeed reaches beyond the individual experience to a shared communal experience. Audiences are asked to fill in the blanks in blues lyrics, to try to understand how the feelings of the singer have come about. The enigmatic quality afforded by the lack of narrative precision, coupled with the intense emotional expression in the vocals and instrumentals, draws the audience in emotionally, inviting the listener to identify with the protagonist of the song.

To the extent that the individual experience in the vocal overcomes its particularity to invite the audience to identify and share the experience, the dialectic between individual and community is set in motion by blues performance. While the blues performance may not represent a coming together of democratic community exactly, it does exhibit some of the hallmarks of the resolution of the dialectical tension between individual and community that Rousseau struggles with throughout his corpus. As I suggested in chapter 2, the practical exigencies of musical performance provide a useful model for thinking through some of the more abstract articulations of his democratic theory. Specifically, I argued that realizing the general will entails not only creating the conditions for a group dynamic, but also overcoming particular interests by each individual member that makes up the group.

I used the model of tuning to reorient our thinking about the general will toward what I called a "relative absolute." The standard set for tuning in some sense is arbitrary: the woodwinds give the A to the orchestra; but once the standard is set, it becomes an absolute normative standard for the group. I argued that this understanding applied to the notion of the general will yields a result that is oriented toward practice and proceduralism, rather than abstract absolutism in democratic theory. Blues music obviously relies on tuning like any other type of live music, but provides an interesting twist for understanding audience engagement.

As I indicated, the blues is generally composed using a pentatonic scale with characteristic "blues notes," or what Evans terms "pitch areas," at certain specific intervals of the scale. Anyone who has listened to the blues immediately recognizes the bending and wailing achieved in the vocals, guitar, harmonica, horns, or even with the trilling of keys on the piano as the signature sound of the blues.[16] The musicians playing the blues generally take turns using the blue note to evoke emotion. It just doesn't sound right if the vocals, guitar, and harmonica, for example, all hit the blue note at the same time. One soloist hits the blue note against the background of the other instruments playing the other notes of the pentatonic scale. In order to create the emotional intensity of the blues, it is necessary to coordinate efforts and subordinate individual interests to the dictates of performance. Each musician has a specific role to play in creating the aesthetic object. The soloist creating the blue note needs the normative standard of the others in order for the note to stand out. In this sense, the blues, like all other musical forms, requires a group dynamic that is helpful in understanding how democratic communities can integrate individual interests and needs within the functioning of the collectivity. Individual forms of expression take shape and express meaning through the coordinated efforts of the group dynamic.

But beyond the interactions of the musicians, the blues example provides a window onto audience experience in relation to the playing out of the relative absolute. The blue notes have an effect on the members of the audience who are engaged in the process of discerning and judging consonant and dissonant sounds. The neutral third (between the major and minor third) often evokes in the listener a kind of squirming or straining as she or he longs for resolution up or down in the pitch. The listener hangs on to the bend in the guitar note or the melisma of the vocals, waiting for the more satisfying feeling of the familiar pitch. The uneasiness and tension that these pitch areas cause relate to the dynamics of tuning that I described in chapter 2. Listeners are made to be a part of this integral aspect of musical performance that is normally reserved for the musician alone. But rather than a technical aspect of music, tuning in the blues becomes an essential part of musical expression. Making the listener aware of the tuning standard through deviation and return helps to further draw him or her into the experience.[17]

I would argue that Rousseau would recognize the ways in which the blues draw the listener into the musical experience and condition the listener to accept the standard of the community through the shared experience of the blue notes. As a concrete example of the will of the community being imposed on the individual—the group feels the need for the major or minor third, while the musician plays the neutral third—the blue note exemplifies the tension and resolution of individual subordination to communal life. The blues also provides evidence of the limitless potential for human beings to overcome obstacles and achieve greatness through communal endeavor. While the individual needs and emotions of the singer are expressed through melisma and lyric content, the group experience of live performance demonstrates the shared quality of the experience and the even greater potential for achievement through coordinated action.

Absolute and Relative Value

Imagining what Rameau would have to say about the blues is beyond the scope of any speculation I would like to attempt. I have little doubt that Rousseau would have a better appreciation for blues than Rameau just based on his anthropological/historical interest in music that allows for flexibility and relativism in musical expression. This having been said, it may prove useful to use the blues as a concrete example to work through some of the theoretical stakes in the disagreement between Rameau and Rousseau.

The debate between Rameau and Rousseau is often characterized as one between harmony and melody. The blues offers a good example of melodically driven music. While the blues has a more-or-less fixed form, there is nonetheless more of an implied harmony in blues than an explicit one. Evans explains,

> many blues really have no harmony, if by this one means chords and chord changes. Blues is usually sung by a single voice, and instruments often play single melodic lines, so that harmony is only suggested by the fact that vocal and instrumental lines happen to occur simultaneously. . . . There is, however, a harmonic pattern that is often sensed by listeners and musicians and that acts for them as a harmonic mental template. One "hears" this pattern in the mind even though it may be only suggested by a note here or there. Some blues conform to the pattern closely and really could be said to have "chord changes," while others conform barely or not at all.[18]

In this respect, the blues may serve as a helpful point of reference in understanding the dispute between the two of them in terms of the placement of emphasis. The blues, with its implied harmony, would definitely represent a form that privileges melody over harmony. Mathematical relations and freedom of movement through a well-defined harmonic system are not part of what drives the blues. Instead, the depth of emotion that can be expressed in the tension of the music relies on the suggestion of harmony, rather than its explicit articulation.

As I discussed the debate between Rameau and Rousseau concerning the interpretation of the monologue from Lully's *Armide*, the stakes deepened from the disagreement over melody and harmony to include a moral dimension in Rousseau's condemnation of the musical handling of the scene. In chapter 3, I argued that Rousseau subscribes to a theory of musical verisimilitude in which there is a moral imperative to express emotion through a musical vehicle that is appropriate to the action. Because the lyrical content of the scene in *Armide* involves the attempt to overcome natural pity—an unnatural act for Rousseau—I argued that it represents a tragic struggle that was not conveyed by the subtle harmonic development in the score. Both for the performer and the listener, there is a disconnect, according to Rousseau, between the intense emotionalism of the content and the formal, aestheticized beauty of the score. The blues offers a striking contrast to this type of formalized notion of aesthetic beauty epitomized in the monologue in *Armide*. Without a developed or even explicitly articulated harmony, the blues expresses emotion through the interwoven relationship between vocals and instruments. Rousseau would likely find the use of melisma and other vocal techniques satisfying in the search to express deeply felt emotion. The response of the instruments to the vocals, echoing the emotion through the use of pitch areas, underscores the passion that gives rise to the aesthetic form.

Behind this moral imperative to make the aesthetic expression match in some sense the emotional intensity of the action, lies both a political and metaphysical agenda. I suggested that, contrary to Rameau, for Rousseau the need to express feeling through song arises from within the community. Whereas for Rameau, human beings seem to make music as part of an instinctual response to the physical environment, based on harmonic relations established by God, for Rousseau the stakes in making music are moral, social, political, and metaphysical in a different way. We feel a need to communicate feeling to our fellow beings. Music becomes a vehicle for this communication. And, indeed, the blues embodies just this type of emotional communication. As I argued above, the vulnerability of the persona of the singer, laying bare raw emotion to the community, sparks a shared feeling of recognition and commonality. As I characterized it in chapter 3, Rousseau seems to call for a form of song that will transmit a kind of transport or rapture throughout the community. The blues definitely qualifies as a secular type of music destined to communicate just such transport. It's not called the "devil's music" for nothing. Many blues songs reference travel and transport, beyond the quotidian traveling from place to place, to the spiritual.[19] From the social, economic, and political position of oppression, this music rises up to give expression to frustration and anger, but also to challenge the injustice and offer hope for the future. There is no doubt that it represents a form of creative expression that springs from the moral passions.

Folk Music

The blues definitely belongs to the category of "authentic," "primitive," "roots" music that Rousseau associates with the ability to stir an emotional response. Rousseau's insights into the socially constructed nature of the response to particular formal properties of music help to explain why the blues is characterized as "primitive" music. The lack of harmony (as we just saw), pentatonic scale, curving melodic lines, and relatively simply rhythmic patterns all condition the listener to hear blues as "simple" music. Furthermore, the African hypothesis—that certain formal properties of the blues may have been adapted from Western African music—lends credence to Rousseau's attempt to blur the distinction between Western and non-Western forms of music.[20] Placed on Rousseau's culturally constructed continuum of music, the blues meet the criteria for "simple," "authentic," "primitive" music.

The emotional charge of simple music, according to Rousseau, derives from the way in which this type of music functions as a sign in memory. Music with particular formal characteristics often triggers emotion in response to memory in a culturally conditioned way. In the case of the blues, for some audiences the songs carry a strong emotional charge associated with particular childhood memories, especially for those who heard the songs played by parents and other family members. For others, like Eric Clapton, cited in the epigraph, hearing the music for the first time makes them feel as though they've heard it before. Not unlike the argument in chapter 1 concerning audience response to *Julie*, the blues tends to evoke feelings of familiarity with the depth of emotion expressed, making listeners identify with the musicians. Rousseau might argue that the formal properties of the blues condition this response. Because the blues are perceived by the culture to be "primitive," they have this effect on the audience, accessing deep emotions linked to memory and childhood.

What does it mean to be moved by the blues? The emotional response to the blues is complex. As we saw in chapter 4, Rousseau recounts with pride in the *Confessions* that audience members were moved to tears during the opening performance of *Le devin du village*. What does this emotional response signal? For the blues, it may be that certain audience members are moved to tears: by the beauty or virtuosity of the performance, by the sentiments expressed, by associations in memory with the song, or by the collective feeling shared by the audience, or a variety of other reasons. Even if they are not moved to tears, most members of the audience will experience some strong emotional pull. I would argue that this emotional response is both a recognition of the suffering, alienation, frustration, and humiliation expressed in the lyrics, as well as of the promise of hope and continued struggle expressed in the tension between fixed form and variation. In other words, the blues pushes the audience to feel simultaneously the depth of negative emotion being laid bare by the vocalist and instrumentalists and the promise of a brighter future articulated in the aesthetic form: at once joy and despair.

While this is not the exact experience that Rousseau describes in the *vendanges* letter in *Julie* celebrating the joys of agricultural labor, the tension between the depth of sorrow and the promise of deliverance from suffering in the blues articulates the power of an aesthetic form that is rooted in a particular class and community. In order to accede to the emotion, it is not necessary to be a member of the community: one does not have to be an African American sharecropper to feel the power of the blues. But the power does derive from the rootedness in the community. To listen to the blues is to become, at least fleetingly, a member of that community.

Perhaps it is in this way that Rousseau would understand the possibility of using music with a strong emotional pull to help shape a better social and political future. While I signaled caution about the potential abuses of the "faux folk" in the service of masking and idealizing what really amount to problematic relations characterized by hierarchy and privilege (as in my discussion of the class tensions in the scenes in *Julie*), I ultimately embraced the notion that music could be used to help engineer a more democratic community. The example of the blues, and specifically Samuel Charters's political gesture of disseminating the blues to a broader audience, helps to fill out what it might mean to use "primitive" music rooted in folk practices for social ends. In order to appreciate new forms of music, the audience must be educated. Educating the public about the form entails raising awareness about the conditions that helped to create that particular form and, ideally, greater cultural understanding. In the abstract, thinking that particular aesthetic forms might work their magic by promoting more democratic communities seems naïve. The actual practice of educating a public to understand the meaning behind the aesthetic expression, in order to better appreciate it and the context that gave rise to it, highlights the promotion of cultural understanding that lies behind the gesture. In this respect, listening to the blues might just move an audience to understand the pain and humiliation of discrimination and segregation, and it might lead to greater social and political justice.

Music's Power of Redemption

As we saw in the final chapter, Rousseau's understanding of the musical object provides the foundation for an aesthetic theory with a decidedly modern bent. The articulation of a theory of self-referential mimesis, the emphasis on the fleeting quality of the present moment, the elegiac relation to the past, but most important, the promise of redemption through the aesthetic realm from the ills of modern life, all point to what I have called a "modernist" aesthetic in Rousseau. The importance accorded to the perception of form in music, coupled with the awakening of moral interest in the listener, indicate that music provides a glimpse of the human community. I have argued that musical performance works against the alienation of modern life by holding out the hope of redemption through communal experience.

In this last respect, the blues offers a striking example of how that musical practice might be put into action. As I have stressed, the blues usually articulates the struggle and adversity of the individual, all the while implicating the audience in an act of communal recognition. The blues audience feels the musicians' pain, but also shares the musicians' hope for the future. In the tension between despair and hope, individual and community, the blues derives its aesthetic energy and force. The post-Reconstruction rural south offered a hostile environment that, in fact, paradoxically fostered the birth of the form. As individuals were displaced from their communities and struggled against oppression, violence, discrimination, and economic hardship, a new aesthetic form arose that articulated the new tension between individual and community. The call and response pattern echoes the dialectic between individual and community: in the new modern world, each individual has to fend for him/herself, and yet the community endures, in spite of the new social reality. Responding to the individual's call, the audience recognizes and identifies with the struggle and holds out hope for the future. For Rousseau, individuals become "interested" and create a community in precisely this way. I like to imagine *Rousseau Among the Moderns* as my way of responding to Rousseau's call.

# NOTES

## INTRODUCTION

1. For a study of Rousseau's influence on the Revolution itself, see Swenson, *On Jean-Jacques Rousseau*. See also Peter Gay's introduction to Cassirer, *Question of Rousseau*. Gay writes, "The influence of Rousseau's doctrines has been immense—they left their mark on the most diverse spirits and movements. Burke execrated Rousseau as the very embodiment of the Age of Reason. De Maistre and Bonald condemned him as the advocate of an irresponsible individualism and as the philosopher of ruinous disorder. Later critics, such as Sir Henry Maine, attacked him for establishing a 'collective despot' and for reintroducing, in the *Contrat social*, 'the old divine right of kings in new dress'" (4; internal quotes from Henry Maine, *Popular Government* [New York: Holt, 1886], 157, 160).

2. In response to Derrida's reading of Rousseau, de Man's *Blindness and Insight* includes a chapter that takes issue with Derrida's reading, especially with respect to Rousseau's account of rhetorical language. Gearhart presents a reading of Rousseau's articulation of the relationship between history and fiction in relation to both de Man and Derrida in *Open Boundary*, 234–84. Other notable contributions to the critical debate include Siebers, "Ethics in the Age of Rousseau"; McDonald, "Derrida's Reading of Rousseau"; Garver, "Derrida on Rousseau"; and Bernasconi, "No More Stories." Finally, for a reading of Rousseau that raises the possibility of accent in written language, see Wyss, *Jean-Jacques Rousseau*.

3. Among the more important early studies of Rousseau's contributions in musicology are Jansen, *Jean-Jacques Rousseau als Musiker* (Berlin: Georg Reimer, 1884); Tiersot, *Jean-Jacques Rousseau*; and Pougin, *Jean-Jacques Rousseau musicien*. There are also important studies that integrate considerations of music, such as Wokler, *Social Thought*, and Robinson, *Rousseau's Doctrine of the Arts*.

4. A few critics have published interdisciplinary studies of Rousseau that cover works in music. See Scott, "Harmony"; O'Dea, *Rousseau*; Lefebvre, *L'esthétique de Rousseau*; Thomas, *Music and the Origins of Language*; Strong, "Theatricality, Public Space"; and Strong, "Music, Politics." Finally, Robert Wokler presents a strikingly original argument that historians looking for the traces of the practical implications of Rousseau's work in the French Revolution ought to look at the writing on music, and specifically the *Lettre sur la musique française* and the *Essai sur l'origine des langues* ("Rousseau on Rameau and Revolution").

5. A characteristic publication born of this uncertainty is an issue dedicated to "The Future of Criticism—A Critical Inquiry Symposium," *Critical Inquiry* 30, no. 2 (2004). As W. J. T. Mitchell points out in the preface to the issue, the *New York Times* and the *Boston Globe* covered this meeting of the journal's board that focused on the "crisis" in theory. Many of the essays in the issue focus on literary theory's potential for political engagement.

6. As the editor of *Eighteenth-Century Studies* from 2004 until 2012, I occupied a privileged vantage point from which to survey the field. Since its creation in 1967, the journal has had an interdisciplinary focus. Nonetheless, the increase of submissions and publications in art history, musicology, and material cultural studies has been noticeable in the last ten years.

7. According to Tiersot, the Geneva Library has a manuscript that looks to be incomplete notes for a treatise on harmony, based largely on Rameau, in Rousseau's hand (*Jean-Jacques Rousseau*, 58).

8. I strongly disagree with critics such as Wokler who insist on attempting to ascertain the "intended meaning" behind Rousseau's texts, gleaned from the historical context that gave rise to them (see *Social Thought*).

9. For a detailed discussion of aesthetic modernity in nineteenth-and twentieth-century thought, see chapter 5 of this volume.

10. For a complete account of the writings in music, see Gagnebin's introduction to Rousseau, *Œuvres complètes*, 5:xiii–xxix (hereafter OC).

11. Wokler asserts that "throughout his life Rousseau was more devoted to the study of music and its theory than to any other subject" (*Social Thought*, 242).

12. For a detailed analysis of this episode from the *Confessions*, see chapter 4 of this volume.

13. See Gagnebin's account in the introduction to OC, 5:xiii–xiv. In the *Confessions*, see esp. 1:11–12, 117–31, 147–51, and 313–16.

14. The last musical composition is likely *Romance du Saule*, one of the ballads in *Consolations des misères de ma vie*. See OC, 1:1316, note 1.

15. For all the document sources on the *querelle des bouffons*, see Launay, *Querelle des bouffons*; for a discussion of the political and ideological stakes of the debate, see Johnson, "Encyclopedists." Heartz offers a contextualization of the *querelle* in relation to the reform of opera in "From Garrick to Gluck," esp. 263.

16. For a detailed discussion of the difficulty of establishing a date of composition for the text, see Oliver Pot's introduction to the *Examen*, in OC, 5:cxlv–clxiv.

17. Jean Starobinski, in the introduction to the Pléiade edition, cites a letter from January 24, 1765, to the publisher Du Peyrou that makes mention of the text along with the *Lettre sur la musique française* and "Réponse à M. Rameau" (likely the "Examen des deux principes") (5:clxv). Starobinski also mentions a 1761 letter to Malesherbes that expresses the desire to publish the *Essai* "à cause de Rameau qui continue à me tarabuster vilainement" (5:clxviii). Although the dates of composition cannot be determined precisely, and significant differences between the *Discours sur l'origine de l'inégalité* and the *Essai* contribute to the confusion, 1761 seems like a fairly safe guess. See also Derrida's speculations about the genesis of the text in dialogue with Starobinski (*Grammatology*, 171–72).

18. Derrida cites *Tristes Tropiques* as well as the account in *Entretiens avec Claude Lévi-Strauss*, translated as *Conversations with Claude Lévi-Strauss*. For a nuanced reading of Derrida's legacy in reading Rousseau and Lévi-Strauss, see Fleming and O'Carroll, "In Memoriam."

19. Lévi-Strauss, *Tristes Tropiques*, 299; Derrida cites the version from the *Conversations*: "the primary function of writing, as a means of communication, is to facilitate the enslavement of other human beings" (292) (*Grammatology*, 130).

20. Rousseau touches only briefly on the use of language in the *Discours*, setting its origin aside as unknowable (3:146–51). He does not specifically mention the use of language to oppress. The *Essai* contains a brief discussion of the persuasive power of spoken language, especially in the context of religious fanaticism (5:409–10), but not for negative political ends. Indeed, the end of the text suggests a need for more

language more favorable to liberty (5:428–29). There is little doubt that the example from Lévi-Strauss's experience among the Nambikwara nonetheless crystallizes an idea that is implicit, if not fully articulated, in Rousseau's texts.

21. See my discussion of the political stakes of singing in chapter 2.

22. It is important to note that while the "lost innocence" characterization is true of the *Second Discourse* and *Essay*, it nonetheless tends to obscure the more negative aspects of the state of nature in Rousseau. For example, it is clear that man's moral and political freedom cannot be fully realized within the natural state.

23. Derrida's pairing of the terms "animality/humanity" in Rousseau seems to suggest that man is an animal in the state of nature. Although this is true in some respects—many characteristic features of humans are only virtual and not yet realized—it is important to recognize that man in the state of nature is still human and not an animal. Rousseau takes great pains to defend natural man's freedom, which distinguishes him from the animals. Likewise, his perfectibility also sets him apart. See *Discours*, 3:141–42.

24. This distinction is discussed in chapter 2 of this volume. For a nuanced reading of the status of the indexical in Rousseau, Lévi-Strauss, and Derrida, see Kavanagh, "Patterns of the Ideal."

25. Derrida cites the Letter to the Prince of Würtemberg in the *Correspondance complète*, 18:118. Sosso's extended reading of the origin of the imagination, which aligns with Derrida's reading, highlights the relationship between pity, the imagination, and desire. Sosso, *Rousseau*, esp. 40–57.

26. See the account of pity in the *Discours sur l'origine de l'inégalité* (3:153–56). See my discussion of the two versions of pity in Rousseau in *Beyond Contractual Morality*, 123–27.

27. See the *Essai* (5:392–93).

28. Derrida's account of mimesis in Rousseau depends on a narrative understanding of mimesis. As we will see in chapter 5, Rousseau has very different conceptions of mimesis that are not based on a narrative structure precisely because they derive from music.

29. Paul de Man also disagrees with Derrida on this point; see *Blindness and Insight*, 126–37.

30. See Kelly's careful differentiation of the different claims about imitation for the visual arts and music in *Rousseau as Author*, esp. 53–55.

31. Ultimately for Derrida speech and writing are indistinguishable in this sense. The *différance* of writing is always already present in speech. In this respect, he would not disagree with my argument here. However, my position would emphasize Rousseau's celebration of something like Derridean *différance* in the performance of music.

32. See also de Man's reading of the appearance of metaphorical language before literal language in *Allegories of Reading*, 135–59.

33. It might be argued that reading scores emphasizes rational thought more than listening to music. Such a position would be consistent with the dispute between Rameau and Rousseau on the value of written music as opposed to live performance. Rameau's insistence on the rational, mathematical properties of music leads to the conclusion that scores are preferable because of the legibility of the system, while Rousseau emphasizes the emotional impact of music through live performance. See my discussion of their debate in chapter 3.

CHAPTER 1

1. For a comprehensive overview of the history of the individualist and collectivist readings of Rousseau up through Ernst Cassirer, see Gay's introduction to Cassirer, *Question of Rousseau*, 3–30.

2. For a detailed discussion of the melody versus harmony debate, see chapter 3 of this volume.

3. Two related critical fields focus on the question of performance. The discipline of "performance studies" tends to focus on events as performance, and, following the influential work in philosophy by J. L. Austin and in sociology by Pierre Bourdieu, there has been an increasing critical awareness of the importance of performance related to performativity and performatives in a number of fields. In literary studies, gender studies, history, anthropology, sociology, linguistics, and many other fields, the notions of "performance," "performativity," and "performatives" have been broadened to enable the questioning of methodological assumptions. For an interesting discussion of the overlap between performance studies and performativity, see J. Hillis Miller, "Performativity as Performance/Performativity as Speech Act." For an excellent overview of the impact in history, see Burke, "Performing History." While my thinking about performance has no doubt been influenced by these enormously important critical trends, for the purposes of this study I have sought to limit my thinking about performance to actual musical practice and not extend the definition into other areas.

4. Rousseau, *Projet concernant de nouveaux signes pour la musique*, OC, 5:133, 138-40.

5. Barry argues that the musical object, depending on level of complexity, may require concretization in the form of a score for a nuanced and detailed perception of structure: "In order to see a musical object altogether, the temporal dimension with its continually disappearing parts must be frozen so that the work can be expressed as a simultaneity—it must be spatialized. Musical time become space is the contraction of performance, as successive time, into score, as simultaneous space. The work is a potentiality as dots on paper, which were referred to previously as the work as storage—a spatial storage which is reconstituted through time in performance. When spatial objects (in score) are time-indexed they acquire all the characteristics of musical time objects discussed above. The score is a spatialization of the work, which allows mobile, time-indexed objects to be caught and become spatialized 'objects'" (*Musical Time*, 58).

6. Rameau specifically criticizes Rousseau for overemphasizing rhythm in *Erreurs sur la musique dans l'Encyclopédie*, in *Complete Theoretical Writings of Jean-Philippe Rameau*, 5:207-11. I discuss the debate with Rameau in detail in chapter 3. In this respect it is interesting to compare Nicholas Cook's discussion of Heinrich Schenker and Arnold Schoenberg to Rameau's privileging of harmony over melody. According to Cook, both Schoenberg and Schenker privilege the work as a totality that reveals a formal structure that is spatial rather than temporal. For Rousseau, by contrast, the essence of music lies in its temporal performance, not in a virtual structure better perceived in the score (Cook, *Music, Imagination, and Culture*, 226-30).

7. Marie-Elisabeth Duchez explains the provenance of the text that has come to be known as "L'origine de la mélodie" in the introduction to the Pléiade edition, 5:cxxxvii–cxliv. The text originally formed part of the unpublished "Principe de la Mélodie ou réponse aux erreurs sur la Musique," which, according to Duchez, is a first version of the "Examen de deux principes."

8. George Houle argues that the eighteenth century bore witness to reforms in musical notation, including attempts to codify time signatures. In France there were some attempts to associate tempo with time signature. Overall, the reform efforts indicate a fair degree of variation in performance practice (*Meter in Music*, 35-38). In addition to considerations of meter, performers also made choices with respect to ornamentation. As Frederick Neumann points out in his study of baroque ornamentation styles, while the eighteenth century saw a general increase in the notation of

ornaments, artistic freedom still conditioned performance practice (*Ornamentation*, esp. 35–36).

9. Rousseau comments in the *Confessions* that Rameau made the most pertinent critique of his system: that while clear and transparent from the point of view of intervals, it requires mental work that might be difficult to execute while playing. In other words, without relative note placement on a staff and, presumably, in groups representing duration, sight-reading becomes more difficult. See *Confessions* in OC, 1:285.

10. For examples of the notation system, see the *Projet*, 5:148–51.

11. In fairness to Rousseau, the working out of complex time signature notations was still an ongoing project during the eighteenth century. See Houle, *Meter in Music*, 35–61.

12. Rousseau argues against the conventional wisdom of his day in asserting that the Greeks developed a conception of meter.

13. Interestingly, this definition is not in the article in the *Encyclopédie*.

14. The emphasis on equality in breaking music into its constituent temporal parts resonates with conceptions of individuals within the legitimate body politic. See my discussion of music and democracy in chapter 2.

15. For a discussion of the history of the effects of music on emotion, see Reiss, *Knowledge, Discovery*.

16. On the history of French declamatory style in relation to prosody, see Anthony, *French Baroque Music*, esp. 78–85.

17. See Thomas, *Music and the Origins of Language*, esp. 138–42, and Verba, *Music and the French Enlightenment*, 31–50.

18. Epstein, *Shaping Time*, 21–47.

19. Another striking example of the way in which the experience of time in music can structure group experience comes from military drills. William H. McNeill describes "something visceral at work" in these drills and the emotional effect that "constitutes an indefinitely expansible basis for social cohesion among any and every group that keeps together in time, moving big muscles together and chanting, singing, or shouting rhythmically" (*Keeping Together in Time*, 2). I am grateful to Zev Trachtenberg for this reference.

20. Compare the discussion of French music in the article "Battre la mesure," in which Rousseau claims that French music has no natural precision (5:663).

21. Bloom, "Rousseau's Critique," 148. Bloom discusses the centrality of virtue as a special kind of passion related to patriotism in Rousseau.

22. Descartes defines the passions as "des perceptions, ou des sentimens, ou des emotions de l'ame, qu'on rapporte particulierement à elle, & qui sont causés, entretenuës, & fortifiées par quelque mouvement des esprits" (*Passions de l'âme*, 86).

23. In order to make sense of the manifold of sense impressions that bombard us every second, Condillac asserts that our attention is fixed on particular sensations: "Les choses attirent notre attention par le côté où elles ont le plus de rapport avec notre temperament, nos passions et notre état" (*Essai sur l'origine des connaissances humaines*, 119).

24. Didier argues that the conception of rhythm in music changed after the *querelle des bouffons*, moving away from considerations of prosody in opera toward something closer to dance or pantomime ("Rythme musical").

25. Compare Lefebvre's claims about the metaphysical and moral dimension of music related to accent and language in Rousseau (*L'esthétique de Rousseau*, 21).

26. Bloom, "Rousseau's Critique," 148.

27. Paul de Man famously takes issue with Derrida's celebrated reading of mimesis and metaphor in the *Essai* in *De la grammatologie*. See Derrida, *Grammatology*, and

de Man, *Blindness and Insight*, 102–41. See my discussion of these theoretical readings in the introduction. Jones argues against the transcendental readings in favor of a more historical reading of Rousseau inspired by his Scottish interpreters. Following Shaftesbury, Smith, and Ferguson, Jones maintains that Rousseau "placed poetic language at the heart of social interaction" to bridge the natural and social worlds ("Language Origins").

28. Compare Strong's discussion of the overcoming of self-consciousness in "public identity" through music festivals in "Theatricality, Public Space," esp. 123–24.

29. Althusser's reading of the social contract emphasizes the reenactment of the initial contract in every act of legislation, signaling a temporal reading of the "moment" of the contract that is repeated. See "Social Contract (The Discrepancies)," esp. 107–8.

30. See *Du contrat social*, 3:364, 368, 373–75; *Discours sur l'origine de l'inégalité*, 3:154–57, 166, 170–71; and *Essai sur l'origine des langues*, 5:395–96, 402–3. See my readings of Rousseauean pity in *Mass Enlightenment*, 31–39, and Kantian aspects of Rousseau in *Beyond Contractual Morality*, 72–74. Bloom's reading owes a debt to Cassirer's Kantian readings in both *Question of Rousseau* and *Philosophy of the Enlightenment*.

31. Compare Strong's discussion of representation in relation to the qualities that make us human in "Music, the Passions." Strong similarly argues that Rousseau's critique of representation in theater and politics is directly related to its inability to represent the unrepresentable, the "moi commun," that is to say, that which we hold in common as humans.

32. Talmon most famously raised the question of the totalitarian implications of the *Social Contract*, especially with respect to the potential for a dictatorship led by a charismatic legislator. See *Origins of Totalitarian Democracy*. For other discussions of the suppression of individual interests in Rousseau's political theory, see Simon, *Mass Enlightenment*, 44–69; Trachtenberg, *Making Citizens*, 131–43; Shklar, *Men and Citizens*, 150–64; and Marejko, *Jean-Jacques Rousseau*.

33. See Trachtenberg's discussion of the problem of will formation in "Subject and Citizen." Neidleman reads the tension as occurring between voluntarism and virtue in "Rousseau's General Will." See also my discussion in chapter 2.

34. Implicitly, my argument relies on reconciliation between Kant's *Critique of Practical Reason* and *Critique of Judgment*. Various postmodern readings of the sublime in Kant have highlighted both the subject's indirect experience of itself through the sublime as well as the relationship between the categorical imperative and the awe inspired by the sublime. See Lyotard, "Sublime à présent," and Nancy, "Offrande sublime." For Rousseau, it is not a question of an experience of the sublime, but rather the stimulation of feeling that leads from the aesthetic to the moral experience.

35. The readings of Rousseau that highlight efforts to engineer social unity through conformity emphasize the homogenizing tendencies of the pronouncements in the *Social Contract*. See note 27 above. Young's feminist reading of the suppression of affectivity, needs, and desires from the civic public of the social contract also emphasizes the effort to impose conformity. See "Impartiality and the Civic Public." See also Strong's defense of Rousseau that asserts that he does not seek to efface difference: "Note that having something in common also requires differentiation, the notion suggested by some, that Rousseau wants us to be identical is false and indeed nonsense" ("Music, the Passions").

36. Osipovich carefully distinguishes between the text of the play, the live performance, and the social practice of theatergoing in his analysis of the *Lettre à d'Alembert*, arguing that it is the live performance aspect that most troubles Rousseau

(360), specifically in relation to enacting particular roles ("What Rousseau Teaches Us," 360). Strong contends that it is the problem of interpretation in relation to the problem of representation the fuels Rousseau's condemnation of theater. See "Theatricality, Public Space."

37. Paige distinguishes the theory articulated in *Lettre à d'Alembert* from a "proto-aesthetic" that understands the communication of passion to the audience through a kind of contagion. Paige reads in Rousseau's theory a departure from the contagion model and a movement toward a reliance on identification. See "Rousseau's Readers Revisited." Paige accounts for the condemnation of theater in Rousseau's belief that spectators will "only make the imaginative leap when the emotions are pleasurable" (135). See also Scott's discussion of the relationship between the theory of language and music and the condemnation of theater in "Play of the Passions."

38. Rousseau maintains that theater stirs emotions that lead to weakness and vice rather than virtue: "Le mal qu'on reproche au théâtre n'est pas précisément d'inspirer des passions criminelles, mais de disposer l'âme à des sentiments trop tendres, qu'on satisfait ensuite aux dépends de la vertu" (5:47). Kelly describes the effect of theatrical experience as "encourag[ing] an easygoing moral smugness, a false sense of having done one's duty simply by having sympathized with the suffering of someone who is innocent" (*Rousseau as Author*, 59).

39. For an analysis of the failure of empathy in the Rousseauean theatergoer in relation to Brecht and Diderot, see Byford, "Figure of the 'Spectator.'"

40. Costelloe argues similarly that these forms of public theater can reinforce communal morality. See "Theatre of Morals."

41. Mostefai compares this section of the *Lettre* to a similar observation made by Diderot in the *Entretiens sur le fils naturel*. See *Citoyen de Genève*, 56.

42. Delaney reads the corrupting effects of the arts and sciences on virtue in the *First Discourse* as symptomatic of the broader problem of individualism, bringing the text in line with the arguments in the *Lettre à d'Alembert*. See *Rousseau and the Ethics of Virtue*, esp. 76–79.

43. Darnton, "Readers Respond to Rousseau." For readings critical of Darnton's contentions concerning eighteenth-century sensibility, see Darnton, "Symbolic Element in History"; LaCapra, "Chartier, Darnton"; and Fernandez, "Historians Tell Tales."

44. Paige, "Rousseau's Readers Revisited," 140.

45. Ibid., 141. The notion that readers would place themselves as observers within the narrative parallels many of Michael Fried's contentions about the positioning of spectators with respect to visual art of the period. See Fried, *Absorption and Theatricality*.

46. Paige, "Rousseau's Readers Revisited," 142.

47. Compare the virtually identical passage from the *Essai*, 5:421.

48. The feeling is familiar because music works through memory. See my discussion of mimesis in music in relation to memory in chapter 4; Dugan and Strong, "Music, Politics," esp. 350; and Waeber, "Jean-Jacques Rousseau's 'unité de mélodie.'"

49. Floyd, *Power of Black Music*, 97.

CHAPTER 2

1. Eighteenth-century notation was a great deal more complex than current systems. See Tiersot's brief discussion in *Jean-Jacques Rousseau*, 63.

2. Buzon points out that Rousseau's notation system, at least in its original version, did not require printers to use anything but standard characters. See "Musique et notation," 29.

3. Kleinman has demonstrated that the method does indeed work by testing it on older learners who had no previous knowledge of scales or intervals. Experimenting with students at New York University using Rousseau's notation system, he reports great success in teaching scales and intervals, moreover in a way consistent with *Emile:* the students learn by doing. See "L'enseignement musical chez Rousseau."

4. The most obvious example of the Enlightenment desire to make technical knowledge more widely accessible is Diderot and d'Alembert's *Encyclopédie.* Although the desire to popularize expert knowledge uneasily coexists alongside certain elitist themes, the *Encyclopédie* nonetheless represents a democratizing spirit in disseminating technical knowledge. From a political standpoint, the desirability of engineering a democratic community by homogenizing interests does not directly engage the issue of the accessibility of technical knowledge, but could encompass such an argument. In this respect, insofar as moderation and equality are seen as positive influences on democratic republics, Rousseau's debt to Montesquieu is undeniable. The most obvious articulation of Rousseau's preference for small territories with pre-existing common cultures is in book 2, chapter 10 of the *Social Contract* (3:389).

5. Rousseau's *Confessions* provides interesting anecdotal evidence to support the notion that he wanted to enable provincial musicians to be able to perform in cities with other musicians. In an amusing episode, Rousseau assumes the identity of Vaussore, a "musician and composer," and attempts to pass himself off as a music teacher in Lausanne. See book 4 of the *Confessions* (1:146–50).

6. Condillac makes a similar distinction between motivated gestural signs and the arbitrary signs of language in the *Essai sur l'origine des connaissances humaines,* although he ultimately rejects arbitrary signs as artificial. For an excellent discussion of eighteenth-century epistemology and linguistic theory in relation to music, including Rousseau's debt to Condillac, see Rumph, "Sense of Touch in *Don Giovanni.*"

7. Rousseau develops the idea further in the *Essai,* asserting, "A mesure que les besoins croissent, que les affaires s'embrouillent, que les lumiéres s'étendent le langage change de caractére; il devient plus juste et moins passionné; il substitüe aux sentimens les idées, il ne parle plus au Cœur mais à la raison. Par-là-même l'accent s'éteint, l'articulation s'étend, la langue devient plus exacte, plus claire, mais plus traînante plus sourde et plus froide" (5:384). It is the infamous privileging of speech over writing by Rousseau that gives rise to Derrida's influential reading of the *Essai* in *Grammatology,* 165–268, and to de Man's critique of Derrida's reading in *Blindness and Insight,* 102–41 (see my discussion in the introduction). For an excellent overview of the critical tradition surrounding the *Essai,* see Thomas, *Music and the Origins of Language,* 85–89.

8. "Comme les sentimens qu'excite en nous la peinture ne viennent point des couleurs, l'empire que la musique a sur nos ames n'est point l'ouvrage des sons. De belles couleurs bien nuancées plaisent à la vüe, mais ce plaisir est purement de sensation. C'est le dessein, c'est l'imitation qui donne à ces couleurs de la vie et de l'ame, ce sont les passions qu'elles expriment qui viennent émouvoir les nôtres, ce sont les objets qu'elles représentent qui viennent nous affecter. . . . La melodie fait précisement dans la musique ce que fait le dessein dans la peinture; c'est elle qui marque les traits et les figures dont les accords et les sons ne sont que les couleurs" (5:412–13).

9. For discussions of Rousseau's conception of mimesis in music in relation to Aristotle and the abbé Dubos, see Verba, "Jean-Jacques Rousseau," 308–26, and Scott, "Harmony." See also my discussion in chapter 5.

10. Compare the distinction between passions and imitations of passions in singing in the article *chant*. It is the imitation of human passion that moves the listener in song.

11. Dauphin argues that Rousseau recognizes two kinds of mimesis in music; the first imitates nature and the second imitates music itself. See *Musique au temps des Encyclopédistes*, 28–40.

12. Rousseau explains music's cultural specificity: "Chacun n'est affecté que des accens qui lui sont familiers; ses nerfs ne s'y prêtent qu'autant que son esprit les y dispose. . . . Les cantates de Bernier ont, dit-on, guéri de la fièvre un musicien françois, elles l'auroient donnée à un musicien de toute autre nation" (5:418).

13. See my discussion of rhythm, meter, pulse, and tempo in chapter 1. For a discussion of the way in which music moves the emotions in Rousseau, see Thomas, *Music and the Origins of Language*, esp. 138–42; Verba, *Music and the French Enlightenment*, 31–50; and Simon, "Music and the Performance of Community in Rousseau," 192–200.

14. For discussions of the concept of pity in Rousseau, see Masters, *Political Philosophy of Rousseau*, 136–46; Simon, *Mass Enlightenment*, 31–35; and Simon, *Beyond Contractual Morality*, 53–57, 124–28.

15. "La pitié qu'on a du mal d'autrui ne se mesure pas sur la quantité de ce mal, mais sur le sentiment qu'on prête à ceux qui le souffrent." *Emile, ou de l'éducation* (5:508).

16. The notion that emotion only hinders democratic deliberations has been used for feminist readings of Rousseau's conception of the public sphere. According to this line of thought, the exclusion of women from the public sphere is related to the exclusion of considerations of needs, affectivity, and desire from the public realm. See Young, "Impartiality and the Civic Public," 57–76; Pateman, *Disorder of Women*; and Pateman, *Sexual Contract*.

17. See Talmon, *Origins of Totalitarian Democracy*. The following passage tends to support this reading of the *Social Contract*: "Afin donc que le pacte social ne soit pas un vain formulaire, il renferme tacitement cet engagement qui seul peut donner de la force aux autres, que quiconque refusera d'obéir à la volonté générale y sera contraint par tout le corps: ce qui ne signifie autre chose sinon qu'on le forcera d'être libre" (3:364).

18. Other passages of the *Social Contract* suggest the heavy hand that the legislator can have in aiding the determination of the general will. For example, "La volonté générale est toujours droite, mais le jugement qui la guide n'est pas toujours éclairé. Il faut lui faire voir les objets tels qu'ils sont, quelquefois tels qu'ils doivent lui paroitre, lui montrer le bon chemin qu'elle cherche, la garantir de la séduction des volontés particulieres, rapprocher à ses yeux les lieux et les tems, balancer l'attrait des avantages présens et sensibles, par le danger des maux éloignés et cachés. Les particuliers voyent le bien qu'ils rejettent: le public veut le bien qu'il ne voit pas. Tous ont également besoin de guides: Il faut obliger les uns à conformer leurs volontés à leur raison; il faut apprendre à l'autre à connoitre ce qu'il veut" (3:380). Such passages have led critics to caution against the absolute nature of the general will—particularly in conjunction with the potential for abuse by a legislator—in the name of the public good. See Shklar, *Men and Citizens*, and Trachtenberg, *Making Citizens*. For a more positive assessment of the role of the legislator, specifically in relation to his use of rhetoric to inspire communal feeling and build popular consent, see Kelly, "'To Persuade Without Convincing.'"

19. Compare Mason's account of a response to an article in the *Chronique de Paris* from 1789: "Responding to an article claiming that the ancient Greeks used the

same word for 'songs' and 'laws' because they knew that one might use songs to govern, the reader protested, 'The Greeks never considered governing with songs; little children know that Mazarin said of the French: *Let them sing, they'll pay anyway*; and what frightens the aristocracy today is that we talk, we write, we arm ourselves, and we do not sing'" (*Singing the French Revolution*, 40; internal citation from *Chronique de Paris*, October 20, 1789).

20. Montesquieu, *Considérations sur les causes*, 50.

21. For an account of the ways in which the social hierarchy of the Ancien Régime was reproduced within the Paris Opéra during the eighteenth century, see Johnson, *Listening in Paris*. Johnson argues that the influence of the court continued through midcentury: "If the Académie Royale de Musique in 1750 was less explicitly the king's spectacle than it had been in the late seventeenth century, it was still a pageant of nobility on display" (34).

22. During the *querelle des bouffons*, arguments over the relative merits of French- and Italian-style opera led to deeper political disputes. Kennedy argues that the aesthetic liberty associated with Italian opera and its partisans was equated with political liberty (*Cultural History of the French Revolution*, 116–18). Similarly, Johnson argues that the *querelle* engaged philosophical and ideological differences that coincided with the appearance of the first volumes of the *Encyclopédie* ("Encyclopedists"). Later, during the Revolution, music gained an explicitly political association that continued throughout the nineteenth century. For a discussion of the political implications of music during the Revolution and nineteenth century, see Donakowski, *Muse for the Masses*. For a specific discussion of the importance of popular song during the Revolution, see Mason, *Singing the French Revolution*.

23. Mason, *Singing the French Revolution*, 15–33.

24. The question of audience reception is addressed in chapters 1 and 3.

25. Althusser, "Social Contract (The Discrepancies)."

26. Elsewhere I have focused on the "social engineering" solution to the problem of dissent, especially in the *Projet de constitution pour la Corse* and *Considérations sur le gouvernement de Pologne*. See Simon, *Mass Enlightenment*, 44–69.

27. Strong articulates the problem slightly differently, making it a hallmark of Rousseau's work: "The nature of the space in which we are when we are in common is a space determined by the actuality of being different. What is the thought of this space? Thinking this thought is, I want to argue, what drives all of Rousseau's thought" (*Jean-Jacques Rousseau*, 34).

28. Neidleman characterizes the tension as between voluntarism and virtue, arguing that the general will never resolves the tension, but instead that modern political life thrives on it. See "Rousseau's General Will."

29. Bloom reads moral behavior as the overcoming of self-interest in favor of the general will, understood as inhering in each individual. See "Rousseau's Critique."

30. See Becker, "Essay on the History of Tuning."

31. See also my discussion of tuning and temperament in chapter 3.

32. Compare Habermas's discussions of the ideal speech situation in "Towards a Theory of Communicative Competence" and "What Is Universal Pragmatics?" See also Dugan and Strong's use of Stanley Cavell's term "categorical descriptive" to characterize the general will ("Music, Politics," 331).

33. Cook explains the relationship between musicians required in performing chamber music relative to tempo. The same argument may be applied analogously to tuning: "A well-established quartet performing a familiar work plays together with a kind of suppleness and mutuality of timing that is altogether different from what happens in the sight-reading session. Rather than abiding by a uniformly agreed beat,

the performers keep together because they are, in a quite literal sense, playing by ear" (*Music, Imagination*, 130).

34. For a comprehensible study of the history of temperament, see Isacoff, *Temperament*. For a discussion of specific mean-tone temperaments, see Neal, "Art and Science of Keyboard Temperament." For a discussion of Rousseau's and Rameau's positions on equal temperament, see my discussion in the following chapter.

35. Rehding discusses the flexibility of the human voice in relation to the enharmonic in "Rousseau, Rameau," esp. 146.

36. Chua, *Absolute Music*, 103.

37. For a discussion of Rousseau's debates with Rameau, and their aesthetic stakes, see Kintzler, *Jean-Philippe Rameau*, and my discussion in chapter 3.

38. Compare Strong's characterization of the distinction between Rousseau's style of writing and Hume's or Kant's. Strong argues that Rousseau's writing, especially in the autobiographical works, reveals "the person." Strong writes, "The personal encounter demands a different quality of response than that which I might call intellectual, in that one cannot as easily hold the person at a distance in the way that one can hold a text, or even the author of a text" ("Self Knowing the Self," 112). According to Rousseau's understanding, music partakes of this same kind of personal encounter that Strong adduces in Rousseau's writing, by overcoming interpersonal distance in the communication of feeling.

39. See Kant, *Critique of Judgment*, 41–45. I will discuss the relationship between Rousseau and Kant in more detail in chapter 5.

40. Exemplary in this respect is the *vendanges* letter in *Julie, ou la nouvelle Héloïse*, detailing the gaiety, including singing, that goes along with the communal work of the grape harvest (part 5, letter 7, 3:602–11). See my discussion of this letter in chapter 4.

CHAPTER 3

1. Some critics, following Rousseau's account in the *Confessions*, would cite the *Projet concernant de nouveaux signes pour la musique*, presented to the Académie des sciences in 1742, as the beginning of the debates between Rousseau and Rameau, given Rameau's critical reception of the project. See *Confessions*, 1:285–86; O'Dea, *Jean-Jacques Rousseau*, 13–14; Pougin, *Jean-Jacques Rousseau*, 27; and Verba, *Music and the French Enlightenment*, 10–11. On Rameau's side, the major works include *Démonstration du principe de l'harmonie* (1750), *Observations sur notre instinct pour la musique, et sur son principe* (1754), *Erreurs sur la musique dans l'Encyclopédie* (1755), and the posthumous "Vérités également ignorées et intéressantes, tirées du sein de la nature."

2. This represents somewhat of an oversimplification of the two sides, as shall be developed in the following pages. For general discussions of the debate between Rousseau and Rameau, see Verba, *Music and the French Enlightenment*, 8–50; O'Dea, *Jean-Jacques Rousseau*, 7–44; Kintzler, *Jean-Philippe Rameau*, 129–73; Scott, "Harmony," esp. 287–90; Christensen, *Rameau and Musical Thought*, 247–51; and Wokler, *Social Thought*, 242–378. For a discussion of the political and ideological stakes of the reception of Rousseau and Rameau, see Paul, "Music and Ideology."

3. Tiersot contrasts the two positions as between science and instinct: "Rameau est ainsi l'incarnation de la musique selon la science, Rousseau, selon l'instinct" (*Jean-Jacques Rousseau*, 83).

4. Isacoff, *Temperament*, 15–16.

5. Mark Lindley writes, "French tuning instructions characteristically required two or three 5ths at the back of the circle of 5ths to be tempered slightly larger than

pure (most probably A-flat–E-flat–B-flat–F . . . ), thus producing a more pronounced difference in size and quality between the 3rds D-flat–F–A-flat–C and the 3rds among the seven diatonic notes. This kind of tuning was often referred to by 18th-century French musicians as the 'ordinary' or 'common' temperament, although some occasionally confused it with regular mean-tone." See "Temperaments," *Oxford Music Online*, http://www.oxfordmusiconline.com/subscriber/article/grove/music/27643?q=temperaments&search=quick&pos=1&_start=1#firsthit (accessed July 14, 2008).

6. See ibid.

7. In the *Nouveau système*, Rameau writes, "LE Temperament consiste à changer la juste proportion d'un Intervale, sans donner atteinte à la satisfaction que l'Oreille doit en recevoir." He goes on to argue in favor of a system of temperament that would allow for consonant chords, proper intervals, and be consistent with harpsichord tuning practice. He stops short of advocating for equal temperament. See Rameau, *Nouveau système de musique theorique*, 107. Available online at http://www.chmtl.indiana.edu/tfm/18th/RAMNOU_TEXT.html (accessed July 14, 2008).

8. All translations are my own. For an interesting discussion of a dispute between Rameau and the academicians in Lyon over equal temperament, see Cohen, "Rameau, Equal Temperament."

9. Christensen argues that Rameau's work represents a dialectic between a speculative or theoretical approach to music and a practical one. In discussing the question of temperament, Christensen maintains that Rameau advocates for equal temperament as "an alteration demanded by both the ear and reason," underscoring the blend of theory and practice in the position (*Rameau and Musical Thought*, 200–203, citation from 202). In a slightly different vein, Rehding emphasizes Rameau's avoidance of microtones in his embrace of equal temperament. See his discussion of microtones and temperament in relation to the enharmonic genus in "Rousseau, Rameau," 155.

10. These objections are similar to those voiced in "Tempérament" in the *Encyclopédie*. See Diderot and d'Alembert, *Encyclopédie*, 16:56, available online at the ARTFL Encyclopédie Project website (http://encyclopedie.uchicago.edu/). All translations from this edition are mine.

11. Rehding summarizes the difference of opinion in the following way: "For Rameau . . . the keyboard instrument stands for a barrier demarcating what our 'ear' is capable of perceiving, or rather, a safeguard to protect what Rameau considered harmonically inadmissible. For Rousseau, by contrast, the keyboard sound seemed to be enough to trigger the memory of an ancient musical culture where melodic inflection was still possible and music still possessed its sublime orphic powers" ("Rousseau, Rameau," 170).

12. Christensen's analysis of Rameau's thought would dispute this distinction, maintaining that Rameau also represents the *esprit systématique*, given his attention to empirical data (see *Rameau and Musical Thought*, 39–40). While Christensen is correct in maintaining Rameau's empiricism in the context of earlier eighteenth-century musical thought, and especially in qualifying the nature of his Cartesianism, in contrast with Rousseau, it will be necessary to shift the conception of the distinction slightly and acknowledge that we are always dealing with matters of degree.

13. D'Alembert, "Discours préliminaire des éditeurs," *Encyclopédie*.

14. For a discussion of d'Alembert's position in the quarrels among the Encyclopedists concerning Rameau's theory, see Isherwood, "Conciliatory Partisan," 95–119.

15. Christensen, *Rameau and Musical Thought*, 30–33.

16. Rameau, *Traité de l'harmonie réduite à ses principes naturels*, unpaginated preface, ii (my emphasis); translations are my own. Kintzler underscores Rameau's dedication to Cartesian method: "Ce ne fut pas une simple manière d'être, une figure

de style, un habit à la mode du temps; ce fut une passion, un amour démesuré des formes intelligibles" (*Jean-Philippe Rameau*, 33). See also Didier's characterization of Rameau's refutation of musical relativism as Cartesian in "Musique primitive," 123–33. Finally, Dauphin's reading of the dispute between Rameau and Rousseau highlights the tension between the Pythagorean aspects of Rameau and the Aristoxenian elements in Rousseau. See "L'origine du conflit Rameau-Rousseau."

17. Christensen explains Rameau's principle of the *corps sonore* in the following terms: "The *corps sonore* (literally the 'sonorous body') was Rameau's term for any vibrating system such as a vibrating string which emitted harmonic partials above its fundamental frequency. Its importance in Rameau's theory can scarcely be exaggerated. Rameau was convinced, the good Cartesian that he was, that music was governed by rational laws, and that these laws could be deduced with geometric rigor from a single principle. He believed the theorist's most critical task was to identify this unique principle and to demonstrate its musical consequences. And in all of his theoretical publications save his first, the *corps sonore* served as this principle" ("Eighteenth-Century Science and the *Corps Sonore*," 23).

18. Christensen would distinguish between the more theoretically oriented works in Rameau's corpus—such as the sections of the *Traité* and *Génération harmonique* that I cite here—and more practically oriented works, such as other sections of the *Traité* and the *Code de musique pratique*. See *Rameau and Musical Thought*, 40–41. Isherwood argues that d'Alembert's account of Rameau's theory in *Elémens de musique théorique et pratique, suivant les principes de M. Rameau* (1752), although largely faithful to Rameau's methodology, nonetheless places more emphasis on the ear and on experience than Rameau does. Isherwood speculates that this move toward experience and away from pure mathematics may have contributed to the rift between the two prior to the polemics about the articles in the *Encyclopédie*. See "Conciliatory Partisan," 98–99.

19. Foucault, *Order of Things*, 58–77.

20. Foucault maintains that *mathesis* and *taxinomia* are linked in the classical *episteme* through their manipulation of sign systems for order and knowledge, despite the tension between the closed calculability of *mathesis* and the empirically motivated *genesis* that fuels *taxinomia* (ibid., 73). For my purposes here, d'Alembert's break with Rameau indicates the split between the older *mathesis*-based systems of the seventeenth century—represented by Rameau's turn away from experience—and the newer *genesis* and *taxinomia*-based systems of the eighteenth century. For discussions of the systems of categorization in the *Encyclopédie* and their nontotalizing tendencies, see Proust, "Diderot et le système des connaissances humaines"; Anderson, "Encyclopedic Topologies"; and Benrekassa, "Pratique philosophique de Diderot."

21. With respect to Rameau's mathematical operations, the word "certainty" should probably be placed in scare quotes. D'Alembert was critical of Rameau's arithmetical gymnastics in his attempts to mathematically ground some of the more problematic aspects of his system. See Christensen's excellent discussion of the epistemological and methodological tensions between d'Alembert and Rameau in *Rameau and Musical Thought*, 162–63, 259–66.

22. Rameau also writes, "Oublions pour un moment tout ce que l'expérience peut suggérer en Musique" (in the opening of chapter 4 of the *Génération*, 38). See also Rehding's discussion of Rameau's analysis of the enharmonic genus. Rehding asserts, "the introduction of the enharmonic genus in Rameau's system leads us into a realm where aural perception and mathematical reason part company: Rameau's calculations on the *corps sonore*—and, ultimately, his aspirations for music theory assume the status of an exact science . . .—make it inevitable that a difference between D-flat

and E-flat exist. But if he were to acknowledge the enharmonic difference, the derivation of the closed system of harmony and melody from 'one natural principle,' Rameau's supreme theoretical achievement, would inevitably be a lost cause," underscoring Rameau's tendency to disregard empirical facts in favor of the closed system. See "Rousseau, Rameau," 149.

23. Reiss comments on this reductionist view in Rameau: "In many ways, the aesthetic rationalization achieved was radically reductionist, as one might support it would have to be, to tune 'affection' to 'mathematics.' In music itself, harmonic rationalization worked to repress all expressive elements that failed to fit its particular notion of calculable intervals. The view was exemplified in Jean-Philippe Rameau's 1722 *Traité*, whose second sentence asserted that 'the [triadic] chord was the basic element of musical discourse, and that melody was therefore based on harmony'" (*Knowledge, Discovery*, 197).

24. The derivation of the minor third poses a consistent problem for Rameau. O'Dea remarks that Rousseau already diagnoses the problem in his article "Dissonance," written for the *Encyclopédie* (*Jean-Jacques Rousseau*, 17–18).

25. Christensen, *Rameau and Musical Thought*, 71.
26. Cohen, "'Gift of Nature,'" 69.
27. Ibid., 71.
28. Ibid., 29, 106.

29. Christensen highlights Rameau's simplification of accompaniment achieved in his thorough-bass pedagogy. See *Rameau and Musical Thought*, 54–61.

30. McDonald argues that opposed to Rameau's scientific and objective conception of nature in music, Rousseau derives a sense of what is "natural" in relation to his conception of "l'homme sensible" ("En-harmoniques," 10).

31. Compare Rousseau's articulation in the *Examen de deux principes avancés par M. Rameau* (written between 1755 and 1766): "Mais outre ces trois sons harmoniques, chaque son principal en donne beaucoup d'autres qui ne sont point harmoniques, et n'entrent point dans l'Accord parfait. Telles sont toutes les aliquotes non reductibles par leurs Octaves à quelqu'une de ces trois premiéres. Or il y a une infinité de ces aliquotes qui peuvent échapper à nos sens, mais dont la résonance est démontrée par induction et n'est pas impossible à confirmer par expérience. L'Art les a rejettées de l'Harmonie, et voila où il commence à substituer ses régles à celles de la Nature" (5:351).

32. O'Dea characterizes the methodological dispute between Rameau and Rousseau as bordering on a *différend* in Lyotard's sense: "The reason for this bald mutual contradiction is that the arguments aligned on each side have no point of contact. Rameau's derive from mathematics and acoustics; Rousseau's from language, aesthetics and (in their final form) from history. Rousseau approaches music as a phenomenon of human culture to be accounted for as such, one in which the natural, physical qualities of musical sound are of only incidental interest. Music emerges out of language, and language is not natural to man: some of the critical, the most original elements of Rousseau's contributions to European thought can be traced back in the end to the quarrel with Rameau" (*Jean-Jacques Rousseau*, 28). Compare Christensen's assessment: "Most of Rousseau's arguments with Rameau were driven by his own ideological agenda, and reflect his maturing thoughts on language, education, society, and politics—an agenda Rameau was fully incapable of recognizing or appreciating" (*Rameau and Musical Thought*, 250).

33. See my discussion of performance relative to time and rhythm in chapter 1.

34. Duchez explains the provenance of the text that has come to be known as "L'origine de la mélodie" in the introduction to the Pléiade edition, cxxxvii–cxliv.

The text originally formed part of the unpublished "Principe de la Mélodie ou réponse aux erreurs sur la Musique," which, according to Duchez, is a first version of the "Examen de deux principes."

35. Rameau discusses time, meter, and syncopation in the *Traité*, 295–99. In the same text, he criticizes the too frequent use of syncopation in the bass (82). In the *Code de musique pratique*, he asserts that rhythm is natural to humans and animals (23). Overwhelmingly, his musical theory is dedicated to harmony, voicing, and chording, with proportionally little time spent on rhythm and time.

36. Compare Gessele's discussion of Rousseau's critique of the fundamental bass with respect to the generation of dissonance. Gessele underlines the disconnect between Rameau's theory of fundamental bass and practice, as Rousseau perceives it. See "Institutionalization of Music Theory in France," 33–38.

37. See *Essai*, 5:381–82, and my discussion in the introduction and chapter 2 of this volume.

38. Some passages in Rameau indicate an awareness of the arbitrariness implied by equal temperament: "Je sçais que l'habitude d'entendre une certaine Concordance d'un côté, et une certaine Discordance de l'autre dans le Tempéramment en usage, peut faire qu'on se révoltera d'abord contre des impressions toutes différentes: mais il suffit qu'il y ait de l'arbitraire, et que la seule habitude puisse faire pancher d'abord plutôt d'un côté que de l'autre, pour qu'on doive opiner pour le plus parfait: accoutumez-vous au nouveau Tempéramment, bien-tôt vous n'y sentirez plus rien de tout ce qui peut vous y déplaire à présent" (*Génération*, 102–3). Compare Cohen's discussion of the "sous-entendu" in Rameau in "'Gift of Nature.'"

39. In this respect, for Rameau, music follows the rules of a language game as defined by Lyotard in *Condition postmoderne*, 22–24.

40. Rousseau differs on his pronouncements on this issue. At times, for example, in the *Lettre sur la musique française*, he acknowledges the constraints of harmonics in line with Rameau. At other times, he is far less sanguine about his belief in the inevitability of the system.

41. The passage continues with a contrast to Rousseau: "For Rousseau, by contrast, the keyboard sound seemed to be enough to trigger the memory of an ancient musical culture where melodic inflection was still possible and music still possessed its sublime orphic powers" ("Rousseau, Rameau," 170).

42. The monologue recitative at the center of the dispute between Rameau and Rousseau is from Jean-Baptiste Lully's *Armide*, with a libretto by Philippe Quinault based on Tasso's *Jerusalem Liberated*. The opera was first performed in 1686. The story concerns a sorceress, Armide, who has taken the knight Renaud captive. In the monologue from act 2, scene 5, Armide stands over the sleeping knight with a dagger in hand, unable to kill him because of her feelings of love for him.

43. Rameau, *Nouveau système*, 41. He returns to the monologue in the *Observations sur notre instinct pour la musique* (1754) and the *Code de musique pratique* (1760) in response to Rousseau. For an excellent explanation of Rameau's analysis of the monologue, see Christensen, *Rameau and Musical Thought*, 120–23.

44. The meaning of the term "modulation" undergoes some transformation during the eighteenth century. As Christensen explains, the older meaning of modulation related back to a seventeenth-century notion of mode "as characteristic intervallic and melodic patterns" (*Rameau and Musical Thought*, 170). In other words, modulation in the older sense meant essentially to reaffirm the key in which a piece is composed. The newer meaning suggests movement among keys. As Christensen notes, "It is really only a small shift in nuance to speak of a modulation 'in' a key and modulation 'to' a key" (174). In effect, because the keys to which one modulates must be related

to the original key, modulation in this sense, when well executed, helps to establish and emphasize the original key.

45. Hyer, "'Sighing Branches,'" 16.

46. See Waeber's discussion of Rousseau's conception of "unité de mélodie" in relation to the notion of "contresens," developed for music by Grimm in the *Lettre sur l'Omphale*. Waeber points out that both Grimm and d'Alembert accepted a notion of "contresens" in which, in essence, the music went against the spirit of the lyrics. Waeber argues that Rousseau's reaction to *Armide* "is entirely aimed at demonstrating how Lully's musical 'contresens' ruined Quinault's text" ("Jean-Jacques Rousseau's 'unité de mélodie,'" 104). In the same vein, Strong argues that Rousseau is concerned with instances of "double representation," particularly in opera, that impede comprehension: "But, in order for this representation to be comprehensible, its signification must be clear and singular. Rousseau repeatedly argues against the danger of 'double representation' in music. This phrase is used, in particular, to describe the contemporary situation in opera, where the sense communicated by the visual spectacle of staging and characters is distinct from the sense of the accompanying music" ("Music, the Passions," 98–99).

47. Rousseau's work on "récitatif obligé" is relevant in this context. In her study of melodrama, Waeber carefully traces the relationship between *récitatif obligé* and the emerging lyrical form. Making reference to Rousseau's *Lettre à M. Burney*, Waeber writes, "le récitatif obligé, dramatiquement justifié par une surenchère de l'expression, joue avec la rupture discursive en 'entreocoupant' le discours du chanteur par des 'ritournelles' instrumentales" (*En musique dans le texte*, 35).

48. Rousseau invokes verisimilitude in the *Lettre* to critique the use of recitatives (5:319). He does not specifically mention verisimilitude in the section devoted to the analysis of *Armide*, but the earlier evocation seems applicable to Lully.

49. This line of argument is actually an attempt at a double stab at Rameau, who does not strongly distinguish between intervals and their inversions, for example, the fifth and the fourth. See, for example, *Traité*, 12–14.

50. This perspective is consistent with the rejection of equal temperament in favor of mean-tone or well temperament in order to preserve the force of particular intervals, as we saw above.

51. The idea that the harmony is "suggested" and not directly articulated is perfectly consistent with Rameau's conception that listeners are able to perceive order in music because of the fundamental bass—whether actually played or not. See Cohen's excellent discussion of "the ear" and "instinct" in "'Gift of Nature,'" esp. 83–90.

52. It is important to note that Rameau did add to Lully's original figuration of the bass to reflect his own understanding of the implied chromatic development of the piece according to his theory of the fundamental bass. For a detailed analysis of Rameau's exegesis, including his retouching of Lully's bass, see Eugène Borrel, *L'interprétation de la musique française*, 196–214.

53. Herbert Schneider, acknowledges Rousseau's errors in the analysis, but nonetheless defends the critique of Lully's recitative as paving the way for Gluck. See "Rameau et la tradition lulliste."

54. Rameau charges Rousseau with not really listening: "Mais les yeux suffisent-ils en Musique? Il y faut des oreilles, et sur-tout un jugement impartial, où la raison ne se laisse point aveugler. Bientôt on verra cette Tonique devenir Dominante, dès qu'on croira pouvoir s'en autoriser" (86–87). The eyes, ears, and the judgment of reason all play a role in appreciating the beauty of music for Rameau.

55. Lully, *Armide*, 138.

56. In the notes to the Pléiade edition, Olivier Pot underscores the fact that Rameau accuses Rousseau of "bad faith" for recognizing and then ignoring the modulation in the passage (5:1488, note 1).

57. Haeringer remarks on the attention paid to librettos by the *philosophes*, especially Rousseau and Diderot, in contrast to their general neglect by an earlier aesthetic. See *L'esthétique de l'opéra en France*, 89.

58. In the preface to the *Discours sur l'origine de l'inégalité*, Rousseau asserts the existence of "deux principes antérieurs à la raison, dont l'un nous intéresse ardemment à nôtre bien-être et à la conservation de nous-mêmes, et l'autre nous inspire une répugnance naturelle à voir perir ou souffrir tout être sensible et principalement nos semblables." He goes on to develop the moral implications of natural pity: "tant qu'il [natural man] ne resistera point à l'impulsion intérieure de la commiseration, il ne fera jamais du mal à un autre homme ni même à aucun être sensible" (3:125–26). The developed discussion of *pitié* occurs in both the *Discours* (3:153–57) and in the *Essai sur l'origine des langues* (5:395–96). For critical readings of pity, see my discussion in *Mass Enlightenment*, 31–35, and *Beyond Contractual Morality*, 53–57, 124–27; and in Trachtenberg, *Making Citizens*.

59. I am suggesting that this scene would be Rousseau's equivalent to the kind of struggle that animates Corneille's *Horace* or Racine's *Phèdre* or *Andromaque*.

60. As Christensen ably summarizes the theory in a general way, "Rameau argued that all music is foundationally harmonic in structure. Every harmony (or chord) is generated from a single fundamental (or what we call today a chord 'root') in some consistent way. In the *Traité*, this way was monochord (string) divisions, while in later writings it was the acoustical phenomenon of harmonic upper partials generated by many vibrating systems (the *corps sonore*). By manipulating the various ratios and proportions of his monochord divisions and *corps sonore*, Rameau was able with more or less success to account for all of the harmonies commonly employed in French Baroque practice" (*Rameau and Musical Thought*, 5).

61. As Strong succinctly summarizes the dispute between Rameau and Rousseau about nature: "Nature for Rameau was not that which spoke to Rousseau's heart; it is rather the nature of geometry and physics" ("Rousseau: Music, Language, and Politics").

62. See Cohen's excellent discussion of "instinct" in Rameau in "'Gift of Nature.'"

63. Jacobi discovered and subsequently published the manuscript in its entirety. For the history of the manuscript and the unfinished text, see Jacobi and De Crue, "A l'occasion du bi-centenaire de la mort de J.-Ph. Rameau, 'Vérités intéressantes.'"

64. See my discussion of musical mimesis in the chapter 5 for a more developed analysis of the way in which music communicates feeling. Compare Chua's characterization of the dispute: "So the implication of Rameau's harmonic theory was an origin of music without voice, without soul, without sentiment and without humanity. As far as Rousseau was concerned, Rameau had mistaken the emptiness of instrumental sounds for the plenitude of vocal signs that issue melodiously from the living soul. In his hands, nature herself had become an instrument playing upon the body and had turned the body into an instrument in the process. And this was not ultimately an academic problem, despite Rousseau's mathematical wrangling with Rameau, but a moral matter that concerned the natural origins of humanity. Rameau had substituted the passionate presence of the voice for the dead calculation of intervals, and had dared to call such articulation and spacing life itself" (*Absolute Music*, 99).

65. See my discussion of the effect of *Le devin du village* on the audience in chapter 4.

66. In the *Social Contract*, Rousseau refers to the "*moi commun*" formed by the pact (3:361, emphasis in the original).

67. Berger, *Bach's Cycle, Mozart's Arrow*, 152. See also my discussion of redemption through aesthetics in chapter 5.

68. Rousseau's own posthumously published collection of romances, *Les consolations des misères de ma vie, ou receuil d'airs, romances et duos*, further indicates that the composer not only communicates passion to eventual performers and listeners, but that the music might serve to comfort and console the composer as well.

69. I acknowledge that it is problematic to equate the vicar's position with Rousseau's, but I nonetheless perceive strong lines of coincidence between the metaphysical and moral positions staked out in *Emile* and the implications of the writings on music. Certainly the kind of mind/body dualism articulated is reinforced in numerous passages of the *Confessions*.

70. Much of Rousseau's attention in the *Lettre à d'Alembert sur les spectacles* is famously turned to the bad ways in which the passions may be stirred by dramatic performance. See *Lettre*, 5:15–43. Compare Chua's discussion of Rousseau's moral condemnation of Rameau in *Absolute Music*, 101.

CHAPTER 4

1. Rousseau, *Confessions*, trans. Cohen; all parenthetical references are to this translation. Tiersot identifies the song and provides lyrics and a transcription based on a manuscript in the library of the Paris Conservatoire (see "Concerning Jean-Jacques Rousseau."). Robinson offers a slightly different transcription of the piece based on an 1833 edition of Rousseau's works (see "Jean-Jacques Rousseau, Aunt Suzanne").

2. For a discussion of the *madeleine* in Proust in relation to affective memory, see Terdiman, *Present Past*, esp. chapter 6. Terdiman provides a useful review of the relevant literature in addition to his insightful and subtle reading of the workings of memory and forgetting in the novel. De Nora's sociological study of the uses of music in everyday life highlights the use of music by couples. De Nora writes, "One of the first things respondents used music for was to remember key people in their lives, for example loved family members who had died." She further documents the high incidence of the use of music for "romantic or intimate" relationships: "Music helped them to recall lovers or former partners and, with these memories, emotionally heightened phases of moments in their lives" (see *Music in Everyday Life*, esp. 63–66; quotation on 63). Finally, on the centrality of memory for the experience of music in Rousseau, see Dugan and Strong, "Music, Politics," and Waeber, "Jean-Jacques Rousseau's 'unité de mélodie.'"

3. Jacques Attali highlights this attribute of music: "On peut réentendre virtuellement un son en mémoire rien qu'en y pensant; on peut en quelque sorte le fredonner dans son esprit: phénomnèse. Lorsqu'on réentend une œuvre mémorisée, on n'entend pas que l'œuvre, mais aussi tout le contexte dans lequel on l'a déjà entendue, réellement et virtuellement" (*Bruits*, 45).

4. De Nora describes a "technology of the self" in which individuals use music for a variety of purposes: to motivate themselves, to concentrate, to calm down, to evoke the past, etc. (see *Music in Everyday Life*, 46–62).

5. See the *Discours sur l'origine de l'inégalité*, 3:145–51; and the *Essai sur l'origine des langues*, 5:375–81. Interestingly, Rousseau credits the child with inventing language in the *Second Discourse*, a line of thinking that runs slightly counter to the argument that he develops in the *Dictionnaire*.

6. For recorded samples of Swiss herdsmen's songs, including "Ranz des vaches," see "Swiss Alpine Music," http://www.swissinfo.ch/eng/Home/Archive/Ranz_des_vaches.html?cid=7685444 (accessed July 25, 2008).

7. As Dugan and Strong have asserted about this same passage, "national musics express the noble memory of self-creation," relating the pull of national music to political formation (see "Music, Politics," 353).

8. Compare the discussion of the physical versus intellectual pleasure of music in chapter 5 of this volume.

9. Didier makes a similar claim that the exotic is always nostalgic in eighteenth-century musical thought (see "Musique primitive," 131).

10. Seeking to define "folk music" in the early twentieth century, Henry Edward Krehbiel wrote, "Folksong is not popular song in the sense in which the word is most frequently used, but the song of the folk; not only the song of the people but, in a strict sense, the song created by the people. It is a body of poetry and music which has come into existence without the influence of conscious art, as a spontaneous utterance, filled with characteristics of rhythm, form and melody which are traceable, more or less clearly, to racial (or national) temperament, modes of life, climatic and political conditions, geographical environment and language. Some of these elements, the spiritual, are elusive, but others can be determined and classifed." Krehbiel, entry in Hughes, *Musical Guide*, quoted in Oliver, *Screening the Blues*, 1.

11. As Nettl defines "ethnic, folk, or traditional" music, it contains "two groups of styles and repertoires: (1) folk music, which is found in those cultures and areas in which there is also a longtime development of urban, professional, cultivated, musical tradition, something that is often called art or classical music, and (2) tribal music, the music of nonliterate cultures, that is, those peoples without a tradition of literate, sophisticated musical culture living alongside the musical folk culture" (*Folk and Traditional Music*, 1). Thus, Rousseau's sample would seem to inaugurate the field of ethnomusicology. In a discussion of Rousseau's own collection of romances, *Consolations des misères de ma vie*, Tiersot notes the presence of Venetian songs: "Ce n'est pas un romantique de 1830 qui nous a apporté cet écho de la lagune; mais c'est le premier des romantiques, Jean-Jacques Rousseau, qui se manifeste ainsi comme évocateur d'impressions d'une intense poésie, en même temps que comme notre premier folkloriste musical" (*Jean-Jacques Rousseau*, 78). The difficulty of separating out the proper objects of musicology and ethnomusicology has become increasingly problematic, given the value judgments that inhere in the distinction and the resulting ethnocentrism. On Rousseau's use of historical/anthropological evidence against Rameau's physicomathematical arguments, including non-European material, see O'Dea, *Jean-Jacques Rousseau*, 43. For a useful collection of early modern accounts of non-Western music, see Harrison, *Time, Place, and Music*.

12. Montesquieu's typology of cultures rests on distinctions between forms of government and the geographical conditions—especially climate and its relation to human psychology—that give rise to these different forms. The discussion of the effects on climate, terrain, and manners and morals on national character leads to a categorization of cultures based on their inclination or disinclination to be governed. See Montesquieu, *De l'esprit des lois*, in OC, vol. 1, books 14–19. See also Didier's discussion of this conflation in "Musique primitive."

13. Agnew discusses the cognitive dissonance that arises when Maori music transcribed during Cook's second voyage is brought back to Germany in the late eighteenth century and deemed too "advanced" for a primitive culture. Agnew cites Friedrich Arnold Klockenbring's 1778 essay, "Etwas über die Musik in den neuerlich entdeckten Südländen." She writes, "he asks how it could be that 'although the New Zealanders are generally much tougher, more warlike, and fiercer in their passions than the inhabitants of islands located closer to the equator in milder latitudes, their

music exceeds that of Tahiti and Anamoka in terms of its complexity and gentle tonality?'" ("Listening to Others," 176). See also Agnew, "Scots Orpheus in the South Seas," and Irving, "Pacific in the Minds."

14. Rousseau, *Social Contract and Discourse on the Origin of Inequality*, 167.

15. This point will be developed in the last section of this chapter on *Julie, ou la nouvelle Héloïse*.

16. Compare the argument in the *Essai sur l'origine des langues* that harmony separates song and speech (5:416).

17. Tiersot hypothesizes a possible connection to Calvin's preference for simple, unison song (*Jean-Jacques Rousseau*, 7).

18. Compare the argument in the *Essai*, 5:416. Gagnebin, in his introduction to the Pléïade edition volume of the *Œuvres complètes* dedicated to the musical writings, characterizes this passage as among those "aberrations éloignées de toute observation musicale" (5:xxii).

19. For a subtle discussion of what Rousseau means by the term "unison," see Kumbier, "Rousseau's *Lettre*."

20. Laborde disputes Rousseau's transcription of the Chinese example, saying that it is pentatonic and that Rousseau got it wrong: "A la mesure 3 de l'air, donné par Rousseau, on trouve deux *fa;* surquoi il faut observer que cet air Chinois, ainsi que plusieurs autres morceaux de Musique Chinoise, n'est composé que de cinq notes, & n'a pour élémens que ce que les Chinois appelent *les cinqs tons,* & qui sont ici *sol la fi re mi,* dans lesquels il n'y a ni *fa,* ni *ut*" (*Essai sur la musique ancienne et moderne*, 1:145).

21. See Agnew, "Scots Orpheus in the South Seas," and Angew, "Listening to Others," esp. 168–69. Rousseau has Colette refer to bagpipes in the lyrics of the final song of *Le devin du village*, "Allons danser": "A la ville on fait bien plus de fracas; / Mais sont-ils aussi gais dans leurs ébats? / Toujours contens, / Toujours chantans; / Beauté sans fard, / Plaisir sans art: / Tous leurs concerts valent-ils nos musettes?" For the complete libretto, see University of Toronto Libraries, Internet Archive, http://archive.org/details/ledevinduvillageoorous (accessed August 23, 2012). See Manning's discussion of the song in "Rousseau's Other Woman," 38. The "ouverture" also contains a second movement that, according to Heartz, "is in the key of D minor; its 6/8 meter, in combination with long pedals, like the drones of rustic pipes, helps suggest the rural setting of the opera" ("Italian by Intention," 34).

22. For a provocative discussion of similarities between the reception of non-Western music in the eighteenth century and the reception of jazz by Europeans in the early twentieth century, see Mercier-Faivre and Seité, "Jazz à la lumière."

23. For a clear discussion of ancient Greek music, see Thomas J. Mathiesen, "Greece: Ancient," *Oxford Music Online*, https://vpn.lib.ucdavis.edu/subscriber/article/grove/music/,DanaInfo=www.oxfordmusiconline.com+11694pg1?q=greece%2C+ancient&search=quick&pos=1&_start=1#firsthit (accessed August 23, 2012). Reiss provides a helpful summary of the history of the tetrachord in relation to early modern tuning (see *Knowledge, Discovery*, esp. 190–91). See also O'Dea's nuanced and contextualized reading of Rousseau's assessments of Greek music in the *Encyclopédie* article "Musique," in *Jean-Jacques Rousseau*, 20–22. Baud-Bovy provides a careful summary of Greek sources on the "enharmonic," and concludes by agreeing with Rousseau's assertion concerning Aristoxenus's contrivance of a new harmonic system (see "Le 'genre enharmonique' a-t-il existé?"). Finally, Rehdig provides a comprehensive analysis of Rameau's and Rousseau's differences on the enharmonic in "Rousseau, Rameau."

24. Diderot and d'Alembert, "Genre," *Encyclopédie*, 7:596.

25. Scott situates the positive valorization of Greek music within the dispute with Rameau, who had characterized the Greek harmonic system as incapable of being as expressive as modern music (see "Harmony," 304).

26. Grove Music Online provides a succinct summary of the historical reception of the pentatonic scale: "Once described variously as the 'Chinese scale' or the 'Scotch scale,' the pentatonic scale has impressed commentators since at least the mid-19th century for its astonishing ubiquity. A significant feature of such diverse musical traditions as those of the British Isles, West Africa and Amerindian America (among countless others), pentatonicism may well be a musical universal (Chailley, 111–28; Nettl, 42), and many have taken for granted its historical primitivism (Helmholtz, 257; Suchoff, 1976, 371; Trân)." Jeremy Day-O'Connell, "Pentatonic," *Oxford Music Online*, https://vpn.lib.ucdavis.edu/subscriber/article/grove/music/,DanaInfo = www.oxfordmusiconline.com + 21263?q = pentatonic&search = quick&pos = 1&_start = 1#firsthit (accessed August 23, 2012).

27. For a discussion of the relationship between time signatures, note values, and indications of tempo in eighteenth-century notation, see Houle, *Meter in Music*, esp. 35–38.

28. Laborde writes, "C'est le même air que Rousseau a donné dans son Dictionaire, planche N, mais qui est étrangement défiguré. 10. D'un morceau de Musique Chinoise, très-lent & très-grave, on a fait, dans le Dictionaire, une sorte d'air de danse, & certainement de très mauvais goût, en y exprimant par des croches, & d'une maniere légere, ce que le P. Amiot traduit par des noires d'une mesure lente" (*Essai sur la musique*, 1:145).

29. The article "Musette" in the *Encyclopédie* (10:895) gives a very detailed description of how bagpipes produce sound, including a reference to the octave drone. The plates to the *Encyclopédie* include both illustrations of various wind instruments (plate 6) (22:14:2) and samples of music similar to plate N in Rousseau's *Dictionnaire* (plate 7) (24:15:9). In the discussion of "Ranz des vaches" in the text accompanying the plates in the *Encyclopédie*, the author notes, "La *fig*. 6. est un air appellé en Suisse le *rans des vaches*, parce qu'en effet les bouviers, vachers, ou pâtres de ce pays, comme dans presque toute l'Allemagne, rappellent leurs animaux au bercail tous les soirs par cette espece de chant, soit avec un cornet ou une cornemuse, ou soit avec un grand roseau évidé, long de huit piés à-peu-près, qu'ils embouchent à la maniere des cors, & qui a le son approchant de celui de ces instrumens. Cette espece de cornet, simple & très-naturel, qui leur sert de houlette dans le jour, est harmonique; une preuve en est en partie dans les *sol* que l'on voit ici dièzés, parce que ce son, comme dans les cors, est en rapport avec celui de la totalité comme re/1. sol/11, & qu'il approche plus de que de; c'est ce qui a obligé d'altérer ainsi cette note au moyen du dieze, quoiqu'exactement elle ne le soit point à ce dégré dans le corps sonore" (24:15:9–10). The commentary on the G-sharp indicates the acknowledgment of a scale altered from the diatonic that is described as simple, natural, and very harmonic because of the scale. The text goes on to cite the text of Rousseau's article "Musique" on the power of "Ranz des vaches."

30. The popularity of *Le devin du village*, as ascertained through its performance history, bears out some of Rousseau's account: the opera saw 350 performances over the next 50 years. Charlotte Kaufman recounts that "the premiere was given at Fontainebleau before the King in October 1752, and *Le Devin* remained in the repertory of the Paris Opéra until 1829." See "Questions and Answers About Rousseau and *Le devin du village*," http://www.areditions.com/rr/embellish/1998_05/rousseau.html (accessed April 3, 2008).

31. Coudreuse and Vila both explore tears in relation to sensibility in Rousseau, focusing primarily on the *Confessions, Julie*, and *Rousseau juge de Jean-Jacques*. See

Coudreuse, *Goût des larmes au XVIIIe siècle*, and Vila, *Enlightenment and Pathology*.

32. Heartz disputes Rousseau's claim of novelty, pointing out that many of the pieces that comprise *Le devin* are based on French models, especially dance pieces. While he finds nothing particularly interesting in Colette's "J'ai perdu tout mon bonheur" (he even refers to it as "limited and repetitive" and "monotonous"), Heartz singles out the fact that the opera begins with "a long, plaintive, and folk-like song in many strophes, sung by the pastoral heroine" ("Italian by Intention," 35). Tiersot also suggests that Rousseau's opera was not entirely different from other light fare being performed at the time (*Jean-Jacques Rousseau*, 102–3).

33. See "Unité de mélodie," 5:1146. Also, compare my discussion of melodic unity in chapter 2 of this volume.

34. Jourdain, one of Rousseau's harsher critics in the pamphlet wars, described the opera as "Une Fête qui ne finit point." See Jourdain, *Seconde lettre*, in *La querelle des bouffons*, 1:583, cited in Heartz, "Italian by Intention," 45. On the history of the pastoral in France, see Anthony, *French Baroque Music*, 60–66.

35. Auld, "'Dealing in Shepherds,'" 54.

36. Waeber persuasively argues that much of the "novelty" of *Le devin* lies in Rousseau's use of "bas comique" and "jeu muet," normally associated with the *théâtre de la foire* and not the opera (see "'Devin de la foire'?").

37. According to the *Calendrier électronique des spectacles sous l'ancien régime et sous la révolution* (http://www.cesar.org.uk/cesar2/home.php), 1752 saw the production of eight operas in various locations, including *Omphale*, *Les fêtes de Thalie*, and Pergolesi's *La serva padrona*, that touched off the *querelle des bouffons*. Most of the operas performed were opéras-comiques, with a few pastoral parodies thrown in. Rousseau's *Devin*, composed in a "simple" style, as I will discuss, contrasts with the "French" style of the other operas. For an excellent discussion of what was at stake in the *querelle des bouffons*, and especially for the philosophical resonances of the debate, see Johnson, "Encyclopedists."

38. Heartz cites the contemporary critic of Rousseau's opera, Jourdain, who lambastes *Le devin* for its lack of originality: "One of his severest critics dismissed *Le devin* as 'a little opera-comique on known vaudevilles, with accompaniments that made every effort to pass for being Italian, but which are not so well disguised'" (Heartz, *Music in European Capitals*, 717; internal cite to Jourdain, *Seconde lettre du correcteur des bouffons à l'écolier de Prague* (Paris, 1753), in *La querelle des bouffons*, 1:582–84). Heartz's own assessment of the *Devin* gives Rousseau a little more credit for having at least composed an opera with a mixture of Italian and French elements, but which owes a great debt to French dances.

39. The effect of the *Devin* on audiences, at least as Rousseau describes it in the *Confessions*, contrasts markedly with his discussion of the negative effects of theater in the *Lettre à d'Alembert sur les spectacles:* "la plus avantageuse impression des meilleures tragedies est de réduire à quelques affections passagéres, stériles et sans effet, tous les devoirs de l'homme, à nous faire applaudir de nôtre courage en loüant celui des autres, de nôtre humanité en plaignant les maux que nous aurions pu guérir, de nôtre charité en disant au pauvre: Dieu vous assiste" (5:24).

40. The debate concerning literature's ability to manipulate readers' emotion is ongoing in the eighteenth-century context, and especially acute with respect to women readers. Rousseau's celebrated first preface to *Julie* makes mocking reference to the scandalous way in which literature is often viewed: "Jamais chaste fille n'a lu de roman" (2:6). For a discussion of eighteenth-century beliefs about the moral impact of literature, see May, *Dilemme du roman au XVIIIe siècles*, 75–138; Mylne,

*Eighteenth-Century French Novel*; and Cook, *Fictional France*, 1–21. The further step of seducing the reader brings to mind Diderot's famous hoax in writing *La religieuse* for his friend the Marquis de Croismare. For a fascinating discussion of the hoax from the perspective of the link between language and material consequences, see Terdiman, *Body and Story*, esp. 30–36.

41. Starobinski reads this letter as part of the overall structure of obstacle and transcendence in Rousseau's thought, specifically that this type of music becomes a kind of "pure sentiment" (*Jean-Jacques Rousseau*, esp. 110–13).

42. Tiersot perceives a possible source of the representation of music in the *vendanges* letter in *Julie* in Rousseau's early childhood (*Jean-Jacques Rousseau*, 14–15). Perry suggests a strong link between women's voices and the Scottish ballad tradition in "'Finest Ballads.'"

43. Rousseau writes, "Les *Voix* graves sont les plus ordinaires aux hommes faits; les *Voix* aiguës sont celles des femmes: les Eunuques et les enfans ont aussi à-peu-près le même Diapason de *Voix* que les femmes; tous les hommes en peuvent même approcher en chantant le Faucet. Mais de toutes les *Voix* aiguës, il faut convenir, malgré la prévention des Italiens pour les Castrati, qu'il n'y en a point d'espèce comparable à celle des femmes, ni pour l'étendue ni pour la beauté du Tymbre" (5:1150). See O'Dea's discussion of this preference in *Jean-Jacques Rousseau*, 83.

44. The paragraph continues, "Nous ne pouvons nous empêcher, Claire de sourire, Julie de rougir, moi de soupirer, quand nous retrouvons dans ces chansons des tours et des expressions dont nous nous sommes servis autrefois. Alors en jettant les yeux sur elles et me rappellant les tems éloignés, un tressaillement me prend, un poids insupportable me tombe tout à coup sur le cœur, et me laisse une impression funeste qui ne s'efface qu'avec peine" (2:609).

45. See Starobinski's discussion of the "illusory" nature of the equality in *Jean-Jacques Rousseau* 121–25.

46. One passage of the letter makes the comparison to the Roman Saturnalia explicitly: "Ces saturnales sont bien plus agréables et plus sages que celles des Romains. Le renversement qu'il affectoient étoit trop vain pour instruire le maitre ni l'esclave: mais la douce égalité qui regne ici rétablit l'ordre de la nautre, forme une instruction pour les uns, une consolation pour les autres et un lien d'amitié pour tous" (2:608).

47. Perry ("'Finest Ballads'") highlights the association between Scotland and the ballad during the eighteenth century, citing Bronson, "Mrs. Brown and the Ballad." The fact that the pentatonic scale is often referred to as the "Scotch scale" (see note 26 above) reinforces this association between ballads and primitivism.

48. Tiersot underscores the popularity of Rousseau's romances: "Ce n'est pas sans raison, il faut bien s'en rendre compte, que ce simple petit acte [*Le devin du village*] écrit d'une main peu experte, est resté au répertoire de l'Opéra pendant trois quarts de siècle et se laisse encore écouter avec agrément: il a donné par là la preuve d'une vitalité fort supérieure à celle de maintes œuvres, peut-être de plus grande envergure, mais froides et vides, qu'on affectait d'admirer davantage en son temps. De même les romances de Jean-Jacques Rousseau ont joui d'une longue popularité qui fut de très bon aloi" (*Jean-Jacques Rousseau*, 3).

49. In the entry for "romance," Marcelle Benoit writes in the *Dictionnaire de la musique en France aux XVIIe et XVIIIe siècles*, "Un des premiers exemples du nouveau genre musical est 'Dans ma cabane obscure' du *Devin du village* (1752) qui connut une immense succès" (619). Similarly, *Oxford Music Online* explains, "The French used the term 'romance' in the first half of the 18th century to denote a strophic poem recounting an ancient story of love and gallantry. . . . Rousseau (*Dictionnaire de Musique*, 1768) presented the first primarily musical definition of the term,

suggesting that the melody should reflect the qualities of the poem: 'point d'ornemens, rien de maniéré, une mélodie douce, naturelle, champêtre.' One of the most important examples of the new genre is Rousseau's 'Dans ma cabane obscure' from *Le devin du village* of 1752. The strophic form, recurring three-bar phrases, thin texture and narrow range reflect the naive, natural state of the young peasant. Rousseau creates a sentimental mood through expressive devices such as the sudden expansion of the melodic range in the second half and the fuller texture and chromatic harmonic shifts near the final cadence." Roger Hickman, "Romance," *Oxford Music Online*, https://vpn.lib.ucdavis.edu/subscriber/article/grove/music/,DanaI nfo = www.oxfordmusiconline.com + 23725?q = romance&search = quick&pos = 1&_start = 1#firsthit (accessed August 23, 2012). Mongrédien documents the disappearance of the romance form during and directly after the Revolution and its reappearance after the Directory (*French Music*, 241).

50. Perry, "'Finest Ballads,'" 10. Compare Love's discussion of "women's music" in relation to forms of political communication (*Musical Democracy*, 67–86).

51. Marie-Antoinette is reported to have performed the role of Collette in *Le devin du village*, in keeping with her "peasant" taste as displayed in the Hameau de la Reine at Versailles. One account of her performance of the role occurs in Smythe, *Guardian of Marie-Antoinette*, 2:675–76. The Karl Baedeker *Paris and Environs* explicitly links the building of the *hameau* to the influence of Rousseau's opera: "The *Hamlet* (restored in 1899), as the nine or ten rustic cottages grouped round an artificial lake are called, was built by *Mique* and *H. Robert* in 1782–87 for the court-ladies who wished to indulge in the idyllic life which became the fashion in consequence of J. J. Rousseau's book [*sic*], 'Le Devin du village' or 'Village Soothsayer'" (370).

52. Rousseau maintains throughout the *Projet de constitution pour la Corse* the importance of agriculture for reforming Corsican manners and morals. He writes near the beginning, "Le gout de l'agriculture n'est pas seulement avantageux à la population en multipliant la subsistance des hommes mais en donnant au corps de la nation un temperament et des mœurs qui les font naitre en plus grand nombre. Par tout pays les habitans des campagnes peuplent plus que ceux des villes soit par la simplicité de la vie rustique qui forme des corps mieux constitués, soit par l'assiduité du travail qui previent le desordre et les vices" (3:904).

53. See my discussions of Rousseau's conception of Polish national identity and military virtue in "Militarisme et vertu chez Rousseau," and *Mass Enlightenment*, 56–69. For a discussion *Lettre à d'Alembert* as a critique of the fostering of "feminine behavior" through the theater, see Dugan and Strong, "Music, Politics," 339–40.

CHAPTER 5

1. Cassirer, *Philosophy of the Enlightenment*, 279. All parenthetical references are to this edition.

2. On the issue of good taste in relation to modulation in Rameau, see Hyer, "'Sighing Branches,'" esp. 16.

3. Cassirer, *Philosophy of the Enlightenment*, 28.

4. Ibid., 297–308.

5. For a discussion of eighteenth-century aesthetics with respect to the effects of the work of art specifically on the reader or spectator, see, for example, Caplan, *Framed Narratives*, and Fried, *Absorption and Theatricality*.

6. On the centrality and import of the *Dictionnaire de musique* as an articulation of aesthetic theory, see Verba, "Jean-Jacques Rousseau," and Scott, "Harmony."

7. It is important to note that Rousseau's choice of music as privileged aesthetic object also runs counter to what have been characterized as Enlightenment trends

toward "ocularization" and the visual. For a discussion of the turn toward the ocular, especially in the American Enlightenment, see Schmidt, "Hearing Loss."

8. Strong argues in a similar vein that "[s]ubsequent to Rousseau, Kant, Hegel, Marx, the German and English and American romantics, as well as some others (even Nietzsche), extend, develop, resist, struggle against Rousseau's presence and his words. Others continue to do so today. Rousseau is not the whole story of modernity, but he is, in ways that others around and before him were not, *modern*." *Jean-Jacques Rousseau*, 3.

9. See Simon, *Mass Enlightenment*.
10. Berger, *Bach's Cycle, Mozart's Arrow*, 152.
11. Jauss, "Literary Process of Modernism," 39.
12. Habermas, "Modernity."
13. Ferry, *Homo Aestheticus*, 8.
14. The appearance of Alexander Gottlieb Baumgarten's *Aesthetica* in 1750 is often cited as marking a significant turning point in the creation of the term "aesthetics" to denote a branch of philosophy specifically dedicated to perception through the senses, for which he used our experience of art as a primary example.
15. During the eighteenth century, music was considered to be both an art—dependent on mimesis—and a science that dealt with the realm of sensory impressions. For a discussion of music's double status as art and science see Verba, "Jean-Jacques Rousseau." Compare the opening remarks in the "Discours préliminaire aux elements de musique théorique et pratique suivant les principes de M. Rameau éclairis, développés et simplifiés par M. D'Alembert": "On peut considerer la musique comme un art qui a pour objet l'un des principaux plaisirs des sens, ou comme une science par laquelle cet art est réduit en principes." Reprinted in Kintzler, *Jean-Philippe Rameau*, 193.
16. Interestingly, these same issues reappear in modernist and avant-garde music. As Kahn has argued, modernist and avant-garde composers of the early twentieth century turned away from the incorporation of prerecorded sounds within their compositions, deeming them too referential and, therefore, too mimetic, particularly for the avant-garde aesthetic (see "Sound of Music").
17. See Verba, "Jean-Jacques Rousseau," and Scott, "Harmony," on imitation in Aristotle and the abbé Dubos in relation to Rousseau.
18. See Dugan and Strong on the relationship between judgment in aesthetics and politics, in "Music, Politics," esp. 354.
19. For a discussion of Rousseau's and Rameau's understandings of nature in relation to music, see chapter 3.
20. Compare Starobinski's discussion of popular song as it is represented in *Julie, ou la nouvelle Héloïse* and its ability to highlight the distance between the past and the present (see *Jean-Jacques Rousseau*, esp. 113–16).
21. See Berger's discussion of Rousseau's emphasis on man's responsibility for his own perdition in *Bach's Cycle, Mozart's Arrow*, esp. 131–76.
22. For a discussion of alienation in Rousseau, see Simon, *Mass Enlightenment*, especially chapter 1–3.
23. *Pygmalion* in and of itself is a paradoxical text from the point of view of genre alone. The alternation between spoken voice and orchestral music indicates a new direction in thinking about opera. For a discussion of *Pygmalion* within the context of *opéra comique*, see Rebejkow, "Rousseau et l'opéra-comique."
24. Weber, "Aesthetics of Rousseau's *Pygmalion*."
25. Coleman, "Rousseau and Preromanticism."
26. Compare Coleman's discussion of secularization in romanticism and Rousseau's own paradoxical relation to Christianity in "Rousseau and Preromanticism."

27. Rousseau never advocates for a rationalization of the aesthetic sphere. Indeed, the emphasis on feeling runs counter to these accounts.

28. In "Literary Process of Modernism," Jauss contends that Rousseau diagnoses the conflict between nature and civilization without offering any solution: "The three means of reform that he had developed in *Emile*, the *Social Contract*, and the *Nouvelle Héloïse* were already inconsistent at the most basic level of their disparate points of departure, leaving, all told, nothing more than an aporia, whose solution was accessible neither to Rousseau nor to the French Enlightenment" (41). I will argue in favor of a reading of Rousseau's music theory that proposes a version of aesthetic modernism that offers aesthetic experience—in the form of music—as an antidote to the alienation of modern life.

29. Foucault cites Baudelaire's *The Painter of Modern Life and Other Essays*, 13, in "What Is Enlightenment?," 310.

30. Habermas, "Modernity," 344. Habermas cites Octavio Paz, *Essays* (Frankfurt am Main: Suhrkamp, 1979), 2:159.

31. Dugan and Strong, "Music, Politics," 331–32.

32. See also Simon, "Music and the Performance of Community in Rousseau."

33. Derrida, *Grammatology*. See my discussion of Derrida and de Man in the introduction to this volume.

34. Although music requires presence for performance, its temporal quality and unrepeatability suggest a highly unstable art form. Rather than the stability that Derrida sees in the privileging of speech over writing in the *Essai*, I would suggest that the privileging of music has everything to do with its unstable dissemination.

35. Jauss suggests that unrepeatability is a characteristic of second-generation avant-gardists such as Apollinaire, Duchamp, or Picasso, noting that their work stresses the "pure contingency" of everyday experience. Although Rousseau's understanding of music does not encompass the quotidian, his emphasis on its sequential/temporal form does highlight what Jauss describes in the avant-garde as "the nonrecoverable character of all temporal experience" ("Literary Process of Modernism," 59).

36. In chapter 3, I carefully lay out the relative and absolute positions of Rameau and Rousseau with respect to their musical systems.

37. Compare the virtually identical passage from the *Essai*, 5:421.

38. Dauphin, *Musique au temps des Encyclopédistes*, 28–40. On this point I disagree with de Man's assertion that music is not mimetic for Rousseau. See de Man, *Blindness and Insight*, esp. 129–31.

39. For a contextualization of the concept of "unité de mélodie" both with respect to Rousseau's thought and eighteenth-century musical thought generally, see Waeber, "Jean-Jacques Rousseau's 'unité de mélodie.'"

40. In this respect, the contrast with Rameau's use of concepts like "the ear" and "instinct" illustrates Rousseau's movement toward Kantian-style judgment in aesthetics. See Cohen's discussion of the limits of cognition in Rameau in "'Gift of Nature.'"

41. Kant, *Critique of Judgment*, 38–45. Subsequent quotations are cited parenthetically in the text.

42. See my discussion of the difference between music's spatial and temporal existence in chapter 1. Of course, Kant would disagree about this assessment of the nature of music. See Bowie's analysis of Kant's aesthetic with respect to music in *Aesthetics and Subjectivity*, 34–36.

43. See Scott, "Harmony," 299.

44. For Kant, the aesthetic object need only be (re)presented through the faculty of the imagination. In this respect, images from dreams could be subject to aesthetic judgment.

45. Rousseau's conception of interest, in this respect, appears to be closer to Condillac's than to Kant's. In the *Essai sur l'origine des connaissances humaines*, Condillac argues that we make sense of the infinite number of perceptions with which we are bombarded by paying attention to those that are most meaningful to us based on our passions and temperaments: "Concluons que nous ne pouvons tenir aucun compte du plus grand nombre de nos perceptions, non qu'elles aient été sans conscience, mais parce qu'elle sont oubliées un instant après.... Les choses attirent notre attention par le côté où elles ont le plus de rapport avec notre temperament, nos passions et notre état" (*Essai sur l'origine des connaissances humaines*, 119).

46. See Lyotard, "Sublime à présent," and Nancy, "Offrande sublime." For Lyotard, the question of the present and time consciousness is central to the sublime in Kant, linking the sublime to his understanding of the break between the modern and the postmodern.

47. For a discussion of "sublime" judgments in Rousseau that also relate to the recognition of the human community, see Simon, "Diverting Water in Rousseau."

48. To frame it from another perspective, aesthetic judgment in Rousseau has been likened by Dugan and Strong to the type of judgment requisite for political action. Dugan and Strong emphasize the distinction between the way in which, for Rousseau, theater removes judgment from the audience, while music provides an occasion for exercising judgment that stresses that which we hold in common. They argue that music "holds our attention because it is a part of who we are." They go on to draw the parallel between music and political theory: "similarly, political theory must find a language that makes its audience know its assertions as the audience's own" ("Music, Politics," 354).

49. Paul Simon, "You Can Call Me Al," *Graceland* (Warner Brothers, 1986).

50. Habermas, "Modernity," 350.

51. Strong broadens the question of the recognition of commonality in Rousseau, characterizing the struggle as one of overcoming narcissism and solipsism. Strong argues for a reading of Rousseau that imagines "in a society whose realities are legitimate and just, a human encounter with others will be to find in those others precisely that which constitutes me, like them, a human being" ("Self Knowing the Self," 115).

CONCLUSION

1. Rousseau was no stranger to arguments grounded in hypotheticals, most famously the rationale for the discussion of the state of nature in the *Discourse on the Origin of Inequality* (3:123).

2. See Evans, "Goin' Up the Country," 33–85. For a detailed description of the socioeconomic context of the rise of the blues, see Lomax, *Land Where the Blues Began*.

3. For a discussion of early African American spirituals, see Floyd, *Power of Black Music*, esp. 39–48. I am grateful to Sandra Graham for her insightful comments on this point.

4. Evans writes, "In 1901 and 1902 Charles Peabody, excavating an archeological site near the Delta community of Stovall, noted that his black workers often sang improvised songs to guitar accompaniment about everyday life, love, hard luck, and good times.... Around the same time, folklorist Gates Thomas heard blues in south Texas, including variants of lines and tunes encountered by Charles Peabody in Mississippi and recalled by Jelly Roll Morton from New Orleans" ("Goin' Up the Country," 34–35).

5. For a very clear presentation of the formal structure of the blues, see Evans, *NPR Curious Listener's Guide*, esp. 83–97. I borrow the term "pitch area" from Evan's very apt description of the neutral third and other "blue notes."

6. Ibid., 94–95.

7. Charters, *Country Blues*. The book was originally released with a selection of songs from "race records," the subsidiaries of large recording companies that originally recorded African American blues artists for an African American audience during the 1920s and 1930s. These recordings were unknown to the majority of white America. In addition to Charters, Alan Lomax, working for the Library of Congress, documented early rural blues in field recordings. He also made this music accessible to a white audience.

8. Among the artists who had second careers late in life because of Charters's work: Son House, Lightnin' Hopkins, Mississippi Fred McDowell, Mississippi John Hurt, Skip James, Robert Wilkins, Sleepy John Estes, and Robert Pete Williams.

9. For a detailed analysis of compositional technique and tradition in the folk blues, see Evans, *Big Road Blues*.

10. In the introduction to *Children of the Blues*, Art Tipaldi credits the people he interviewed. They "allowed me to hear how musical conversations breathe. They have demonstrated the blues paradox that less is fundamentally more. They have opened my eyes to understand how the more spaces you leave, the more impact it has when you do play. They have laid bare that musically the blues is focused on tension and release" (8).

11. Evans, *Curious Listener's Guide*, 95.

12. For an example of this style, listen to "Death Letter," music and lyrics Eddie "Son" House, recorded April 1965, New York City. Son House, *Son House: The Original Delta Blues* (Columbia, 1998).

13. One indication of the community of listeners implied by blues is the use of shifting forms of address. Lyrics often move from second- to third-person forms. One example is in Memphis Minnie's "Me and My Chauffeur," in which she sings: "Won't you be my chauffeur; (2) / I wants him to drive me, / I wants him to drive me downtown; / Yes he drives so easy / I can't turn him down." The signifying is emphasized by the change of address.

14. The famous opening of the *Confessions* underscores both his uniqueness and the worthiness of laying his soul bare to his "semblables" (1:5).

15. The lyrics to Leroy Carr's "Blues Before Sunrise" provide a good example of the lack of narrative detail in blues. "I have the blues before sunrise, tears standing in my eyes; (2) / It was a miserable feeling, now babe, a feeling I do despise. / I have to leave, leave you baby, because you know you done me wrong (2) / I'm gonna pack up and leave you darling and break up my happy home."

16. For the uninitiated listener, I recommend the opening guitar solo on Stevie Ray Vaughan's "Texas Flood" as a good example of obvious blue notes. *Stevie Ray Vaughan and Double Trouble: Greatest Hits* (Epic, 1995).

17. The guitarist Bob Brozman attributes a similar kind of tension in the blues to the play between diatonic and modal scales: "The 12-bar blues, with the three chords as we know them today, did not develop overnight. It took literally a generation for black guitarists in Mississippi to figure that out. African musicians came from a modal culture, not a diatonic one. So the earliest blues, like Charley Patton's 'When Your Way Gets Dark' and stuff like that, are one-chord blues. You can feel the 12-bar structure, and you can actually take the melodies he sings and put the three chords of the blues under them, but in fact, it's just one chord and it's modal. So I look at the history of the blues as kind of a struggle of a modal people to get their heads around the idea of a diatonic instrument and diatonic music." Quoted by Matt Blackett in *Guitar Player*, May 2009, 19.

18. Evans, *Curious Listener's Guide*, 89.

19. Robert Johnson provides among the best examples of the combination of secular and spiritual transport in early blues. See the lyrics of "Cross Roads Blues," for example: "I went down to the crossroad, fell down on my knees (2) / Asked the lord above 'Have mercy now, save poor Bob if you please' / Yeeooo, standin' at the crossroad, tried to flag a ride (2) / Didn't nobody seem to know me babe, everybody pass me by." *Robert Johnson: The Complete Recordings* (Columbia, 1999).

20. See Oliver, *Yonder Come the Blues*.

# BIBLIOGRAPHY

Agnew, Vanessa. "Listening to Others: Eighteenth-Century Encounters in Polynesia and Their Reception in German Musical Thought." *Eighteenth-Century Studies* 41, no. 2 (2008): 165–88.
———. "A Scots Orpheus in the South Seas: Encounter Music on Cook's Second Voyage." *Journal for Maritime Research* 3, no. 1 (2001): 1–27.
Althusser, Louis. "The Social Contract (The Discrepancies)." In Bloom, *Jean-Jacques Rousseau*, 83–117.
Anderson, Wilda. "Encyclopedic Topologies." *MLN* 101, no. 4 (1986): 912–29.
Anthony, James R. *French Baroque Music from Beaujoyeulx to Rameau*. New York: W. W. Norton, 1974.
Attali, Jacques. *Bruits: Essai sur l'économie politique de la musique*. Paris: Presses universitaires de France/Fayard, 2001.
Auld, Louis E. "'Dealing in Shepherds': The Pastoral Ploy in Nascent French Opera." In Cowart, *French Musical Thought*, 53–79.
Barry, Barbara R. *Musical Time: The Sense of Order*. Harmonologia Series No. 5. Stuyvesant, N.Y.: Pendragon, 1990.
Baud-Bovy, Samuel. "Le 'genre enharmonique' a-t-il existé?" *Revue de musicologie* 72, no. 1 (1986): 5–21.
Baudelaire, Charles. *The Painter of Modern Life and Other Essays*. Translated by Jonathan Mayne. London: Phaidon, 1964.
Becker, Skip. "An Essay on the History of Tuning—Part IX." *Piano Technicians Journal* 41, no. 5 (1998): 31–34.
Bemetzrieder, Anton. *Leçons de clavecin et principes d'harmonie* (1771). New York: Broude Brothers, 1966.
Benoit, Marcelle. *Dictionnaire de la musique en France aux XVIIe et XVIIIe siècles*. Paris: Fayard, 1992.
Benrekassa, Georges. "La pratique philosophique de Diderot dans l'article 'Encyclopédie' de *l'Encyclopédie*." *Stanford French Review* 8, nos. 2–3 (1984): 189–212.
Berger, Karol. *Bach's Cycle, Mozart's Arrow: An Essay on the Origins of Musical Modernity*. Berkeley: University of California Press, 2007.
Bernasconi, Robert. "No More Stories Good or Bad: De Man's Criticisms of Derrida on Rousseau." In *Derrida: A Critical Reader*, edited by David Wood, 137–66. Oxford: Blackwell, 1992.
Bloom, Allan, ed. *Jean-Jacques Rousseau*. New York: Chelsea House, 1988.
———. "Rousseau's Critique of Liberal Constitutionalism." In *The Legacy of Rousseau*, edited by Clifford Orwin and Nathan Tarcov, 143–67. Chicago: University of Chicago Press, 1997.
Borrel, Eugène. *L'interprétation de la musique française (de Lully à la révolution)*. Paris: Félix Alcan, 1934. Reprint, New York: AMS, 1978.

Bowie, Andrew. *Aesthetics and Subjectivity from Kant to Nietzsche.* 2nd ed. Manchester: Manchester University Press, 2003.
Bronson, Bertrand. "Mrs. Brown and the Ballad." In Bertrand Bronson, *The Ballad as Song*, 64–78. Berkeley: University of California Press, 1969.
Burke, Peter. "Performing History: The Importance of Occasions." *Rethinking History: The Journal of Theory and Practice* 9, no.1 (2005): 35–52.
de Buzon, Frédéric. "Musique et notation: Remarques sur le *Projet concernant de nouveaux signes pour la musique.*" In *Rousseau et les sciences*, edited by Bernadette Bensaude-Vincent and Bruno Bernardi, 21–32. Paris, L'Harmattan, 2003.
Byford, Andy. "The Figure of the 'Spectator' in the Theoretical Writings of Brecht, Diderot, and Rousseau." *Symposium* 56, no. 1 (2002): 25–42.
Caplan, Jay. *Framed Narratives: Diderot's Genealogy of the Beholder.* Minneapolis: University of Minnesota Press, 1985.
Cassirer, Ernst. *The Question of Jean-Jacques Rousseau.* 2nd ed. Edited and translated by Peter Gay. New Haven: Yale University Press, 1989.
———. *The Philosophy of the Enlightenment.* Translated by Fritz C. A. Koelln and James P. Pettegrove. Princeton: Princeton University Press, 1951.
Charters, Samuel. *The Country Blues.* New York: Da Capo Press, 1975.
Chartier, Roger. "Texts, Symbols, and Frenchness." *Journal of Modern History* 57, no. 4 (1985): 682–95.
Christensen, Thomas. "Eighteenth-Century Science and the *Corps Sonore*: The Scientific Background to Rameau's Principle of Harmony." *Journal of Music Theory* 31, no. 1 (1987): 23–50.
———. *Rameau and Musical Thought in the Enlightenment.* Cambridge: Cambridge University Press, 1993.
Chua, Daniel K. L. *Absolute Music and the Construction of Meaning.* Cambridge: Cambridge University Press, 1999.
Clapton, Eric. *Clapton: The Autobiography.* New York: Broadway, 2007.
Cohen, Albert. "Rameau, Equal Temperament, and the Academy of Lyon: A Controversy Revisited." In Cowart, *French Musical Thought*, 121–27.
Cohen, David E. "The 'Gift of Nature': Musical 'Instinct' and Musical Cognition in Rameau." In *Music Theory and Natural Order from the Renaissance to the Early Twentieth Century*, edited by Suzannah Clark and Alexander Rehding, 68–92. Cambridge: Cambridge University Press, 2001.
Coleman, Patrick. "Rousseau and Preromanticism: Anticipation and Oeuvre." *Yale French Studies* 66 (1984): 67–82.
Condillac, Etienne Bonnot de. *Essai sur l'origine des connaissances humaines précédé de l'archéologie du frivole.* Paris: Galilée, 1973.
Cook, Malcolm. *Fictional France: Social Reality in the French Novel, 1775–1800.* Oxford: Berg, 1993.
Cook, Nicholas. *Music, Imagination, and Culture.* Oxford: Oxford University Press, 1990.
Costelloe, Timothy M. "The Theatre of Morals: Culture and Community in Rousseau's *Lettre à M. d'Alembert.*" *Eighteenth-Century Life* 27, no. 1 (2003): 52–71.
Coudreuse, Anne. *Le goût des larmes au XVIIIe siècle.* Paris: Presses universitaires de France, 1999.
Cowart, Georgia, ed. *French Musical Thought, 1600–1800.* Ann Arbor: UMI Research Press, 1989.
D'Alembert, Jean LeRond. "Discours préliminaire aux éléments de musique théorique et pratique suivant les principes de M. Rameau éclaircis, développés et simplifiés par M. D'Alembert." Reprinted in Kintzler, *Jean-Philippe Rameau*, 193–207.

Darnton, Robert. *The Great Cat Massacre and Other Episodes in French Cultural History.* New York: Vintage Books, 1985.
———. "The Symbolic Element in History." *The Journal of Modern History* 58, no. 1 (1986): 218–34.
Dauphin, Claude. *La musique au temps des Encyclopédistes.* Paris: Centre international d'étude du XVIIIe siècle, 2001.
———. "L'origine du conflit Rameau-Rousseau dans les théories de Pythagore et Aristoxène." In Grant and Stewart, *Rousseau and the Ancients,* 57–67.
Delaney, James. *Rousseau and the Ethics of Virtue.* New York: Continuum, 2006.
de Man, Paul. *Allegories of Reading: Figural Language in Rousseau, Nietzsche, Rilke, and Proust.* New Haven: Yale University Press, 1979.
———. *Blindness and Insight: Essays in the Rhetoric of Contemporary Criticism.* 2nd ed. Minneapolis: University of Minnesota Press, 1983.
De Nora, Tia. *Music in Everyday Life.* Cambridge: Cambridge University Press, 2000.
Derrida, Jacques. *Of Grammatology.* Translated by Gayatri Chakravorty Spivak. Baltimore: Johns Hopkins University Press, 1974.
Descartes, René. *Les passions de l'âme.* Edited by Geneviève Rodis-Lewis. Paris: Vrin, 1964.
Diderot, Denis, and Jean LeRond d'Alembert, eds. *Encyclopédie ou dictionnaire raisonné des sciences, des arts et des métiers.* 17 vols. Online at ARTFL, http://artfl.uchicago.edu/cgibin/philologic31/getobject.pl?c.120:150:2.encyclopedie1207.
Didier, Béatrice. "Musique primitive et musique extra-européenne chez Rousseau et quelques écrivains du XVIIIe siècle." In *L'homme des Lumières et la découverte de l'autre,* edited by D. Droixhe and P.-P. Gossiaux, 123–33. Brussels: Editions de l'Université de Bruxelles, 1985.
———. "Le rythme musical dans *l'Encyclopédie* et chez Rousseau." *Studies on Voltaire and the Eighteenth Century* 265 (1989): 1405–9.
Donakowski, Conrad L. *A Muse for the Masses: Ritual and Music in an Age of Democratic Revolution, 1770–1870.* Chicago: University of Chicago Press, 1972.
Dugan, C. N., and Tracy B. Strong. "Music, Politics, Theater, and Representation." In Riley, *Cambridge Companion to Rousseau,* 329–64.
Epstein, David. *Shaping Time: Music, the Brain, and Performance.* New York: Schirmer, 1995.
Evans, David. *Big Road Blues: Tradition and Creativity in the Folk Blues.* Berkeley: University of California Press, 1982.
———. "Goin' Up the Country: Blues in Texas and the Deep South." In *Nothing but the Blues: The Music and the Musicians,* edited by Lawrence Cohn, 33–85. New York: Abbeville Press, 1993.
———. *The NPR Curious Listener's Guide to the Blues.* New York: Pedigree Books, 2005.
Fernandez, James. "Historians Tell Tales: Of Cartesian Cats and Gallic Cockfights." *Journal of Modern History* 60, no. 1 (1988): 113–27.
Ferry, Luc. *Homo Aestheticus: The Invention of Taste in the Democratic Age.* Translated by Robert de Loaiza. Chicago: University of Chicago Press, 1993.
Finn, Neil, and Tim Finn. "Chocolate Cake." *Woodface.* Crowded House. Hollywood: Capitol Records, 1991.
Fleming, Chris, and John O'Carroll. "In Memoriam: Jacques Derrida (1930–2004)." *Anthropological Quarterly* 78, no. 1 (2005): 137–50.
Floyd, Samuel A., Jr. *The Power of Black Music: Interpreting Its History from Africa to the United States.* New York: Oxford University Press, 1995.
Foucault, Michel. *The Order of Things: An Archeology of the Human Sciences.* New York: Vintage, 1970.

---. "What Is Enlightenment?" In *Ethics: Subjectivity and Truth*, edited by Paul Rabinow, translated by Robert Hurley and others, 303–19. New York: The New Press, 1997.
Fried, Michael. *Absorption and Theatricality: Painting and Beholder in the Age of Diderot*. Berkeley: University of California Press, 1980.
Garver, Newton. "Derrida on Rousseau on Writing." *The Journal of Philosophy* 74, no. 11 (1977): 663–73.
Gearhart, Suzanne. *The Open Boundary of History and Fiction: A Critical Approach to the French Enlightenment*. Princeton: Princeton University Press, 1984.
Gessele, Cynthia. "The Institutionalization of Music Theory in France: 1764–1802." Ph.D. diss., Princeton University, 1989.
Grant, Ruth, and Philip Stewart, eds. *Rousseau and the Ancients / Rousseau et les Anciens*. Pensée Libre No. 8. Montreal: North American Association for the Study of Jean-Jacques Rousseau, 2001.
Habermas, Jürgen. "Modernity: An Unfinished Project." In *Critical Theory: The Essential Readings*, edited by David Ingram and Julia Simon-Ingram, 342–56. New York: Paragon House, 1991.
---. "Towards a Theory of Communicative Competence." *Inquiry* 13 (1970): 360–75.
---. "What Is Universal Pragmatics?" In *Communication and the Evolution of Society*, translated by Thomas McCarthy, 1–68. Boston: Beacon, 1979.
Haeringer, Etienne. *L'esthétique de l'opéra en France au temps de Jean-Philippe Rameau*. Oxford: Voltaire Foundation, 1990.
Harrison, Frank. *Time, Place, and Music: An Anthology of Ethnomusicological Observation, c. 1550 to c. 1800*. Amsterdam: Frits Knuf, 1973.
Heartz, Daniel. *From Garrick to Gluck: Essays on Opera in the Age of Enlightenment*. Edited by John A. Rice. New York: Pendragon, 2004.
---. "Italian by Intention, French of Necessity: Rousseau's *Le devin du village*." In *Echos de France et d'Italie: Liber amicorum Yves Gérard*, edited by Marie-Claire Mussat, Jean Mongrédien, and Jean-Michel Nectoux, 31–46. Paris: Buchet/Chastel Société française de musicologie, 1997.
---. *Music in European Capitals: The Galant Style, 1720–1780*. New York: W. W. Norton, 2003.
Houle, George. *Meter in Music, 1600–1800: Performance, Perception, and Notation*. Bloomington: Indiana University Press, 1987.
Hughes, Rubert, ed. *The Musical Guide*. New York: McClure Phillips, 1903.
Hyer, Brian. "'Sighing Branches': Prosopopoeia in Rameau's 'Pigmalion.'" *Music Analysis* 13, no. 1 (1994): 7–50.
Irving, David. "The Pacific in the Minds and Music of Enlightenment Europe." *Eighteenth-Century Music* 2, no. 2 (2005): 205–29.
Isacoff, Stuart. *Temperament: The Idea That Solved Music's Greatest Riddle*. New York: Alfred A. Knopf, 2002.
Isherwood, Robert M. "The Conciliatory Partisan of Musical Liberty: Jean LeRond d'Alembert, 1717–1783." In Cowart, *French Musical Thought*, 95–119.
Jacobi, Erwin R., and Robert E. De Crue. "A l'occasion du bi-centenaire de la mort de J.-Ph. Rameau, 'Vérités intéressantes': Le dernier manuscrit de Jean-Philippe Rameau († à Paris, le 12-IX-1764)." *Revue de musicologie* 50, no. 128 (1964): 76–109.
Jauss, Hans Robert. "The Literary Process of Modernism from Rousseau to Adorno." *Cultural Critique* 11 (Winter 1988–89): 27–61.
Johnson, James H. "The Encyclopedists and the *Querelle des bouffons*: Reason and the Enlightenment of Sentiment." *Eighteenth-Century Life* 10 (1986): 12–27.

———. *Listening in Paris: A Cultural History*. Berkeley: University of California Press, 1995.
Jones, Tom. "Language Origins and Poetic Encounters in Rousseau, Shaftesbury, Smith, and Ferguson." *Forum for Modern Language Studies* 42, no. 4 (2006): 395–411.
Kahn, Douglas. "The Sound of Music." In *The Auditory Culture Reader*, edited by Michael Bull and Les Back, 77–90. Oxford: Berg, 2003.
Kant, Immanuel. *Critique of Judgment*. Translated by J. H. Bernard. New York: Hafner, 1951.
Kavanagh, Thomas M. "Patterns of the Ideal in Rousseau's Political and Linguistic Thought." Reprinted in Scott, *Jean-Jacques Rousseau*, 4:7–24.
Kelly, Christopher. *Rousseau as Author: Consecrating One's Life to the Truth*. Chicago: University of Chicago Press, 2003.
———. "'To Persuade Without Convincing': The Language of Rousseau's Legislator." *American Journal of Poltical Science* 31, no. 2 (1987): 321–35.
Kennedy, Emmet. *A Cultural History of the French Revolution*. New Haven: Yale University Press, 1989.
Kintzler, Catherine. *Jean-Philippe Rameau: Splendeur et naufrage de l'esthétique du plaisir à l'âge classique*. Paris: Minerve, 1988.
Kintzler, Catherine, and Jean-Claude Malgoire, eds. *Jean-Philippe Rameau: Musique raisonnée*. Paris: Stock, 1980.
Kleinman, Sidney. "L'enseignement musical chez Rousseau: Sur la voie de la composition." In *Rousseau, l'Emile, et la Révolution*, edited by Robert Thiéry, 525–34. Paris: Universitas, 1992.
Kumbier, William A. "Rousseau's *Lettre sur la musique française*." *Stanford French Review* 1–2 (Fall–Winter 1982): 221–37.
Laborde, Jean Benjamin de. *Essai sur la musique ancienne et moderne*. 1780. 3 vols. New York: AMS, 1978.
LaCapra, Dominique. "Chartier, Darnton, and the Great Symbol Massacre." *Journal of Modern History* 60, no. 1 (1988): 95–112.
Lanson, Gustave. *Histoire de la littérature française*. 8th ed. Paris: Hachette, 1903.
Launay, Denise, ed. *La querelle des bouffons: Textes de pamphlets*. 3 vols. Geneva: Minkoff, 1973.
Lefebvre, Philippe. *L'esthétique de Rousseau*. Paris: Sedes, 1997.
Lévi-Strauss, Claude. *Conversations with Claude Lévi-Strauss*. Translated by John and Doreen Weightman. London: Cape, 1970.
———. *Tristes Tropiques*. Translated by John and Doreen Weightman. New York: Penguin, 1973.
Lomax, Alan. *The Land Where the Blues Began*. New York: New Press, 1993.
Love, Nancy. *Musical Democracy*. Albany: State University of New York Press, 2006.
Lully, Jean-Baptiste. *Armide*. New York: Broude Brothers, 1971.
Lyotard, Jean-François. *La condition postmoderne: Rapport sur le savoir*. Paris: Minuit, 1979.
———. "Le sublime à présent." *PO&SIE* 34 (1985): 97–116.
Manning, Rita C. "Rousseau's Other Woman: Collette in 'Le devin du village.'" *Hypatia* 16, no. 2 (2001): 27–42.
Marejko, Jan. *Jean-Jacques Rousseau et la dérive totalitaire*. Lausanne: Editions de l'age d'homme, 1984.
Mason, Laura. *Singing the French Revolution: Popular Culture and Politics, 1787–1799*. Ithaca: Cornell University Press, 1996.
Masters, Roger D. *The Political Philosophy of Rousseau*. Princeton: Princeton University Press, 1968.

May, Georges. *Le dilemme du roman au XVIIIe siècle: Etude sur les rapports du roman et de la critique (1715–1761)*. New Haven: Yale University Press, 1963.
McDonald, Christie V. "En-harmoniques: L'anagramme de Rousseau." *Etudes françaises* 17, nos. 3/4 (1981): 7–21.
———. "Jacques Derrida's Reading of Rousseau." *Eighteenth Century: Theory and Interpretation* 20 (1979): 82–95.
McNeill, William H. *Keeping Together in Time: Dance and Drill in Human History*. Cambridge: Harvard University Press, 1995.
Mercier-Faivre, Anne-Marie, and Yannick Seité. "Le jazz à la lumière de Jean-Jacques Rousseau." *L'Homme* 158–59 (2001): 35–52.
Miller, J. Hillis. "Performativity as Performance / Performativity as Speech Act: Derrida's Special Theory of Performativity." *South Atlantic Quarterly* 106, no. 2 (2007): 219–35.
Mitchell, W. J. T. Preface to "The Future of Criticism—A Critical Inquiry Symposium." *Critical Inquiry* 30, no. 2 (2004): 324–35.
Mongrédien, Jean. *French Music from the Enlightenment to Romanticism, 1789–1830*. Translated by Sylvain Frémaux. Portland, Ore.: Amadeus Press, 1996.
Montesquieu, Charles Secondat, Baron de. *Considérations sur les causes de la grandeur des Romains et de leur décadence*. Paris: Garnier, 1967.
———. *Œuvres complètes*. 2 vols. Paris: Gallimard, 1949–51.
Mostefai, Ourida. *Le citoyen de Genève et la République des lettres*. New York: Peter Lang, 2003.
Mylne, Vivienne. *The Eighteenth-Century French Novel: Techniques of Illusion*. 2nd ed. Cambridge: Cambridge University Press, 1981.
Nancy, Jean-Luc. "L'offrande sublime." *PO&SIE* 30 (1984): 76–103.
Neal, Simon. "The Art and Science of Keyboard Temperament." *Contemporary Music Review* 19, no. 4 (2000): 159–71.
Neidleman, Jason. "Rousseau's General Will: Anachronism, Contradiction, Tragedy." In Grant and Stewart, *Rousseau and the Ancients*, 198–211.
Nettl, Bruno. *Folk and Traditional Music of the Western Continents*. 3rd ed. Englewood Cliffs, N.J.: Prentice Hall, 1990.
Neumann, Frederick. *Ornamentation in Baroque and Post-Baroque Music with Special Emphasis on J. S. Bach*. Princeton: Princeton University Press, 1978.
O'Dea, Michael. *Jean-Jacques Rousseau: Music, Illusion, and Desire*. New York: St. Martin's Press, 1995.
Oliver, Paul. *Screening the Blues: Aspects of the Blues Tradition*. New York: Da Capo, 1968.
———. *Yonder Come the Blues: The Evolution of a Genre*. Cambridge: Cambridge University Press, 2001.
Osipovich, David. "What Rousseau Teaches Us About Live Theatrical Performance." *The Journal of Aesthetics and Art Criticism* 62, no. 4 (2004): 355–62.
Paige, Nicholas. "Rousseau's Readers Revisited: The Aesthetics of *La Nouvelle Héloïse*." *Eighteenth-Century Studies* 42, no. 1 (2008): 131–54.
Pateman, Carole. *The Disorder of Women: Democracy, Feminism, and Political Theory*. Stanford: Stanford University Press, 1989.
———. *The Sexual Contract*. Stanford: Stanford University Press, 1988.
Paul, Charles B. "Music and Ideology: Rameau, Rousseau, and 1789." *Journal of the History of Ideas* 32, no. 3 (1971): 395–410.
Perry, Ruth. "'The Finest Ballads': Women's Oral Traditions in Eighteenth-Century Scotland." *Eighteenth-Century Life* 32, no. 2 (2008): 81–97.
Pougin, Arthur. *Jean-Jacques Rousseau, musicien*. Paris: Librairie Fischbacher, 1901.

Proust, Jacques. "Diderot et le système des connaissances humaines." *Studies on Voltaire and the Eighteenth Century* 256 (1988): 117–27.
Rameau, Jean-Philippe. *Code de musique pratique* (1760). New York: Broude Brothers, 1965.
———. *The Complete Theoretical Writings of Jean-Philippe Rameau*. Edited by Erwin R. Jacobi. 6 vols. New York: American Institute of Musicology, 1967–72.
———. *Génération harmonique*. Paris: Prault fils, 1737. Reprint, New York: Broude Brothers, 1966. Online at http://www.chmtl.indiana.edu/tfm/18th/RAMGEN_TEXT.html.
———. *Nouveau systême de musique theorique, où l'on découvre le principe de toutes les regles necessaires à la pratique, pour servir d'introduction au Traité de l'harmonie*. Paris: L'Imprimerie de Jean-Baptiste-Christophe Ballard, 1726. Reprinted in Rameau, *Complete Theoretical Writings*, vol. 2. Online at http://www.chmtl.indiana.edu/tfm/18th/RAMNOU_TEXT.html.
———. *Observations sur notre instinct pour la musique, et sur son principe, où les moyens de reconnoître l'un par l'autre, conduisent à pouvoir se rendre raison avec certitude des différens effets de cet art*. Paris: Prault fils, 1754. Reprinted in Jean-Philippe Rameau, *Complete Theoretical Writings*, vol. 3. Online at http://www.chmtl.indiana.edu/tfm/18th/RAMOBS_TEXT.html.
———. *Traité de l'harmonie réduite à ses principes naturels*. Paris: Jean-Baptiste-Christophe Ballard, 1722. Reprint, New York: Broude Brothers, 1965. Online at http://www.chmtl.indiana.edu/tfm/18th/RAMTRA1_TEXT.html.
Rebejkow, Jean-Christophe. "Rousseau et l'opéra-comique: Les raisons d'un rejet." *The Romanic Review* 89, no. 2 (1998): 161–85.
Rehding, Alexander. "Rousseau, Rameau, and Enharmonic Furies in the French Enlightenment." *Journal of Music Theory* 49, no. 1 (2005): 141–80.
Reiss, Timothy J. *Knowledge, Discovery, and Imagination in Early Modern Europe: The Rise of Aesthetic Rationalism*. Cambridge: Cambridge University Press, 1997.
Riley, Patrick, ed. *The Cambridge Companion to Rousseau*. Cambridge: Cambridge University Press, 2001.
Robinson, Philip. "Jean-Jacques Rousseau, Aunt Suzanne, and Solo Song." *The Modern Language Review* 73, no. 2 (1978): 291–96.
———. *Jean-Jacques Rousseau's Doctrine of the Arts*. Bern: Peter Lang, 1984.
Rousseau, Jean-Jacques. *The Confessions*. Translated by J. M. Cohen. New York: Penguin, 1953.
———. *Des consolations des misères de ma vie, ou recueil d'airs, romances, et duos*. Paris: De Roullede de la Chevardienne, 1781.
———. *Correspondance complète*. Edited by R. A. Leigh. 15 vols. Geneva: Institut et musée Voltaire, 1965–98.
———. *Essay on the Origin of Language and Writings Related to Music*. Translated and edited by John T. Scott. In *The Collected Writings of Rousseau*, edited by Roger D. Masters and Christopher Kelly, 289–336. 8 vols. Hanover: University Press of New England, 1998.
———. *Œuvres complètes*. Edited by Bernard Gagnebin. 5 vols. Paris: Gallimard, 1959–95.
———. *The Social Contract and Discourse on the Origin of Inequality*. Edited by Lester G. Crocker. New York: Simon and Schuster, 1967.
Rumph, Steven C. "The Sense of Touch in *Don Giovanni*." *Music and Letters* 88, no. 4 (2007): 561–88.

Schmidt, Leigh Eric. "Hearing Loss." In *The Auditory Culture Reader*, edited by Michael Bull and Les Back, 41–59. Oxford: Berg, 2003.
Schneider, Herbert. "Rameau et la tradition lulliste." In *Jean-Philippe Rameau: Colloque international organisé par la Société Rameau Dijon—21–24 septembre 1983*, edited by Jérôme de la Gorce, 287–306. Paris: Champion-Slatkine, 1987.
Scott, John T. "The Harmony Between Rousseau's Musical Theory and His Philosophy." *The Journal of the History of Ideas* 59, no. 2 (1998): 287–308.
———, ed. *Jean-Jacques Rousseau: Critical Assessments of Leading Political Philosophers*. 12 vols. London: Routledge, 2006.
———. "The Play of the Passions: Music, Mores, and Rousseau's *Lettre à d'Alembert*." In *Rousseau on Arts and Politics / Autour de la Lettre à d'Alembert*, edited by Melissa Butler, 77–89. Ottawa: North American Association for the Study of Jean-Jacques Rousseau, 1997.
Shklar, Judith. *Men and Citizens: A Study of Rousseau's Social Theory*. Cambridge: Cambridge University Press, 1969.
Siebers, Tobin. "Ethics in the Age of Rousseau: From Lévi-Strauss to Derrida." *MLN* 10, no. 4 (1985): 758–79.
Simon, Julia. *Beyond Contractual Morality: Ethics, Law, and Literature in Eighteenth-Century France*. Rochester: University of Rochester Press, 2000.
———. "Diverting Water in Rousseau: Technology, the Sublime, and the Quotidian." *The Eighteenth Century: Theory and Interpretation* 53, no. 1 (2012): 73–97.
———. *Mass Enlightenment: Critical Studies in Rousseau and Diderot*. Albany: State University of New York Press, 1995.
———. "Militarisme et vertu chez Rousseau." In *Jean-Jacques Rousseau, politique et nation: Actes du IIe colloque international de Montmorency*, edited by Robert Thiéry, 337–42. Paris: Honoré Champion, 2001.
———. "Music and the Performance of Community in Rousseau." In *Musique et langage chez Rousseau*, edited by Claude Dauphin, 192–200. Oxford: Voltaire Foundation, 2004.
Smythe, Lillian C. *The Guardian of Marie-Antoinette: Letters from the Comte de Mercy-Argenteau, Austrian Ambassador to the Court of Versailles, to Marie Thérèse, Empress of Austria, 1770–1780*. 2 vols. 2nd ed. London: Hutchison, 1902.
Sosso, Paola. *Jean-Jacques Rousseau: Imagination, illusions, chimères*. Paris: Honoré Champion, 1999.
Starobinski, Jean. *Jean-Jacques Rousseau: La transparence et l'obstacle*. Paris: Gallimard, 1971.
Strong, Tracy B. *Jean-Jacques Rousseau: The Politics of the Ordinary*. Thousand Oaks, Calif.: Sage Publications, 1994.
———. "Music, Politics, Theater, and Representation." In Riley, *Cambridge Companion to Rousseau*, 329–64.
———. "Music, the Passions, and Political Freedom in Rousseau." In *Rousseau and Freedom*, edited by Stanley Hoffmann and Christie McDonald, 92–110. Cambridge: Cambridge University Press, 2010.
———. "Rousseau: Music, Language, and Politics." In *Speaking of Music: Addressing the Sonorous*, edited by Keith Chapin and Andrew H. Clark. New York: Fordham University Press, 2013.
———. "The Self Knowing the Self in the World of Jean-Jacques Rousseau." In *Liberalism Without Illusions: Essays on Liberal Theory and the Political Vision of Judith N. Shklar*, edited by Bernard Yack, 111–23. Chicago: University of Chicago Press, 1996.

———. "Theatricality, Public Space, and Music in Rousseau." *SubStance* 25, no. 2, special issue 80, "Politics on Stage" (1996): 110–27.
Swenson, James. *On Jean-Jacques Rousseau: Considered as One of the First Authors of the Revolution*. Stanford: Stanford University Press, 2000.
Talmon, J. L. *The Origins of Totalitarian Democracy*. New York: Frederick A. Praeger, 1960.
Terdiman, Richard. *Body and Story: The Ethics and Practice of Theoretical Conflict*. Baltimore: Johns Hopkins University Press, 2005.
———. *Present Past: Modernity and the Memory Crisis*. Ithaca: Cornell University Press, 1993.
Thomas, Downing A. *Aesthetics of Opera in the Ancien Régime, 1647–1785*. Cambridge: Cambridge University Press, 2002.
———. *Music and the Origins of Language: Theories from the French Enlightenment*. Cambridge: Cambridge University Press, 1995.
Tiersot, Julien. "Concerning Jean-Jacques Rousseau, the Musician." *The Musical Quarterly* 17, no. 3 (1931): 341–59.
———. *Jean-Jacques Rousseau*. Paris: Félix Alcan, 1920.
Tipaldi, Art. *Children of the Blues: Forty-nine Musicians Shaping a New Blues Tradition*. San Francisco: Backbeat Books, 2002.
Trachtenberg, Zev. *Making Citizens: Rousseau's Political Theory of Culture*. London: Routledge, 1993.
———. "Subject and Citizen: Hobbes and Rousseau on Sovereignty and Self." In *Jean-Jacques Rousseau and the Sources of the Self*, edited by Timothy O'Hagan, 85–105. Brookfield: Avebury, 1997.
Verba, Cynthia. "Jean-Jacques Rousseau: Radical and Traditional Views in the *Dictionnaire de musique*." *The Journal of Musicology* 7, no. 3 (1989): 308–26.
———. *Music and the French Enlightenment: Reconstruction of a Dialogue, 1750–1764*. Oxford: Clarendon Press, 1993.
Vila, Anne C. *Enlightenment and Pathology: Sensibility in the Literature and Medicine of Eighteenth-Century France*. Baltimore: Johns Hopkins University Press, 1998.
Waeber, Jacqueline. "'Le devin de la foire'?: Revaluating the Pantomime in Rousseau's *Devin du village*." In *Musique et geste en France de Lully à la Révolution: Etudes sur la musique, le théâtre, et la danse*, edited by Jacqueline Waeber, 149–72. New York: Peter Lang, 2009.
———. *En musique dans le texte: Le mélodrame de Rousseau à Schoenberg*. Paris: Van Dieren, 2005.
———. "Jean-Jacques Rousseau's 'unité de mélodie.'" *Journal of the American Musicological Society* 62, no. 1 (2009): 79–144.
Weber, Shierry. "The Aesthetics of Rousseau's *Pygmalion*." In Bloom, *Jean-Jacques Rousseau*, 65–81.
Wokler, Robert. "Rousseau on Rameau and Revolution." Reprinted in Scott, *Jean-Jacques Rousseau*, 4:25–56.
———. *Social Thought of J. J. Rousseau*. New York: Garland, 1987.
Wyss, André. *Jean-Jacques Rousseau: L'accent de l'écriture*. Boudry-Neuchâtel: Editions de la Baconnière, 1988.
Young, Iris Marion. "Impartiality and the Civic Public: Some Implications of Feminist Critiques of Moral and Political Theory." In *Feminism as Critique*, edited by Seyla Benhabib and Drucilla Cornell, 57–76. Minneapolis: University of Minnesota Press, 1987.

# INDEX

*Abrégé de la musique* (Descartes), 82
accent
   effect on moral being, 32–33
   in language: emotion carried by, 30–32; and melody of speech, 70–71; types of, 30
   in music: coordinating with accent of language, 30–31; emotion carried by, 30–32, 70–71, 120
Adorno, Theodor, 157
*Aesthetica* (Baumgarten), 211 n. 14
aesthetic experience, Rousseau on role of
   anticipation of moderns in, 148
   as healing force in society, 147–48
aesthetic judgment, Kant on, 167
aesthetic judgment of music
   Rameau's standard for, 104, 108
   Rousseau's standard for, 102–3, 108–9, 110–11, 167, 213 n. 48
aesthetic modernity
   celebration of ephemeral in, 157
   emergence of, 148–50, 152–53
   features of in Rousseau's aesthetic theory, 4, 150, 153–58, 160–65, 185
   and individual point of view, emphasis on, 149–50, 153, 159
   redefinition of music's formal qualities required by, 154, 160–65
   as response to elegiac view of present, 156–57, 158–59
   self-consciousness of, 159
   view of nature in, 154
   view of present in, 155–57
aesthetic reception, 38–44
   creation of group response as goal of, 38–39
   of novels, and self-recognition, 42–44
   of theatrical productions, as destructive of general will, 39–42, 192–93 nn. 31, 36–38

aesthetics, as term, 211 n. 14
aesthetic theory
   privileging of specific genres by, 150
   of Rousseau: elegiac view of present in, 9, 115, 117, 122, 125, 155–57, 159; features of aesthetic modernity in, 4, 150, 153–58, 160–65, 185; privileging of music in, 150, 159, 210–11 n. 7
African American music, pre-Civil War, 174. *See also* blues music
Agnew, Vanessa, 128, 205–6 n. 13
agricultural work, in *vendanges* letter in *Julie*
   emotional charge carried by, 135–36, 184
   social harmony of, 135–36, 139–40, 184; singing as source of, 140–43
Alembert, Jean-Baptiste le Rond d', 81–82, 85, 199 n. 20. *See also Encyclopédie* (Diderot and d'Alembert)
Althusser, Louis, 58
animality/humanity dichotomy in Rousseau, Derrida on, 9–10, 189 n. 23
aristocracy, political impact of music on, 143, 144
Aristoxenus, 128
*Armide* (Lully)
   Rameau on instinctive composition ability of, 105
   Rameau-Rousseau debate on, 95–103, 108–9, 111, 181–82, 202 n. 46
   synopsis of, 201 n. 42
arts. *See also* painting and music; performing arts
   Rousseau on corrupting power of, 147
   and values spheres, differentiation of, 156, 169
Attali, Jacques, 204 n. 3
audience response. *See also* group experience of music

audience response (*continued*)
  call and response in blues music, 174, 177–78, 185
  creation of group response as goal of music, 38–39
  to *Le devin du village*, 131–32, 133–34; erotic component of for Rousseau, 134–35; factors affecting, 132–33
  tropes of authenticity and, 131–35
Auld, Louis, on pastoral setting, 133
Austin, J. L., 190 n. 3
authenticity, tropes of in music, 131
  Rousseau's *Le devin du village* and, 131–35
avant-garde aesthetic
  emphasis on unrepeatability in, 212 n. 35
  and mimesis, 211 n. 16

Barry, Barbara, 23–24, 190 n. 5
Baudelaire, Charles, 157
Baumgarten, Alexander Gottlieb, 211 n. 14
Bemetzrieder, Anton, 75
Berger, Karol, 110, 151
Bloom, Allan, 31, 33, 35
blue notes, 174, 179–80
blues music
  call and response in, 174, 177–78, 185
  characteristic structure and lyrics of, 174, 214 n. 17
  community emphasis in: Rousseau's likely sympathy with, 176–78, 179, 185; shifting forms of address and, 214 n. 14
  and creation of social harmony through folk music, 183–85
  emotional power, sources of, 183–84
  as folk music, 183–85
  history and origin of, 173–74, 214 n. 17
  as metaphor for creation of general will, 178–81
  as performance-oriented, 176–77
  privileging of melody over harmony in, 181
  and redemption of individual through art, 185
  social justice themes, Rousseau's likely sympathy with, 175
  tension and release in, 176–77, 214 n. 10
  as vehicle for communication of emotion, 182–83
  as vocal genre, 178–79
Bonald, Louis Gabriel Ambroise, Vicomte de, 187 n. 1

botany, Rousseau's love of, 5
Bourdieu, Pierre, 190 n. 3
Brozman, Bob, 214 n. 17
Burke, Edmund, 187 n. 1

*cabinets de curiosités*, increasing interest in, 3
Cartesian rationalism. *See also esprit de système*
  and aesthetic modernity, 149–50
  of Rameau, Rousseau's critique of, 76
  rise of, 148–49
Cassirer, Ernst, 80–81, 148–49
catharsis, Aristotelian theory of, Rousseau's critique of, 40
Charters, Samuel, 175, 184, 214 n. 7
childhood of Rousseau, emotional charge carried by songs from, 115–16
chord inversion, systematization of by Rameau, 86
Christensen, Thomas, 82, 86, 198 nn. 9, 12, 199 nn. 17–18, 201–2 n. 44, 203 n. 60
Chua, Daniel. K. L., 70, 203 n. 64
Clapton, Eric, 173, 183
classical *episteme*, Foucault on, 84–85, 199 n. 20
*Code de musique pratique* (Rameau), 201 n. 35
Cohen, David E., 86–87
Coleman, Patrick, 155–56
community. *See also* general will
  creation of through music, 74, 168, 177–78; blues music and, 176–78, 179, 185; as communication between moral beings, 52–53, 69–70, 72–73, 167–68, 169–71, 177–78, 185
  origin of music in need for, 35–36, 109–10, 116–17, 118–20, 182–83, 185
  prioritization of in *Du contrat social*, 19
  singing in group and, 69, 74
composition of music
  emotional impact as basis of, in Rousseau, 92, 94, 198
  harmonization of accents of discourse with constraints of harmonic systems in, 30–31
  motives for: Rameau on, 107, 111; Rousseau on, 107, 111–12
  and music as art rather than science, 154
  Rameau on, 104–7, 111
Condillac, Étienne Bonnot de, 31, 191 n. 23, 194 n. 6, 213 n. 45

Index   229

*Confessions* (Rousseau)
  on childhood of Rousseau, emotional charge carried by songs from, 115–16
  on *Le devin du village*, audience response to, 131–32
  as first modern biography, 147
  implicit community underlying, 178
  on Rousseau's love of music, 5–6
  on Rousseau's masquerade as music teacher, 194 n. 5
*Considerations on the Government of Poland* (Rousseau), 36, 39, 143–44
*Consolations des misères de ma vie* (Rousseau), 141–42, 156, 178, 204 n. 64
contentment
  as goal of human existence, 38
  music as avenue to, 38
Cook, Nicholas, 190 n. 6
Copy Register of copied music, 5
*The Country Blues* (Charters), 175, 214 n. 7
Couperin, François, 79
critical reception of Rousseau, history of, 1–2
Crowded House, 75
cultural relativism of music, 52
  Rousseau on, 89, 94–95, 195 n. 12
cultural understanding, music as vehicle for, 184–85
cultures, Montesquieu's topology of, 205 n. 12

"Dans ma cabane obscure" (Rousseau), 141–42, 209–10 n. 49
Darnton, Robert, 42
Dauphin, Claude, 164–65
*De la grammatologie* (Derrida)
  influence on critical reception of Rousseau, 1–2
  on Lévi-Strauss's critique of writing as form of power, 7–8
  on Rousseau's *Essai sur l'origine des langues*, 7–14; impact of, 2, 7, 14–15; on political uses of writing, 7–8; and presence of visual within speech, 14; on privileging of speech over writing in Rousseau, 9–12, 13–14; on song as analogous to painting, 11–12; on structure of supplementarity in Rousseau, 9–10, 13
  and theory wave of 18th-century studies, 2

de Man, Paul
  on Derrida's reading of Rousseau, 187 n. 2, 191–92 n. 27
  and theory wave of 18th-century studies, 2
democracy. *See also* egalitarian society, Enlightenment vision of; social harmony, creation of through folk music
  difficulty of practical application, 47, 48
  idealism of, 47
  Rousseau on, 48
  Rousseau's political use of music and, 56–57, 143
  Rousseau's support for: blues music and, 175; and inclusiveness of musical experience, 8–9, 19, 20, 48, 49–50, 56–57, 66
De Nora, Tia, 204 n. 2
Derrida, Jacques. *See De la grammatologie* (Derrida)
Descartes, René, 82
*Le devin du village* (Rousseau)
  audience response to, 131–32, 133–34; erotic component of for Rousseau, 134–35; factors affecting, 132–33
  "Dans ma cabane obscure" from, 141–42, 209–10 n. 49
  novelty of, 208 nn. 32, 37
  pastoral setting of, 132–33
  reception of, 208 n. 38, 210 n. 51
  tropes of authenticity in music and, 131–35
  use of *romances* in, 141–42
*Dictionnaire de musique* (Rousseau)
  on accent, 30
  "Chanson" article, 55–56
  "Chant" article, 68–69, 118
  "Composition" article, 94
  "*Entonner*" article, 61
  "Genre" article, 128
  "Harmonie" article, 88, 90, 93
  on imitation of emotion in music, 44–45, 163–64
  "Mélodie" article, 70–71
  "Mesure" article, 24–25
  on mimetic power of music, 163–64
  "Musique" article, 120–25
  "Musique" article and Plate N folk airs, 124; and continuum of musical complexity, 130; as primitive form of music, 123–25, 128–30; relative naturalness of, 127–28; shared characteristics of, 122–23, 127–30

Dictionnaire de musique (*continued*)
  "*Rhythme*" article, 26
  "*Romance*," 141
  and Rousseau debate with Rameau, 76
  as Rousseau's last work on music, 5, 87
  "*Tempérament*" article, 67–68, 78–79
  "*Tems*" article, 27
  "*Ton*" article, 62–63
  on tropes of authenticity in music, 131
Didier, Béatrice, 191 n. 23
*Discours sur les sciences et les arts* (Rousseau), 147, 155, 156, 169
*Discours sur l'origine de l'inégalité* (Rousseau)
  Derrida's reading of, 8
  elegiac view of present in, 155
  on emergence of modernity, 156
  genetic logic in, 124–25
  on independence and isolation, 19
  on language and music, origin of, 118, 188 n. 20
  on morality and self-overcoming, 35
  on origin of community, 170
  on pity, 10–11, 53, 203 n. 58
  on transformation from animal to human, 9–10
disinterestedness in aesthetic judgment, in Kant *vs.* Rousseau, 167–68, 213 n. 45
*Dissertation sur la musique moderne* (Rousseau), in chronology of Rousseau's works, 6
dualism in Rousseau
  moral force of music and, 112–13
  and self-overcoming, need for, 37–38
Duchez, Marie-Elisabeth, 190 n. 7
*Du contrat social* (Rousseau)
  critiques of, 187 n. 1
  on democracy, 48
  on general will: and body politic as harmonious group, 55; enforcement of, 195 n. 18; formation of, 34–35, 36, 58–60, 192 nn. 32, 35
  on human limitations, 69
  on individual will, overcoming of, 35, 39
  as origin of modern political theory, 147, 211 n. 8
  primacy accorded to state in, 19
  on transformation from animal to human, 9–10
Dugan, C. N., 157, 213 n. 48

egalitarian society, Enlightenment vision of, 194 n. 4. *See also* democracy

blues music and, 175
and democratizing influence of music, 50
18th century, *esprit systématique* in, 80–81
18th-century studies, theory wave of, 2
elegiac view of present
  in aesthetic theory of Rousseau, 9, 115, 117, 122, 125, 155–57, 159
  as inherent feature of music, 161
  in modernity, 155–57, 212 n. 28; aesthetic modernity as response to, 156–57, 158–59; redemption from, in Rousseau, 147–48, 155–56, 168–71; Rousseau's recognition of, 168–69
*Emile, ou de l'éducation* (Rousseau)
  elegiac view of present in, 155
  on pity, 53
emotion
  carried by language: in accent, 30–32; in rhythm, 29–32
  effect of motion on, 29, 53, 214 n. 17
  in folk music, sources of, 125–27
  impact of music on: accent and, 30–32, 70–71, 120; as basis of composition, 92, 94, 198; blues music and, 182–83; convention-based aspects of, 52; in group experience of musical time, 28–30, 34–38, 45–46, 180–81, 191 n. 19; inability of mathematics to explain, 107–8; and modulation in Lully's *Armide*, 96–103, 182–83, 202 n. 46; musical rhythm/meter as imitation of emotions, 26–33, 44–46, 52, 163–64, 165–66, 176–77; necessity of consonance with theme, 102–3, 108–9; and power to uplift or degrade, 113; primal origin of music and, 51, 112–13, 116–17, 119–20, 203 n. 64; Rameau on, 100–101; and self-recognition, 45; through evocation of memories, 117, 120–22, 125
  transfer of through fiction, 42–44
*Encyclopédie* (Diderot and d'Alembert)
  articles on music by Rousseau: in chronology of Rousseau's works, 6; on rhythm/meter in music, 25
  *Discours préliminaire*, on Rameau, 81–82, 85
  and Enlightenment democratization of knowledge, 194 n. 4
  "*Genre*" article (Rousseau), 128
  "*Musette*" article, 207 n. 29
  and Rousseau debate with Rameau, 76
Enlightenment
  and aesthetic modernism, development of, 152–53, 159

vision of egalitarian society, 194 n. 4; blues music and, 175; and democratizing influence of music, 50
Epstein, David, 28–29, 31–32
equal temperament system, 68
  Rameau as supporter of, 77–78, 80, 92–93, 198 n. 9, 201 n. 38
  Rousseau on, 79–80
*Erreurs sur la musique dans l'Encyclopédie* (Rameau), 6
*esprit de système*
  vs. *esprit systématique*, Rameau debate with Rousseau and, 80–81
  in Rameau, 82–87, 92–93, 198–99 n. 16, 200 n. 32
*esprit systématique*
  vs. *esprit de système*, Rameau debate with Rousseau and, 80–81
  role of explanatory systems in, 107
  in Rousseau, 93, 200 n. 32
*Essai sur l'origine des langues* (Rousseau)
  in chronology of Rousseau's works, 6
  Derrida's reading of, 7–14; impact of, 2, 7, 14–15; on political uses of writing, 7–8; and presence of visual within speech, 14; on privileging of speech over writing in Rousseau, 9–12, 13–14; on song as analogous to painting, 11–12; on structure of supplementarity in Rousseau, 9–10, 13
  elegiac view of present in, 155
  on emotional charge carried by music, 116–17
  on formation of social cohesion, 35–36
  on imitation of emotion in music, 44–45
  on imitation of nature in music, 154
  on language and music as conventional signs, 51, 194 n. 6
  on language as political force, 188–89 n. 20
  on morality and self-overcoming, 35
  on music and painting: Derrida on analogy between, 11–12; Rousseau on distinction between, 12, 22–23
  on music as present-oriented temporal form, 160–61
  music as theme in, 2
  on music's power to move listeners, 23–24
  on origin of language and music, 51, 118–19, 170
  on pity, and capacity for suffering, 53
  privileging of speech over writing in: analogy with performed vs. written music and, 12–14; Derrida's reading of, 9–12, 13–14
  privileging of temporal quality of music in, 22–23
  on sound, ignition of passion through, 31–32
  and speech, instability of, in analogy with performed music, 12–13
ethnomusicology
  vs. musicology, as issue, 205 n. 11
  Rousseau and, 123, 205 n. 11
Evans, David, 174, 177, 179, 213 n. 4
*Examen de deux principes avancés par M. Rameau* (Rousseau), 6, 200 n. 31
experience of music, as group experience in 18th century, 33–34. *See also* emotion, impact of music on

feminist readings of Rousseau, 195 n. 16
Ferry, Luc, 153
fiction, transfer of emotion through, 42–44
*First Discourse* (Rousseau). *See Discours sur les sciences et les arts* (Rousseau)
Floyd, Samuel, Jr., 19, 46
folk music
  blues music as, 183–85
  and continuum of musical complexity, 127–28, 130
  creation of social harmony through: blues music and, 183–85; possibility of in Rousseau, 143–45, 184; in *vendanges* letter in *Julie*, 140–43
  definition of, 205 nn. 10–11
  droning as characteristic of, 130
  emotional content, sources of, 125–27
  as expression of social harmony, in *vendanges* letter in *Julie*, 137–38, 142–43
  naturalness of, 127–28
  as primitive form of music, 123–25
  privileging of melody over harmony in, 126–28
  privileging of pentatonic scale in, 128–29
  rhythms characteristic of, 129–30
  Scottish bagpipe music as example of, 130
  shared characteristics of, 122–23
  in *vendanges* letter in *Julie*: creation of social harmony through, 140–43; erotic component in, 138; as expression of social harmony, 137–38, 142–43; privileging of melody over harmony in, 138–40; as vehicle for correct values, 136–37, 138–40

Foucault, Michel
  on classical *episteme*, 84–85, 199 n. 20
  on *genesis* and *taxinomia*, 89
  on modernist aesthetic, 159
  view of present in, 157
French Revolution
  and critical reception of Rousseau, 1
  Rousseau's influence on, 187 n. 1
fundamental base, Rameau's proposition of, 86–87, 93, 202 nn. 51–52

Gagnebin, Bernard, 5
general will. *See also* community
  as analogous to musical group, 55, 60–66
  Bloom on, 35
  collapse of, and decline of the state, 58
  and conflict, mechanisms for resolving: harmonious union of dissident voices as, 74, 75; metaphors for in music theory, 63–65, 74, 75; public interest as touchstone principle and, 63–65, 75; Rousseau's recognition of need for, 60
  conflicts with individual will, 19, 36–37, 39, 54, 57–60; and forced compliance, 195 n. 18; parallels with tension between melody and harmony, 19–20; periodic attitude adjustments necessary to avoid, 63–65; resolution of, blues music as model for, 179–81; Rousseau's framing of as internalized struggle, 59–60; taming of by group experience of music, 36–38, 45–46
  creation of: aesthetic reception and, 38–44; blues music as metaphor for, 178–81; *Du contrat social* on, 34–35; group experience of musical time and, 34–38, 45–46, 180–81, 191 n. 19; and self-overcoming, 35, 39, 60; shared moral experience as basis of, 35; and suppression of dissent, as issue, 36–37, 39, 54, 57–60; through shared emotional experiences, 36, 38, 45–46
  as general standard analogous to orchestral tuning, 60–65, 179
  as incapable of error, 54
  scholarly debate on, 36, 54
  *vs.* will of all, 54, 57, 65
*Génération harmonique* (Rameau), 78, 83, 92–93
  Rousseau on, 88
genetic logic of cultural development, 124–25

God, role in creation, Rameau on, 106–7
Greeks, ancient
  musical scales, Rousseau on, 128–29
  singing of laws by, 55–56, 195–96 n. 19
group cohesion. *See* general will
group experience of music
  and creation of general will, 34–38, 45–46, 180–81
  and Enlightenment vision of egalitarian society, 50
  as norm in 18th century, 20, 33–34
*The Grove Dictionary of Music*, 141–42

Habermas, Jürgen, 152–53, 156, 157, 159, 169
harmonic theory, Rousseau on, 94, 99, 127, 201 n. 40
harmonic theory of Rameau, 83–87, 199 n. 17, 199–200 n. 22, 200 n. 23, 203 n. 60
  as Cartesian rationalism, 148
  and delimiting of allowable combinations, 94
  flexibility of, 87, 101
  on fundamental base, 86–87, 93, 202 nn. 51–52
  grounding of in nature, 83, 94, 105–7
  metaphysics underlying, 103–7; Rousseau on, 107–8
  privileging of epistemology over aesthetics in, 103–4
  role of composition in, 104–7
  on role of instinct in composition, 105–7, 111
  Rousseau's critique of, 88–92, 94, 98, 101, 126, 200 n. 31
  as standard for assessment of music, 104, 108
  as uncovering of order of nature, 105–7
harmony
  as analogy for political cooperation, 19, 73–74, 75
  appeal of as sensual, 71–72
  as basis of emotion in music, in Rameau, 100–101
  in blues music, as implied template, 181
  as conventional sign system, 126–27
  as European invention, 127
  privileging of melody over: in ancient Greek music, 128–29; in folk music, 126–28
  Rousseau's definition of, 126
  Rousseau's privileging of melody over, 19, 71–72, 73; blues music and, 181;

and conventional nature of music, 52;
and debate on temperament, 76–80;
and Lully's *Armide*, critique of,
99–101; Rameau's harmonic theory
and, 90–93
as unification of multiple elements into
melody, 73–74
as unnatural, 126–27
harpsichord, tuning of, 67–68, 76–77
Heartz, Daniel, 208 n. 32
Hegel, Georg Wilhelm Friedrich, 151
Houle, George, 190 n. 8
human voice. *See also* singing
as free to all, 66
infinite capacity for modulation, 66–67,
68–69
moral response evoked in listeners,
69–70
Hume, David, 150
Hyer, Bryan, 96

imagination
instinct as source of, in Rameau, 107
and mimetic power of music, 163
modern loss of, Rousseau on, 155
and music as art rather than science, 154
and pity, in Rousseau, 10–11
imitation. *See* mimesis
individual rights, emphasis on in *Discours sur l'origine de l'inégalité*, 19
individual will, conflicts with general will,
19, 36–37, 39, 54, 57–60. *See also* self-interest
and forced compliance, 195 n. 18
parallels with tension between melody
and harmony, 19–20
periodic attitude adjustments necessary
to avoid, 63–65
resolution of, blues music as model for,
179–81
Rousseau's framing of as internalized
struggle, 59–60
taming of by group experience of music,
36–38, 45–46
instinct, role of in musical composition,
Rameau on, 105–7, 111
interdisciplinary studies
increasing interest in, 2–3
limited involvement of music in, 3
of Rousseau, appropriateness of, 3–4
interest/imagination dichotomy in
Rousseau, Derrida on, 10–11
interest in music, as moral human interest,
167–68, 185
Isacoff, Stuart, 76–77

Jauss, Hans Robert, 151, 212 nn. 28, 35
Johnson, James, 56
*Julie, ou la nouvelle Héloïse* (Rousseau). *See
also vendanges* letter in *Julie*
and aesthetic reception, 38, 42–44
and aesthetic theory of Rousseau, larger
context of, 3, 4–5
elegiac view of present in, 155

Kant, Immanuel
on aesthetic judgment, 167
anticipations of in Rousseau, 35, 73, 151,
165–68
on experience of self through the sublime,
170, 192 n. 34
on transcendental subject, and stability of
knowledge, 170
keyboard instruments, tuning of
compromises necessary in, 60–62,
67–68, 76–77
equal temperament system, 68, 77–80,
92–93, 198 n. 9, 201 n. 38
as issue in Rameau-Rousseau debate,
76–80, 92–93, 95, 198 nn. 7, 9, 11,
201 n. 38
mean-tone temperament system, 68,
77–80, 92
ordinary (common) temperament system,
197–98 n. 5
Rousseau on, 68, 77–79, 79–80, 93, 95,
198 n. 11
well temperament system, 68
Krehbiel, Henry Edward, 205 n. 10

Laborde, Jean-Benjamin de, 130
language. *See also* speech
accent in: emotion carried by, 30–32; and
melody of speech, 70–71; types of, 30
early, as indistinguishable from song,
119–20
expressive, mimesis of in musical
performance, 29–31
modern, loss of emotion in, 52, 120, 194
n. 7
and music, analogic relationship
between, 25–26, 92
origin of: *Discours* on, 188 n. 20; in need
for communication/community,
35–36, 116–17
as political force, 188–89 n. 20
prosody: French, musical limitations
imposed by, 29–31; parallel with
rhythm/meter in music, 25, 26–27

language (*continued*)
  rhythm of: emotion carried by, 29–32; ignition of passion through, 31–32
Leibnitz, Gottfried Wilhelm von, 150
*Lettre à d'Alembert sur les spectacles* (Rousseau)
  on aesthetic reception, 38, 39, 41
  on aesthetics and politics, link between, 56
  and aesthetic theory of Rousseau, larger context of, 3, 4–5
  on corrupting effect of theater, 143, 208 n. 39
*Lettre à Grimm au sujet de ses remarques sur Omphale* (Rousseau), 6
*Lettre d'un symphoniste de l'Académie royale de musique à ses camarades de l'orchestre* (Rousseau), 6
*Lettre sur la musique française* (Rousseau), 201 n. 40
  in chronology of Rousseau's works, 6
  on Lully's *Armide*, 95–96, 102
  on musical limitations imposed by French prosody, 29–31
  on music and language, analogic relationship between, 25–26
  and Rousseau debate with Rameau, 76
*Lettre sur l'opéra italien et français* (Rousseau), 6
Lévi-Strauss, Claude
  *Tristes Tropiques*, 7–8
  on writing as form of power, 7–8
*liasion*, in creation of melody, Rousseau on, 25, 90
"Literary Process of Modernism" (Jauss), 212 n. 28
literature, and manipulation of audiences, 208 n. 40
Locke, John, 150
Lully, Jean-Baptiste. *See Armide* (Lully)
Lyotard, Jean-François, 168, 170

Maine, Henry, 187 n. 1
Maistre, Joseph-Marie, comte de, 187 n. 1
major triad
  in Rameau's harmonic theory, 85–86
  Rousseau on, 89
Marsalis, Wynton, 47
Mason, Laura, 56
material culture, increasing interest in, 3
meaning in music, Rousseau on, 25, 72–74, 90–93. *See also* emotion, impact of music on; moral effect of music

mean-tone temperament system, 68
  Rameau on, 78
  Rousseau as supporter of, 68, 77–79, 79–80, 92
measure, *Dictionnaire de musique* article on, 24–25
melody
  analogy with individual rights, 19
  and contresens, 202 n. 46
  as conveyor of moral meaning, 25, 72–74, 90–93
  as conveyor of passion, 71–72
  *Dictionnaire de musique* on, 70–71
  emotion as basis for creating, 92
  harmonious unification of multiple elements in, 73–74; as analogy for political cooperation, 19, 74, 75
  privileging of over harmony: in ancient Greek music, 128–29; in folk music, 126–28
  relative naturalness of, 127–28
  Rousseau's privileging of over harmony, 19, 71–72, 73; blues music and, 181; and conventional nature of music, 52; and debate on temperament, 76–80; and Lully's *Armide*, critique of, 99–101; Rameau's harmonic theory and, 90–93
  of speech, accent and, 70–71
memory, music evoking emotion through, 117, 120–22, 125, 183
metaphysics
  of Rameau's harmonic theory, 103–7; Rousseau on, 107–8
  of Rousseau, and origin of music, 110–11
meter. *See* rhythm/meter
methodological innovation necessitated by interdisciplinary studies, 3
microtones, Rameau's harmonic theory and, 95, 198 n. 9
military drills, and experience of musical time as type of motion, 191 n. 19
mimesis
  aesthetic modernity and, 153
  and avant-garde aesthetic, 211 n. 16
  of expressive language, in musical performance, 29–31
  song as analogous to painting in, 11–12, 52
mimetic power of music
  debate on capacity for, 153–54
  imagination and, 163

judgment required of composer and
    performer in, 166
judgment required of listener in, 166–67
movement in music and, 163–65
musical rhythm/meter as imitation of
    emotion, 26–33, 44–46, 52, 163–64,
    165–66, 176–77
music as conventional sign system and,
    162–63
technical imitation, 164–65
mind/body dualism in Rousseau
moral force of music and, 112–13
and self-overcoming, need for, 37–38
modern European music, lack of force and
    energy in, 126–27
modernity
    aesthetic: celebration of ephemeral in,
        157; emergence of, 148–50, 152–53;
        features of in Rousseau's aesthetic
        theory, 4, 150, 153–58, 160–65, 185;
        and individual point of view, emphasis
        on, 149–50, 153, 159; redefinition of
        music's formal qualities required by,
        154, 160–65; as response to elegiac
        view of present, 156–57, 158–59; self-
        consciousness of, 159; view of nature
        in, 154; view of present in, 155–57
    alienation of individual in, 155–57, 212
        n. 28; aesthetic modernity as response
        to, 156–57, 158–59; and redemption
        of individual through art, 147–48,
        155–56, 168–71; Rousseau's recog-
        nition of, 168–69
    Habermas on, 152–53
    musical: emergence of, 150; Rousseau's
        aesthetic as, 150
    Rousseau as critic of, 147
    of Rousseau's aesthetic theory, 4, 150,
        153–58, 160–65, 185
    of Rousseau's social and political
        thought, 151–53, 157
    scientific, emergence of, 149
modulation
    in Lully's *Armide*, Rameau-Rousseau
        debate on, 96–103, 202 n. 46
    Rameau's definition of, 96
    Rousseau's definition of, 96
    as term, 201–2 n. 44
Montesquieu, 47, 55–56, 194 n. 4, 205
    n. 12
moral effect of music, 32–33
    as communication between sentient
        moral beings, 52–53, 69–70, 72–73,
        167–68, 169–71, 177–78, 185

consolation as, 204 n. 64
contentment and, 38
melody as conveyor of moral meaning,
    25, 72–74, 90–93
mind/body dualism and, 112–13
as motive for composition, in Rousseau,
    109–13
and power to uplift or degrade, 113
and self-recognition, 45, 53, 171
singer's voice and, 69–70
social cohesion created by group expe-
    rience of music, 35, 37–38
as standard for aesthetic judgment,
    102–3, 108–9, 110–11
moral life, self-overcoming and, 35
motion
    effect of on emotion, 29, 53, 214 n. 17
    experience of musical time as type of,
        28–29, 191 n. 19
    in music, and power of mimesis, 163–65
museum culture, nascent, increasing
    interest in, 3
music
    as conventional sign system, 52–53, 70,
        88–89, 92, 118–20; as memorative
        sign, 117, 120–22, 125, 183; natu-
        ralness in music and, 130; and power
        of mimesis, 162–63
    elegiac view of present as inherent feature
        of, 161
    formal qualities, redefinition of required
        by modernist aesthetic, 154, 160–65
    as human art, 163
    as inherently relational art, 161–62
    as inherently social activity in 18th
        century, 20, 33–34
    mathematical properties of, Rameau on,
        189 n. 33
    mimetic ability of, debate on, 153–54
    as natural expression of emotion, 50–51
    origin of: blues music, 173–74, 214 n. 17;
        in need for communication/
        community, 35–36, 109–10, 116–17,
        118–20, 182–83, 185; in primal
        passions, 51, 112–13, 116–17,
        119–20, 203 n. 64; Rameau on,
        103–7, 203 n. 64; Rousseau on,
        107–13
    as present-oriented temporal form, 12,
        14, 160–61, 176–77, 177–78, 212 nn.
        34–35; as privileging of temporal over
        spatial, 20, 22–23
    redemptive power of, Rousseau on, 110,
        147–48, 151–52, 155–56, 168–71

music (continued)
  Rousseau's love of, 1, 5–6
  self-recognition experienced in, 45, 53, 171
  as self-referential art form, 164–65
  status as art *vs.* science, debate on, 153–54, 211 n. 15
musical modernity
  emergence of, 150
  Rousseau's aesthetic as, 150
musical notation
  18th century reform efforts, 190 n. 8
  Rousseau's simplified form of: cultural hierarchy embodied by, 9; as democratizing effort, 8–9, 19, 20, 48, 49–50, 66; effectiveness of, 194 n. 3; Rameau's critique of, 191 n. 9; simplicity of, 194 n. 2; simplified meter system in, 21–22
  traditional, Rousseau on, 49
musical texts of Rousseau
  characteristics of, 4
  integration of into Rousseau corpus, benefits of, 2–3, 6–7
  limited critical attention to, 2
  overview of, 5–6
*Musical Time* (Barry), 23–24, 190 n. 5
music and painting
  Derrida on analogy between, 11–12
  music as memorative sign and, 117
  Rousseau on distinctions between, 12, 22–23, 52
music of 18th century
  gulf between theory and practice in, 48
  as inherently social activity, 20, 33–34
music theory, as term, 4
music theory of Rousseau. *See also specific topics*
  anticipations of Kant in, 35, 73, 151, 165–68
  arbitrariness of musical signs in, 52–53, 70, 88–89, 92, 118–20; memorative signs, 117, 120–22, 125, 183; naturalness in music and, 130; and power of mimesis, 162–63
  emphasis on music as experience rather than object, 167–68
  *esprit systématique* in, 93, 200 n. 32
  features of aesthetic modernity in, 4, 150, 153–58, 160–65, 185
  on harmonic theory, 94, 99, 127, 201 n. 40
  and judgment required in creation and perception of music, 166–67
  lack of systematicity in, 87
  moral impact of music as fundamental principle in, 111
  privileging of performance and reception in, 89–93
  Rameau as interlocutor in, 87, 200 n. 32
  rigidity with regard to temperament issue, 95
  verisimilitude as fundamental value in, 98–99, 103, 108, 202 n. 48

Nancy, Jean-Luc, 168, 170
naturalness in music
  continuum of musical complexity and, 127–28, 130
  as cultural convention, 130
need/passion dichotomy in Rousseau, Derrida on, 10
Nettl, Bruno, 205 n. 11
Neumann, Frederick, 190–91 n. 8
*Nouveau système de musique théorique* (Rameau), 78, 95
novels, aesthetic reception of, and self-recognition, 43–44

*Observations sur notre instinct pour la musique, et sur son principe* (Rameau), 99
O'Dea, Michael, 200 n. 32
order in music, perception of, Rameau on, 87
ordinary (common) temperament system, 197–98 n. 5
"L'origine de la mélodie" (Rousseau), 21, 90–91, 107–8, 109
origin of music
  blues music, 173–74, 214 n. 17
  in need for communication/community, 35–36, 109–10, 116–17, 118–20, 182–83, 185
  in primal passions, 51, 112–13, 116–17, 118–20, 203 n. 64
  Rameau on, 103–7, 203 n. 64
  Rousseau on, 107–13
Osipovich, David, 192–93 n. 36

Paige, Nicholas, 42, 43, 193 n. 37
painting and music
  Derrida on analogy between, 11–12
  music as memorative sign and, 117
  Rousseau on distinctions between, 12, 22–23, 52
Paris Opéra, and *querelle des bouffons*, 56

passion
  Aristotelian theory of catharsis, Rousseau's critique of, 40
  and democratic deliberation, 54, 195 n. 16
  ignition of through sound, 31–32, 72
  melody as conveyor of, 71–72
  music's power to uplift, 113
  origin of music in, 51, 112–13, 116–17, 119–20, 203 n. 64
  Rousseau's conception of, 31, 72
  virtue as special, other-oriented form of, 33
pastoral settings
  of *Le devin du village*, 132–33
  as old-fashioned, in 18th century, 133
Paz, Octavio, 157
pentatonic scale
  historical reception of, 207 n. 26
  as primitive musical form, 128–29
  privileging of in folk music, 128–29
performance of music
  interpretation of rhythm/meter in: artistic liberty in, 21; as imitation of emotion, 26–33, 44–46, 52, 163–64, 165–66, 176–77; as imitation of expressive language, 29–31; impact on moral sentiments, 33; levels of rhythm and, 23–24; limitations of French prosody and, 29–31; as medium for meaning in music, 25, 72–74, 90–93
  ornamentation choices in, 190–91 n. 8
  Rousseau's privileging of, 89–93; analogy to privileging of speech over writing, 12–13; and emotion *vs.* reason, 189 n. 33; and music as temporal form, 12, 14, 160–61, 176–77, 177–78, 212 nn. 34–35; as privileging of temporal over spatial, 20, 22–23
  wide gap between score and, in 18th century, 20
performance studies, 190 n. 3
performing arts, political functions of. *See also* social harmony, creation of through folk music
  in 18th century, 56
  Rousseau's democratic uses of music, 56–57, 143
  theater as destructive of general will, 39–42, 192–93 nn. 31, 36–38
Perry, Ruth, 142
pitch pipes, variations in tones produced by, 62–63

pity
  and imagination, in Rousseau, 10–11
  in Lully's *Armide*, Rousseau on, 102–3, 108–9
  and recognition of suffering in others and, 53, 70
  Rousseau on, 203 n. 58
political functions of performing arts. *See also* social harmony, creation of through folk music
  in 18th century, 56
  Rousseau's democratic uses of music, 56–57, 143
  theater as destructive of general will, 39–42, 192–93 nn. 31, 36–38
*The Power of Black Music* (Floyd), 19
present
  elegiac view of: aesthetic modernity as response to, 156–57, 158–59; in aesthetic theory of Rousseau, 9, 115, 117, 122, 125, 155–57, 159; as inherent feature of music, 161
  elegiac view of, in modernity, 155–57, 212 n. 28; redemption from, in Rousseau, 110, 147–48, 151–52, 155–56, 168–71; Rousseau's recognition of, 168–69
  emphasis on in Rousseau, 157–58
  view of in aesthetic modernity, 155–57
primal passions, 116–17
primitive cultures, music of
  as representative of earlier European culture, 124–25, 205–6 n. 13
  as similar to western folk music, 122–24
"Profession de foi du vicaire Savoyard" (Rousseau), 37–38, 112–13
*Projet concernant de nouveaux signes pour la musique* (Rousseau). *See also* musical notation, Rousseau's simplified form of
  presentation of to Académie des sciences, 20
  as Rousseau's earliest work on music, 5, 6, 87
  simplified musical notation proposal in, 8–9
*Projet de constitution pour la Corsica* (Rousseau)
  and folk music as political force, 143–44, 210 n. 52
  on general will, formation of, 36
  on individual will, overcoming of, 39
prosody
  French, musical limitations imposed by, 29–31

prosody (*continued*)
parallel with rhythm/meter in music, 25, 26–27
*Pygmalion* (Rousseau)
and aesthetic theory, 159
elegiac view of present in, 155–56

*querelle des bouffons*
political implications of, 56, 196 n. 22
Rousseau's participation in, 6

Rameau, Jean-Philippe
and chord inversion, systematization of, 86
debate with Rousseau on music theory, 6; blues music and, 181–83; complexity of positions in, 101–2; as conflict of *esprit de système vs. esprit systématique*, 80–81; as *différend*, 111, 200 n. 32; issues at stake in, 75–76; on Lully's *Armide*, 95–103, 108–9, 111, 202 n. 46; on mathematical *vs.* emotive properties of music, 80, 189 n. 33; on prioritization of harmony *vs.* melody, 71, 73, 99–101, 190 n. 6; temperament as issue in, 76–80, 198 n. 7
*Encyclopédie* on, 81–82, 85
*esprit de système* in, 82–87, 92–93, 103, 198–99 n. 16, 200 n. 32
harmonic theory of, 83–87, 199 n. 17, 199–200 n. 22, 200 n. 23, 203 n. 60; as Cartesian rationalism, 148; and delimiting of allowable combinations, 94; flexibility of, 87, 101; on fundamental base, 86–87, 93, 202 nn. 51–52; grounding of in nature, 83, 94, 105–7; privileging of epistemology over aesthetics in, 103–4; role of composition in, 104–7; on role of instinct in composition, 105–7, 111; Rousseau's critique of, 88–92, 94, 98, 101, 200 n. 31; as standard for assessment of music, 104, 108; as uncovering of order of nature, 105–7; willingness to bend rules of, 95
harmonic theory of, metaphysics underlying, 103–7; Rousseau on, 107–8
importance to understanding Rousseau, 4
on instinctual enjoyment of music, 99
on rhythm/meter, limited theorization of, 90–91, 201 n. 35
on Rousseau's musical notation scheme, 191 n. 9

on temperament, 78, 92–93, 95, 198 nn. 7, 9, 11, 201 n. 38
tension between Cartesianism and empiricism in, 81–82, 83, 85, 198 n. 12
"Ranz des vaches" (traditional Swiss song)
as example of music of primitive folk culture, 120–22, 128–30, 207 n. 29
relative naturalness of, 127–28
Rousseau on emotional content carried by, 120–22, 125–28
rationalism, Cartesian. *See also esprit de système*
and aesthetic modernity, 149–50
of Rameau, Rousseau's critique of, 76
rise of, 148–49
reason/passion dichotomy in Rousseau, Derrida on, 11
reception of music, as primary focus of Rousseau, 91–93. *See also* emotion, impact of music on; moral effect of music
redemption
in aesthetic modernity, 158–59
of individual through music: blues music and, 185; Rousseau on, 110, 147–48, 151–52, 155–56, 168–71
Rehding, Alexander, 95, 198 nn. 9,11, 199–200 n. 22
Reiss, Timothy J., 200 n. 23
*Rêveries du promeneur solitaire* (Rousseau), 155, 158, 159
rhythm/meter. *See also* time, musical
as analogous to syntax in language, 25–26
*Dictionnaire de musique* article on, 26
as essential element in music, 24–26
of folk music, 129–30
history of, 24–25
as imitation of expressive language, 29–31
as internal structure of music, 25–26
interpretation of, in music performance: artistic liberty in, 21; convention-based aspects of, 52; as imitation of emotion, 26–33, 44–46, 52, 163–64, 165–66, 176–77; as imitation of expressive language, 29–31; impact on moral sentiments, 33; levels of rhythm and, 23–24; limitations of French prosody and, 29–31; as medium for meaning in music, 25, 72–74, 90–93
of language, emotion carried by, 29–32
Rameau's limited theorization of, 90–91, 201 n. 35

Rousseau's lack of sophistication
  concerning, 22
 in Rousseau's simplified musical
  notation, 21–22
 as soul of song, 27
 as type of motion, 28–29
*romances* (ballads)
 class overtones of, 142
 definition of, 209–10 n. 49
 old fashioned sweetness of, 141
 Rousseau's use of, 141–42
*Rousseau juge de Jean-Jacques* (Rousseau), 155

Schenker, Heinrich, 190 n. 6
Schoenberg, Arnold, 190 n. 6
sciences, Rousseau on corrupting power of, 147
scientific modernity, emergence of, 149
score, musical
 as concretization of harmonic system, 20–21, 23, 189 n. 33, 190 n. 5
 as pre-musical form, 23
 Rousseau's privileging of performance over: analogy to privileging of speech over writing, 12–13; and emotion *vs.* reason, 189 n. 33; and music as temporal form, 12, 14, 160–61, 176–77, 177–78, 212 nn. 34–35; as privileging of temporal over spatial, 20, 22–23
 wide gap between performance and, in 18th century, 20
Scott, John, 167
Scottish bagpipe music, as example of music of primitive folk culture, 130
*Second Discourse* (Rousseau). See *Discours sur l'origine de l'inégalité* (Rousseau)
self-interest. *See also* individual will, conflicts with general will
 French theater's stirring of, 39–42, 192–93 nn. 36–38, 192 n. 31
 overcoming of: in group experience of music, 36–38, 45–46; human mind/body dualism and, 37–38; need for, in submission to general will, 35, 36, 60; as origin of moral life, 35, 37–38
 Rousseau on destructive power of, 40–41
self-recognition
 in hearing music, 45, 53, 171
 in reading fiction, 42–44
17th century, *esprit de système* in, 80–81
*Shaping Time* (Epstein), 28–29

shared moral experience, as basis of social cohesion, 35. *See also* group experience of music; moral effect of music
signs, conventional, music as. *See* music, as conventional sign system
singing. *See also* human voice
 as conveyor of moral meaning, 72–74
 as conveyor of passion, 71–72
 as democratic form of music, 66
 feeling of community fostered by, 74
 of folk music, in *vendanges* letter in *Julie*; creation of social harmony through, 140–43; erotic component in, 138; as expression of social harmony, 137–38, 142–43; privileging of melody over harmony in, 138–40; as vehicle for correct values, 136–37, 138–40
 in group: tuning and key adjustments necessary for, 66–67; as type of community, 69, 74
 Rousseau on history of, 55–56
 as social convention, 118–20
*The Social Contract* (Rousseau). See *Du contrat social* (Rousseau)
social harmony, creation of through folk music. *See also* general will
 blues music and, 183–85
 possibility of in Rousseau, 143–45, 184
 in *vendanges* letter in *Julie*, 140–43
soul, Rousseau's conception of, 31
sound
 effect on moral being, 32–33
 ignition of passion through, 31–32, 72
sound palette in music, impact of *vs.* rhythm/meter, 26–27
sovereignty, Rousseau on, 157
speech
 modern, loss of emotion in, 52, 120, 194 n. 7
 origin of in emotion, 51
 tinge of emotion inherent in, 30, 31–32, 51–52
Starobinski, Jean, 2, 188 n. 17
state of nature in Rousseau, 189 nn. 22–23
 Derrida on, 9, 189 n. 23
Strong, Tracy B., 157, 192 n. 31, 197 n. 38, 202 n. 46, 213 nn. 48, 51
structure of supplementarity in Rousseau, Derrida on, 9–10, 13

Talmon, J. J., 54, 192 n. 31
technical imitation, in music, 164–65
tempo, variations in during performance, and subjugation of individual to group will, 65–66, 196–97 n. 33

theatrical productions
  aesthetic reception of as destructive of general will, 39–42, 192–93 nn. 31, 36–38
  political uses of in 18th century, 56
theory wave of 18th-century studies, 2–3
Tiersot, Julien, 205 n. 11, 209 n. 48
time, musical. *See also* rhythm/meter
  *Dictionnaire de musique* article on, 27
  experience of as type of motion, 28–29, 191 n. 19
  group experience of, bonding created by, 34–38, 45–46, 180–81, 191 n. 19
  levels of, 23–24
  Rousseau's conception of, 24–25
  spacialization of in musical score, 190 n. 5
Tipaldi, Art, 214 n. 10
*Traité de l'harmonie* (Rameau), 82, 104–5
transcendent realm, absence of in Rousseau, 110, 151
*Tristes Tropiques* (Lévi-Strauss), 7–8
tuning of instruments
  blue notes and, 180
  keyboard instruments: compromises necessary in, 60–62, 67–68, 76–77; equal temperament system, 68, 77–80, 92–93, 198 n. 9, 201 n. 38; as issue in Rameau-Rousseau debate, 76–80, 92–93, 95, 198 nn. 7, 9, 11, 201 n. 38; mean-tone temperament system, 68, 77–80, 92; ordinary (common) temperament system, 197–98 n. 5; Rousseau on, 68, 77–79, 79–80, 93, 95, 198 n. 11; well temperament system, 68
  in orchestra, general will as analogous to, 60–65, 75, 179
  Rousseau on, 61–63
  Rousseau's practical experience with, 60–61, 67–68, 93

"Unité de mélodie" (Rousseau), 71–72, 166
unity of melody, 73–74, 90, 166, 167

values spheres, differentiation of, 156, 169
*vendanges* letter in *Julie*, 135–43
  on agricultural work: emotional charge carried by, 135–36, 184; social harmony of, 135–36, 139–43, 184
  singing of folk music in: creation of social harmony through, 140–43; erotic component in, 138; as expression of social harmony, 137–38, 142–43; privileging of melody over harmony in, 138–40; as vehicle for correct values, 136–37, 138–40
"Vérités intéressantes" (Rameau), 105–7
virtue
  awakening of, through accent, 32–33
  as special, other-oriented passion, 33

Waeber, Jacqueline, 202 nn. 46–47
Weber, Shierry, 155–56
well temperament system, 68
women's voices
  Rousseau's preference for, 137–38
  in *vendanges* letter in *Julie*, as expression of social harmony, 137–38, 142–43
works of Rousseau. *See also* musical texts of Rousseau
  broadening of critical interests over time, 1–2
  range of disciplines spanned by, 2
writing, and loss of emotional content of language, 52
Young, Iris Marion, 192 n. 35

www.ingramcontent.com/pod-product-compliance
Lightning Source LLC
Chambersburg PA
CBHW021400290426
44108CB00010B/323